A Primer on

SINGLE-
SUBJECT
DESIGN

for Clinical Social Workers

A Primer on

SINGLE-SUBJECT DESIGN

for Clinical Social Workers

by Tony Tripodi

NASW PRESS

National Association of Social Workers
Washington, DC

Ann A. Abbott, PhD, ACSW, *President*
Sheldon R. Goldstein, ACSW, LISW, *Executive Director*

First printing October 1994
Second printing December 1995
Third printing May 1998

Linda Beebe, *Executive Editor*
Nancy Winchester, *Editorial Services Director*
Marcia Roman, *Production Editor*
Laurel Rumpl, *Copy Editor*
Susan Harris, *Proofreader*
Sandi Schroeder, *Indexer*

Library of Congress Cataloging-in-Publication Data

Tripodi, Tony
    A Primer on Single-Subject Design for Clinical Social Workers/ by Tony Tripodi

Includes bibliographical references and index.
ISBN 0-87101-238-3

1. Social case work—Research. 2. Psychiatric social work—Research.
3. Single-subject research. I. Title.
[DNLM: 1. Social work, Psychiatric—methods. 2. Research design. 3. Statistics.
WA 20.5 T835p 1994]
HV43.T75 1994
361.3'2—dc20
DNLM/DLC
for Library of Congress   94–19703
                                                           CIP
⊜ 3

Printed in the United States of America

To

Kathy Germak
Phil Newhart
Barcie Panevics
and
Ernie Waite

CONTENTS

CHAPTER 4

PHASE 2: INTERVENTION

CHAPTER 5

PHASE 3: FOLLOW-UP

CHAPTER 6

DESIGN VARIATIONS

APPENDIX 1

APPENDIX 2

FOREWORD

It has been 20 years since Howe's (1974) review of single-subject design outlined the potential applications of this emergent research tool for social work practice. In the 1960s, the groundbreaking work of applied behavior analysts such as Allen and Wolf and their colleagues (1964, 1966) in a therapeutic nursery school program at the University of Washington illustrated the clinical-diagnosis benefits of single-subject design in isolating the antecedents and consequences of troublesome and self-injurious behavior among very young children. Earlier still, Ayllon and Michael (1959) documented the rich clinical potential of a variety of single-subject designs in understanding the dynamics of puzzling behavior in a mental health unit. Although it is generally acknowledged that the critical; early work on single-subject design was carried out by psychologists, Howe's article, following the early work of Edwin Thomas and other scholars of practice, precipitated the introduction of this particular set of research tools to social work research, practice, and professional education. In fact, single-subject designs became a key element in a movement, recently chronicled by Reid (1994), called "empirical–clinical practice," which had and continues to have a major impact on social work knowledge development.

To a certain extent, the acceptance of single-subject design methodology has been hampered by its identification with behavioral methods and by the absence of agency-based systems designed to support and encourage information-driven practice. Happily, Tony Tripodi's clear, straightforward, and practical volume arrives at an opportune moment. On the clinical practice level, much of the sharpness and polarization around behavioral–nonbehavioral practice has given way to a more eclectic orientation to practice. On the level of practice evaluation, there is a more sophisticated understanding of the multiple uses of research to inform practice. Thus, the context in which practitioners view single-subject design envisions a host of potential uses from more accurate diagnosis to validation of specific treatment techniques to evaluation of treatment effectiveness.

On the organizational level, the major movement toward managed health (and soon child welfare) creates a need for intervention that is outcome-oriented, information-based, and consumer-driven. These facts and concomitant growth of agency-based client information systems argue for a second look at single-subject design as an important methodology for communicating with clients as well as assuring quality of service processes and outcomes.

This tightly written volume by one of social work's leading practice researchers explores the varieties of single-subject designs, their different uses, and the arguments for and against different evaluation pathways. Suitable for both beginning and advanced practitioners, this primer provides an excellent focal point for discussion in staff training and group supervisory sessions. Its lessons, if carefully adapted to meet the particular demands of differing agency contexts and community settings, will aid social work in reclaiming ownership of its own knowledge development function as opposed to accepting research that is all too often externally imposed. Ultimately, much of what Dr. Tripodi writes about will become incorporated into what is considered "best practice." For his view of quality, goal-oriented, information-driven practice, fully attuned to consumer feedback applied in a manner consistent with the core values of social work, we are in the author's debt.

JAMES K. WHITTAKER
University of Washington

REFERENCES

Allen, K. E., & Harris, F. R. (1966). Elimination of a child's excessive scratching by training the mother in reinforcement techniques. *Behavior Research and Therapy, 4,* 79–74.

Allen, K. E., Hart, B., Buell, J. S., Harris, F. R., & Wolf, M. M. (1964). Effects of social reinforcement on isolate behavior of a nursery school child. *Child Development, 35,* 511–518.

Ayllon, T., & Michael, J. (1959). The psychiatric nurse as a behavioral engineer. *Journal of the Experimental Analysis of Behavior, 2,* 323–334.

Howe, M. (1974). Casework self-evaluation: A single-subject approach. *Social Service Review, 48,* 1–23.

Reid, W. (1994). The empirical practice movement. *Social Service Review, 68,* 165–184.

PREFACE AND ACKNOWLEDGMENTS

The purpose of this book is to provide for clinical social workers an introduction to the use of single-subject design in clinical practice. The book shows how this methodology can serve as a frame of reference for making clinical decisions relevant to assessment, implementation, and evaluation of treatment and client follow-up through the use of statistical procedures and graphic analysis. The utility of single-subject design is illustrated in a variety of clinical situations.

This book also was written for social work students and their supervisors in field practice so that the accreditation standards for evaluating a worker's practice, established by the Council on Social Work Education, can be adequately implemented.

I wish to acknowledge colleagues and students at the University of Michigan, the University of Pittsburgh, and Florida International University for their discussions of the topic of single-subject design. Many thanks to Dolores Ogle and Kathleen Cordon for typing the manuscript. Special thanks to Dr. Suzanne Stonbely, who provided the graphic illustrations.

TONY TRIPODI

INTRODUCTION

The Board of Directors of the National Association of Social Workers (NASW) in June 1984 approved the following 11 standards for clinical social workers:

Standard 1. Clinical social workers shall function in accordance with the ethics and the stated standards of the profession, including its accountability procedures. . . .

Standard 2. Clinical social workers shall have and continue to develop specialized knowledge and understanding of individuals, families, and groups and of the therapeutic and preventive interventions. . . .

Standard 3. Clinical social workers shall respond in a professional manner to all persons who seek their assistance. . . .

Standard 4. Clinical social workers shall be knowledgeable about the services available in the community and make appropriate referrals for their clients. . . .

Standard 5. Clinical social workers shall maintain their accessibility to clients. . . .

Standard 6. Clinical social workers shall safeguard the confidential nature of the information obtained within that relationship. . . .

Standard 7. Clinical social workers shall maintain access to professional case consultation. . . .

Standard 8. Clinical social workers shall establish and maintain professional offices and procedures. . . .

Standard 9. Clinical social workers shall represent themselves to the public with accuracy. . . .

Standard 10. Clinical social workers shall engage in the independent private practice of clinical social work only when qualified to do so. . . .

Standard 11. Clinical social workers shall have the right to establish an independent private practice. . . . (Minahan, 1987, pp. 966–970)

Implicit in these standards is the notion that clinical social workers should be accountable to their clients and conduct ethical practice, their goal being to improve the quality of services. Toward this end, the standards help to establish professional expectations that can assist social workers to monitor and evaluate clinical practice. In particular, an interpretation of standard 2 is that clinical social workers should have knowledge and skills from research to evaluate the effectiveness of their work (Minahan, 1987, pp. 966–967).

Approaches for using research to assist in the assessment and evaluation of clinical practice include interviews with clients, systematic observation, use of forms and questionnaires, content analysis of case records and taped recordings, surveys, use of rating scales, and the collection of information before treatment begins and after termination (Tripodi & Epstein, 1980). Because clinical social workers cannot use only one approach to evaluate the effectiveness of work with all clients, they must have a repertoire of available methodologies. One methodology clinical psychologists and social workers have used is single-subject design (Barlow & Hersen, 1984; Bloom, Fischer, & Orme, 1993; Jayaratne & Levy, 1979; Kazdin, 1992). Every clinical social worker should be familiar with the basic notions and procedures of this methodology. Moreover, clinical social workers can use single-subject designs to assess and evaluate as well as to provide input for clinical decisions (Hayes, 1992).

PURPOSE

This book is an introduction to single-subject design methodology for clinical social workers, students, and supervisors. The intent is to provide clinical social workers a perspective on the application of the methodology and the types and levels of knowledge it can generate to enable social workers to assess clinical problems and to evaluate practice. However, single-subject design methodology cannot replace information obtained in clinical interviews and observations.

The three major objectives are

1. to present a basic model of single-subject design methodology and selected variations from the model
2. to show how the basic model can serve as a frame of reference for making clinical decisions with respect to assessing and evaluating the effectiveness of practice interventions
3. to illustrate the utility of single-subject design methodology in a variety of clinical settings.

The book refers to the term *single-subject design*, rather than *single-case design* or *single-system design*, for the following reasons:

- Single-subject design was the preferred term when researchers first applied the methodology to social work in the 1970s (see, for example, Jayaratne, 1977).

- The term *subject* refers to a single unit of analysis, that is, an individual, a couple, a family, or a group. These units coincide with the client units for clinical social workers.

- The term *case* is ambiguous because it can refer to more than one unit of analysis, for example, the client and his or her family. Case, however, is preferred by psychologists who developed the methodology in detail (see Hersen & Barlow, 1976). For purposes of this book, case and subject are synonymous.

- Bloom et al. (1993) used *single-system* to refer to "one individual, group, or collectivity" (p. 11), but their usage throughout the text appears to be synonymous with subject or case. Moreover, *system* implies an analysis of much more than a single unit, that is, an interrelationship among units. Single-subject design methodology does not involve the study of interactions among units.

Authors, for example, Barlow and Hersen, (1984), Bloom et al. (1993), have adequately explained single-subject designs in books from behavioral psychology and social work. However, although the authors have provided a comprehensive presentation of many complex designs, they have not distinguished between those few designs that are useful to clinical social workers and those that are impractical. Moreover, their examples generally pertain to behavioral psychology and often appear inapplicable to much of clinical practice. Furthermore, the authors' presentations appear to be more complex than necessary. The authors do not adequately distinguish the levels of knowledge produced, leading readers to believe that causal knowledge is more obtainable than it is. In addition, the authors do not clearly show how to make inferences from single-subject designs to inform the assessment and evaluative decisions of clinical social workers.

CLINICAL SOCIAL WORK

The following definition of clinical social work was accepted in January 1984 by the Board of Directors of NASW:

Clinical social work shares with all social work practice the goal of enhancement and maintenance of psychosocial functioning of individuals, families, and small groups. Clinical social work practice is the professional application of social work theory and methods to the treatment and prevention of psychosocial dysfunction, disability, or impairment, including emotional and mental disorders. It is based on knowledge of one or more theories of human development within a psychosocial context.

The perspective of person-in-situation is central to clinical social work practice. Clinical social work includes interventions directed to interpersonal interactions, intra-psychic dynamics, and life-support and management issues. Clinical social work services consists of assessment; diagnosis; treatment, including psychotherapy and counseling; client-centered advocacy; consultation; and evaluation. The process of clinical social work is undertaken within the objectives of social work and the principles and values contained in the *NASW Code of Ethics*. (Minahan, 1987, pp. 965–966)

This definition is broad and encompasses a variety of clinical services in public and private settings; a diversity of client populations with respect to such factors as income, race, social class, and so forth; a range of psychosocial problems; and use of different theories and assumptions about the relationship of the person to her or his situation.

Clinical social workers may work in mental health agencies—hospitals, clinics, after-care services; employee assistance programs (EAPs) for business, education, hospitals, factories, and so on; family therapy and family counseling agencies; criminal justice and juvenile institutional, probation, and parole facilities; child guidance clinics; and medical and public health facilities. Clinical social workers may engage in private practice either by themselves or in collaboration with other professionals such as psychiatrists, psychologists, and family counselors. Overall, clinical social workers are functioning in a number of diverse human services agencies and organizations, as well as providing treatments or interventions (these terms are interchangeable) in private practice arrangements.

It therefore follows that clinical social workers deal with clients who represent different cultural and ethnic backgrounds and social classes. However, not all clinical social workers work with a vast range of clients. Some social workers in private practice may work exclusively with particular populations, for example, with male adolescents from middle-income families, focusing on problems of phobias, school adjustments, family relationships, and self-esteem. In contrast, clinical social workers employed in a mental health clinic may work with a more diverse population. The eligibility requirements of the agency or setting in which social workers are employed tend to define client populations. Hence, clinical social workers in a Veterans Affairs (VA) neuropsychiatric hospital will work with veterans from the military who have psychiatric diagnoses and with their families; social workers in a medical hospital may work primarily with cancer patients and their families, dealing with the realities and fears of cancer and its consequences; and clinical social workers in an EAP may focus on individual and small group interventions aimed at reducing stress in the workplace. Furthermore, clinical social workers in the child welfare system may focus on specific interventions, for example, family preservation services as provided by states such as Michigan, designed to prevent out-of-home placements, to increase the child management skills of parents and to eliminate child abuse and neglect; and clinical social workers may work in teams with other mental health professionals to provide counseling when disasters occur, such as Hurricane Andrew in southern Florida, adolescent suicide and its impact on the adolescent's schoolmates, and public acts of homicide and the fear they generate.

Collectively, clinical social workers use different theories about personality and the environment and about changes or the prevention of changes in knowledge, feelings, attitudes, behaviors, skills, and interpersonal interactions. Some social workers are eclectic and use a range of techniques depending on the client, problem, and situation. They may use behavior modification techniques, cognitive interventions, and ego psychological perspectives within an ecological framework. Other social workers may use one major approach stemming from a particular theoretical point of view. For example, they may specialize in the use of group techniques for teaching clients interpersonal skills or they may focus on the therapeutic transaction, providing a means for their clients to understand the dynamics of human relationships with the clinical social worker, their families, and other significant groups.

Tasks

Much of clinical social work practice progresses through interrelated phases. These phases or stages follow a problem-solving model that authors have incorporated into books about social work practice (Blythe & Tripodi, 1989; Hudson & Thyer, 1987; Tripodi & Epstein, 1980). The practice phases used by Tripodi and Epstein—assessing the problem and formulating the treatment, treatment implementation and monitoring, and treatment evaluation—are used here because they are complementary to the basic single-subject design model of baseline, implementation, and follow-up.

In the initial phase of practice with a client, the clinical social worker typically is involved in a number of tasks that are preliminary to the implementation of a treatment or intervention. The social worker gathers information about the client; the source of referral; the client's family, employment, and school history; and the nature and extent of the problems for which the client is referred, either by self or by others in voluntary or involuntary conditions such as mandatory treatment for child abusers or probationers. It is especially important for the clinical social worker to determine whether he or she can provide services appropriate to the client's problems. Hence, the social worker seeks information to make a judgment about what the problems are and whether he or she can engage the client in dealing with the problems. Many clients have a number of problems related to finances, housing, and other basic needs as well as with particular forms of illness, disease, and interpersonal communication and interactions. Hence, the clinical social worker must set priorities to the problems and deal first with those that are more immediately life-threatening or those that are

more pressing because of environmental constraints through the courts and other community agents of control. During this phase, the clinical social worker uses his or her knowledge of theory, research about the effectiveness of interventions, and experience to formulate a treatment plan in cooperation with the client. The social worker devises a contractual arrangement, oral or written, to represent the mutual obligations of the clinical social worker and the client and operationalizes to the extent possible the treatment objectives and the means of achieving them. For example, treatment objectives for a client might include the reduction of anxiety and depression and an increase in positive interactions with his or her mother. The intervention may involve systematic desensitization for the client and counseling sessions with the client and his or her mother that include role plays about negative interactions and discussion about the ways in which both individuals might increase positive interactions.

Having decided which problems to deal with and determined an intervention plan, the clinical social worker, during the second practice phase, attempts to implement the treatment and to monitor compliance of the social worker and the client with the treatment contract. The social worker implements treatment procedures and makes observations about the degree to which the treatment is implemented as planned. Furthermore the social worker makes judgments about the degree to which he or she should continue the treatment or intervention procedures if the social worker and the client attain treatment objectives. The third practice phase involves the termination of treatment as well as follow-up to determine whether the effects of treatment, if obtained, are persistent. This is the evaluation phase in which the clinical social worker discontinues the intervention if the social worker and client attain the treatment objective but plan to observe any changes that occur with the disruption of treatment. The clinical social worker may withdraw an intervention because he or she has accomplished one objective but still work with the client on another problem (Blythe & Tripodi, 1989). For example, systematic desensitization might reduce a client's anxiety, and the clinical social worker may withdraw that intervention; however, the social worker may continue to work with the client and the client's mother through counseling and role plays to increase positive interactions between client and mother. On the other hand, the social worker may terminate social worker–client contacts if there are no further problems. However, the social worker may continue services in long-term care facilities where the purpose of treatment is not to change feelings and behaviors but to maintain the client's state of feelings and attitudes about care.

Decisions

Clinical social workers make decisions—answers to questions pertaining to their major tasks—throughout the treatment phases. In the assessment and treatment formulation phase, the social worker answers questions such as the following:

- What is the client unit—an individual, a couple, a family, a group, and so forth?

- What is the client unit's current status—living arrangements, occupation or student status, identifying demographic variables, and social and psychological assets and deficits?

- How was the client referred to the social worker? Was the referral appropriate or should the client have been referred elsewhere?

- What are the client's problems and needs?

- Is the client sufficiently motivated to engage in the treatment process with the social worker?

- Can the social worker help the client resolve his or her problems and does the clinical social worker have in his or her repertoire a social work intervention that will meet the client's needs?

- Can the social worker assist the client to prioritize his or her problems or needs and can the social worker and the client agree on which problems to deal with?

- What are the treatment objectives for the designated problems? Do the clinical social worker and the client agree with those objectives?

- Can the social worker procure information to assess the nature and severity of the designated problems?

- Does it appear that the problem will continue and even become exacerbated without intervention? (Questions were adapted and modified from Tripodi & Epstein, 1980, p. 12.)

Decisions in the treatment implementation and monitoring phase focus on the delivery of the intervention, its appropriateness for the client, and whether progress occurs in realizing the treatment objectives. The social worker answers questions such as the following:

- Do the client, the clinical social worker, and others important for successful implementation understand what is expected in and between treatment sessions?

- Has the social worker implemented the intervention according to professional standards and the provisions of the treatment contract?

- Does the client appear to want to participate in the intervention plan? Is the intervention appropriate for the particular client? If not, should the social worker use another intervention?

- Are there any barriers to implementation? Can the social worker overcome these barriers?

- Should the social worker revise the initial assessment?

- If implementation of the intervention is inadequate, should the social worker modify the intervention?

- Has there been progress in achieving the treatment objectives? If the social worker and the client have attained treatment objectives, should they terminate the treatment (or intervention)?

- If the social worker terminates the intervention, should he or she plan to follow-up the client to determine whether the attainment of treatment objectives persists? (Questions were adapted and modified from Tripodi & Epstein, 1980, p. 99.)

The final phase of evaluation continues with questions about the achievement of treatment objectives, termination, and follow-up. The second and third phases are interrelated, but the third phase focuses more on the degree to which the intervention has been effective and continues to be effective. However, the clinical social worker also uses this phase to verify the initial assessment and possibly to uncover new problems that originally were not manifest. The social worker then makes decisions based on responses to questions such as the following:

- To what extent have the social worker and the client achieved the treatment objectives?
- If they have not achieved the treatment objectives, are there any discernible reasons why not? Was the treatment appropriate for the client?
- Was termination appropriate? Is there any evidence of client relapse?
- Has client progress persisted in follow-up with the withdrawal of the intervention?
- What level of knowledge did the intervention produce with respect to its relationship to the client's problems? Will this knowledge be useful in the work with other clients?
- Did new problems emerge during the follow-up period?
- Should the social worker reinstitute the intervention (or another one) for the client? (Questions were adapted and modified from Tripodi & Epstein, 1980, pp. 161–162.)

SINGLE-SUBJECT DESIGN METHODOLOGY

Single-subject design methodology includes the specification and measurement of variables that indicate the client's problems; the systematic recording of the extent and severity of the problems before the social worker offers interventions; the systematic recording of the extent of the problems during and after the treatment or intervention; the use of designs, graphic procedures, pattern analysis, or statistical analysis; and a conception of levels of knowledge and necessary evidence to make inferences about the attainment of knowledge levels. In its simplest expression, the complete basic model involves three successive phases: (1) baseline, (2) intervention, and (3) follow-up. In each phase, the researcher takes repeated measurements of variables that indicate the client's problems or needs at specified intervals over time. The researcher then observes patterns of variation in the variables in each of the phases and between phases.

At baseline, there are measurements without an intervention, and analyses of those observations can provide information to assist in the assessment of a client's problems. The baseline phase provides a benchmark of where the client is without intervention; it can indicate the extent and severity of problems as well as the degree to which they may be spontaneously increasing or remitting to a nonproblem state. The intervention phase provides information about the extent of changes in the frequency of the problem as the social worker provides intervention for the client. During the intervention phase, the clinical social worker observes the degree to which he or she implements the planned intervention and whether the measurement patterns of the problem variables are similar to or different from those at baseline. This observation allows the clinical social worker to infer the effectiveness of intervention in relation to intervention goals and indicates whether a problem is stabilizing, increasing, or decreasing. The social worker can implement the intervention phase in most practice situations in which repeated measurements over time are possible (see Chapter 4): after-care treatment, residential treatment, psychotherapy in private practice, medical social work in hospital care facilities, probation and parole supervision, marital counseling, group therapeutic paradigms, and so forth. The social worker also can implement the intervention phase in short-term treatment, but it is impractical in one-shot crisis interviews, such as emergency intervention in natural disasters, traveler's aid, and so forth. In the follow-up phase, the clinical social worker continues to record the problem variables but terminates the intervention. This phase presumes that the clinical social worker has ethically withdrawn the intervention because of the interventions both the client and clinical social worker have agreed on or because the client has achieved therapeutic goals. Obtaining follow-up information requires planning and the use of extra resources by the social worker or the organization or agency in which the social worker is employed. This model of baseline, intervention, and follow-up is consistent with the phase model of direct practice, which incorporates a problem-solving approach, including assessment, planning interventions, implementation, interventions, termination, and follow-up (Blythe & Tripodi, 1989).

The model presented in this book, a basic A-B-A design (Barlow & Hersen, 1984), is used because it is a logical extension of Cook and Campbell's (1979) interrupted time-series design applied to single subjects, which may permit stronger inferences about the effectiveness of an intervention than the A-B design. The A refers to a phase without intervention, whereas B refers to intervention. Hence, the A-B-A design includes baseline, intervention, and return to baseline (the follow-up phase). The A-B design does not have a follow-up phase; hence, it does not permit analysis of what happens to the client after termination or withdrawal of the intervention. Because the clinical social worker can examine much information within the baseline, interven-

tion, or follow-up phase for making decisions within the phases in addition to comparisons among phases, this book refers to those phases, rather than to the letters A and B.

This book intends to introduce readers to the A-B-A design model in detail; clinical examples in subsequent chapters illustrate procedures for analysis. However, the following example illustrates aspects of the model as well as potential problems in its application.

Example

Suppose a clinical social worker in private practice is working with Jim, a 15-year-old male, who is depressed and who thinks critically of himself in relation to others each day. Jim also has low self-esteem and does not engage in ordinary school activities with his classmates. As part of the diagnostic or assessment process, which also includes interviews with Jim's family and study of referral documents and protocols, the clinical social worker, for example, concentrates on the problems of depression and self-critical thoughts.

In discussions with Jim, the clinical social worker devises two variables: (1) frequency of self-critical thoughts and (2) degree of depression. A self-critical thought is one in which he thinks about how incompetent he is compared with others. The clinical social worker asks Jim to tally the number of times he has self-critical thoughts each day and to record those numbers for one week. Jim would count a second self-critical thought only if other thoughts that are not self-critical intervene. The social worker also devises a self-anchored rating scale of depression in consultation with Jim. The scale ranges from 0 to 10; 0 = no depression, 2 = very little depression, 4 = some depression, 6 = moderate depression, 8 = very much depression, and 10 = extreme depression. The social worker also asks Jim to rate his feelings of depression every day for one week. At the end of one week—the second session with the clinical social worker—the social worker constructs graphs to show baseline patterns of self-

figure 1

Severity of Depression for One Week

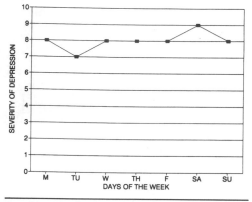

NOTE: M = Monday, TU = Tuesday, W = Wednesday,
TH = Thursday, F = Friday, SA = Saturday, SU = Sunday.

critical thoughts and severity of depression (Figures 1 and 2).

Clearly, Jim perceives he is depressed. He indicates very much depression (8) or higher every day of the week except Tuesday, which he rated 7. Furthermore, the same pattern exists for the frequency of self-critical thoughts, which Jim rated 10 or higher every day except Tuesday. Thus, there apparently is a strong association between the number of self-critical thoughts and depression. However, it is unclear whether self-critical thoughts come before or after the depression; Jim, though, indicated in an interview that he tends to become depressed after he is self-critical. Within the social worker's overall treatment plan, which includes discussions of incidents at home and at school as well as Jim's relationships with peers and family, the social worker decides to use an intervention designed to reduce Jim's self-critical thoughts and, in turn, to possibly reduce depression. The intervention is a cognitive intervention aimed at thought stopping and includes reframing the context of self-critical decisions. The social worker instructs Jim to change the comparisons from himself with others to only with himself whenever he has a self-critical thought and to think of successful performances he has had at school and in sports events. In addition, the social worker asks

Jim to continue to record the frequency of self-critical remarks and perceived depression. After two weeks of intervention, the clinical social worker produces graphs to show the comparisons of intervention with baseline (Figures 3 and 4).

Obviously, the frequency of self-critical thoughts (Figure 4) is reduced to 0 during Friday, Saturday, and Sunday, the last three days of the two weeks of intervention. However, the social worker notes that Jim's feelings of depression continue to exist (Figure 3) and essentially are unchanged. The clinical social worker learns that there is no simple relationship between depression and control of self-critical thoughts, contrary to what Jim believes. This observation implies that assessment of factors that might lead to depression should continue. Moreover, the social worker can reduce the cognitive intervention directed toward Jim's self-critical thoughts in comparison with others.

If Jim no longer invokes the intervention, he and the social worker can determine, by obtaining measurements of self-critical remarks on a daily basis during the follow-up period, whether there is a persistent change in the reduction of self-critical remarks.

As illustrated in the preceding example, single-subject design methodology is

figure 2

Self-Critical Thoughts for One Week

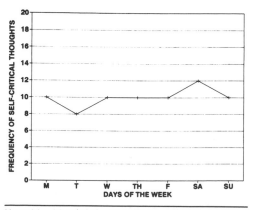

NOTE: M = Monday, T = Tuesday, W = Wednesday,
TH = Thursday, F = Friday, SA = Saturday, SU = Sunday.

figure 3

Severity of Depression over Time, before and after Intervention

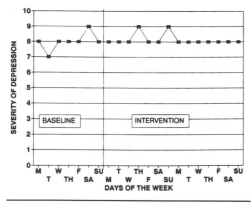

NOTE: M = Monday, T = Tuesday, W = Wednesday, TH = Thursday, F = Friday, SA = Saturday, SU = Sunday.

figure 4

Frequency of Self-Critical Thoughts over Time, before and during Intervention

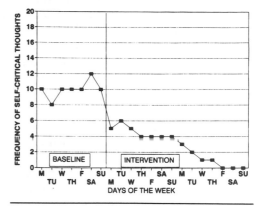

NOTE: M = Monday, T = Tuesday, W = Wednesday, TH = Thursday, F = Friday, SA = Saturday, SU = Sunday.

merely a tool, but it can aid the social worker in making decisions pertinent to assessment and practice effectiveness. When the clinical social worker uses the full single-subject design model and adds other design variations (see Chapter 6), he or she can make inferences that approximate causal relationships between the intervention and designated outcomes or planned results. The emphasis in this book is on using the model and variations of it as a framework for making clinical decisions. However, the clinical social worker ultimately bases the decisions on his or her previous experiences, theory, and knowledge of interventions and on other information derived from clinical observations and interviews.

Levels of Knowledge

Single-subject designs produce or approximate three levels of knowledge: (1) descriptive, (2) correlational, and (3) causal (Tripodi, 1983). Descriptive knowledge consists of simple facts. For example, Jim's ratings of perceived depression for each day of the week constitute descriptive knowledge about the severity of his depression. Correlational knowledge is the description of a relationship between variables. In comparing baseline to intervention on self-critical remarks for Jim, it is apparent that, at baseline without intervention, there is a

greater frequency of self-critical remarks, but during the administration of the intervention, there is a reduction in the number of self-critical remarks; hence, there is a correlation between the intervention and the number of self-critical remarks. The relationship can be more aptly described as inverse or negative: As intervention is introduced, the frequency of self-critical remarks is reduced. If self-critical remarks increased as the intervention were introduced, the relationship would be considered direct or positive. The highest level of knowledge is causal, which includes correlational knowledge between an intervention and changes in a problem variable as well as evidence that no variables other than the intervention are responsible for the changes. Single-subject designs cannot achieve causal knowledge with complete certainty; it can only be approximated. If the clinical social worker could withdraw the intervention for Jim and if the intervention were a reversion to baseline when Jim had a relatively high number of self-critical remarks, the clinical social worker might obtain evidence for causality. This evidence would show that Jim would again eliminate self-critical remarks when the cognitive intervention is introduced again. A fourth level of knowledge is the development of hypotheses by conjecture, observation, or interview. The social worker more likely will obtain this kind of knowledge through qualitative research.

What evidence does the clinical social worker need to obtain different levels of knowledge? The social worker can only have descriptive knowledge if there is evidence of reliability (consistency) and validity (accuracy) for the variables the social worker is measuring. These concepts are discussed in detail in Chapter 2. Correlational knowledge exists when there are reliable and valid variables and when there is graphic or statistical evidence of a relationship among the variables. Procedures to determine the existence of correlational knowledge are discussed in Chapter 4. Causal knowledge about an intervention depends on the following three criteria:

1. The intervention precedes changes in problem variables, for example, the social worker introduces the cognitive intervention for Jim before he makes reductions in self-critical remarks.
2. There is a correlation or association between the intervention and the variables that indicate change. It is standard practice to conceive of the intervention as an independent variable and the change variables as dependent variables.
3. No other variables are responsible for observed changes in the dependent variables. These other variables are internal validity threats (Cook & Campbell, 1979) (see Chapter 4).

RELATIONSHIP BETWEEN CLINICAL PRACTICE AND SINGLE-SUBJECT DESIGN METHODOLOGY

Single-subject design methodology is insufficiently comprehensive to provide the basic information for all practice decisions. Rather, single-subject design provides information that clinical social workers can use to make key decisions in practice. Figure 5 shows the relationship between information obtained from single-subject designs and decisions clinical social workers make in practice. The baseline occurs during the assessment and treatment formulation phase; intervention (treatment), during the treatment implementation and monitoring phase; and follow-up, during the treatment evaluation phase. However, the decisions designated for the practice phases do not include all of the decisions clinical social workers make. Instead, they show that there is a direct relationship between information obtained from single-subject design methodology and critical practice decisions. For example, at baseline, the social worker can obtain information about the measurement of a problem and its nature, severity, and persistence over time without intervention.

The clinical social worker makes inferences in single-subject design methodology by comparing measurements between phases (see Figures 3 and 4). For example, the social worker compares measurements he or she made during intervention with measurements on the same variable at baseline. If there are significant changes from problem severity to the reduction or elimination of the problem, the social worker infers that there is a relationship between the reduction of the problem and the introduction of treatment.

ARGUMENTS FOR THE USE OF SINGLE-SUBJECT DESIGN METHODOLOGY

Bloom et al. (1993) have discussed a number of advantages to using single-subject (single-system) designs, for example, social workers can use the designs to assess problems and evaluate practice, and they can implement the designs in practice. However, some of the arguments appear overstated and insufficiently geared to different levels and types of practice situations. According to Bloom & Fischer (1982), single-subject designs can do the following:

1. They can be built into every practitioner's practice with each and every case/situation without disruption of practice.
2. They provide the tools for evaluating the effectiveness of our practice with

figure 5 *Relationship of Clinical Practice Decisions and Information Provided by Single-Subject Design Methodology*

	Phases		
Clinical Social Work Practice	Assessment and Treatment Formulation	Treatment Implementation and Monitoring	Treatment Evaluation: Termination and Follow-up
Decisions	Is the designated problem severe and persistent and is treatment required?	Has the social worker implemented treatment and has the severity and nature of the client's problem changed?	Should the social worker withdraw treatment? Will the social worker and client successfully attain treatment objectives following withdrawal of the treatment?

	Phases		
Single-Subject Design Methodology	Baseline	Intervention (Treatment)	Follow-up
Information	Specification of treatment objectives into measurable problems. Measurement of nature, severity, and persistence of problem without intervention.	Measurement of changes in nature and severity of problem over time. Inferences about the attainment of objectives. Observations of treatment implementation.	Measurement of maintenance of changes. Provision of descriptive, correlational, and approximations to causal knowledge. Observations of the emergence of new problems.

each client, group, or system with which we work.

3. They focus on individual clients or systems. If there is any variation in effect from one client or system to another, single system designs will be able to pick it up. (pp. 14–15)

Bloom et al. (1993) claimed that clinical social workers can use single-subject designs in practice but not with every client. But this has not been the experience of those clinical social workers who have used this methodology. One of the underlying themes in a recent conference on clinical research was that social workers did not use the methodology or could not apply it to all practice situations. (Videka-Sherman & Reid, 1990). An approach offered by Gambrill and Barth (1980) is more moderate in perspective and indicates the potential utility of single-subject designs with respect to the levels of knowledge produced. Social workers can extend this approach by considering the levels of knowledge the designs can generate within and between phases of the components baseline, intervention, and follow-up (Table 1). For example, social workers can obtain descriptive knowledge of the severity of the problem within each of the three phases. They can obtain correlational knowledge of the intervention and problem severity by comparing observations in the intervention phase with

	Levels of Knowledge	Components of Single-Subject Design
	Descriptive	Obtained within any of the components: baseline, intervention, follow-up
	Correlational	Obtained by comparing observations between intervention and either baseline or follow-up
	Causal	Inferred by comparing observations among all three components and between additional design variations, such as the reinstitution of intervention, and by interviews

table 1 *Levels of Knowledge and Components of Single-Subject Design*

baseline or with follow-up observations. Clinical social workers can infer causal knowledge, which is only approximate, based on information on all components plus other information, such as interviewing, to help rule out alternative explanations for positive changes associated with the intervention. Causal knowledge also contains correlational and descriptive knowledge, and correlational knowledge also includes descriptive knowledge (Tripodi, 1983). Hence, a major argument for the use of single-subject designs is that they can provide different levels of knowledge that practitioners can use to assist them in making decisions about assessment, treatment implementation, and treatment evaluation (see Figure 5).

A second basic argument for the use of single-subject design methodology is that clinical social workers can use the resultant information to inform themselves, clients and their families, and the social workers' supervisors. Clinical social workers obtain information to use in practice decision making. Furthermore, social workers can use the information to show the client the extent to which he or she has progressed in relation to agreed on goals in the social worker–client contract, for example, by referring to simple graphs showing changes, positive or negative, over time. In addition, supervisors can learn which problems social workers are focusing on and whether

social workers have made progress in reducing or maintaining the extent of those problems. Supervisors might then use this information as a stimulus for discussing a particular client: Why is the intervention working? Is it appropriate for this client? Is the information reliable? What is the client's response when he or she sees a graph showing progress?

A third argument for the use of single-subject design methodology is that it produces information for the profession. Clinical social workers can accumulate a log of similar cases in which a particular intervention has or has not been effective. For example, a social worker may use a method of providing health information and knowledge about operations for close friends and relatives of a patient to reduce both the patient's and their anxiety. The social worker may find that 18 of 20 people showed a reduction in anxiety; hence, he or she justifiably retains that particular intervention in the clinical repertoire. In this way, clinical social workers also can systematize their experiences in using different interventions for their clients. Blythe and Briar (1985) have suggested that practitioners can use single-subject designs to develop models of empirically based practice, that is, prescriptions of what should be done and what is likely to be effective in specific practice situations.

As Bloom and Fischer (1982) indicated, clinical social workers can use information from single-subject designs to demonstrate accountability to clients and, if so employed, to the agency in which they work. Clinical social workers also can use this information for talks to community groups, for other presentations and conferences, and perhaps for publication of clinical cases.

ARGUMENTS AGAINST THE USE OF SINGLE-SUBJECT DESIGN METHODOLOGY

Thomas (1978), who has used single-subject designs and has advocated for their use in practice, argued that there are conflicts between practice and research in practice that uses single-subject designs. He has discussed the use of single-subject designs to produce causal knowledge by providing a number of experimental arrangements, the priority of which is more important than the immediate practice situation. By definition, he has set up a conflict between practice and research and then has proceeded to discuss their differences. In contrast to Thomas's discussion, the view presented in this book is more flexible in that the designs generate different levels of knowledge, following the ideas of Gambrill and Barth (1980). Moreover, the perspective in this book is that practice issues and decisions to help clients are the basic priorities; clinical social workers will use single-subject design methodology if it follows natural occurrences of practice and if the social workers can incorporate it as a tool within practice. For example, social workers routinely use procedures such as manipulation of one variable at a time, withholding of intervention, withdrawal of intervention before the client achieves treatment goals, short intervention periods, and extended baseline observations in experimentation to attempt to produce causal knowledge. However, social workers cannot invoke many of the approaches to produce knowledge. This does not mean clinical social workers cannot obtain useful knowledge; rather, they can obtain descriptive and correlational knowledge and approximations to causal knowledge in many practice situations.

Although single-subject design methodology does not fit all situations, this by no means is an indictment of the methodology. Not even all practice methods fit all practice situations. For example, medication and psychoeducational modalities might be applicable to people with chronic schizophrenia, but not to college students with situational anxiety during periods of examination. Differential diagnosis in practice is the basis on which one may decide to use or not use a particular intervention. Analogously, clinical social workers may more appropriately use different research methods, such as single-subject designs. Grasso and Epstein (1992) have discussed different procedures for using a variety of research methods other than single-subject design methodology.

However, a more difficult argument to overcome is one that affects many practice situations and evaluations of practice: How can social workers study the effects of a particular intervention when the client may be receiving other interventions from other sources? In multidisciplinary settings—for example, in a medical or psychiatric hospital—the client has contact with many professionals from which the client may receive intervention. In a neuropsychiatric hospital, a patient may receive occupational therapy, group counseling, individual counseling from a psychiatrist, or counseling from a clinical social worker. Interventions may overlap, precluding study of one intervention. Social workers can deal with this problem by assessing the degree to which the evaluation methodology (for example, single-subject design methodology) is appropriate. (See Chapter 4 for a discussion on the procedures for discerning the context of interventions.) In assessing the problem, the social worker may find that

- no other discernible intervention conflicts with the one he or she is evaluating; that is, the intervention is unique and the social worker can evaluate it using single-subject design methodology.

- the intervention and one or more other interventions overlap, so the social worker can only evaluate the joint effects of the interventions.

- the intervention and other interventions overlap, and the nature of the intervention is so ambiguous and diffuse that evaluation is unwarranted until the social worker can specify the interventions more precisely.

Another argument against the use of single-subject design methodology is that it is too mechanistic—it does not present the whole view of the person. Although the social worker uses systematic procedures, such as the repeated measurement of variables at baseline, those measures do not represent the whole person. Measurements are indices of the client's problems, selected for assessment and potential change through intervention. Any specification of a phenomenon, whether in practice (by prioritizing and focusing on specific features of a client in his or her situation) or in research (by systematically obtaining repeated measurements over time for a particular problem variable), reduces the phenomenon to a segment of its totality. However, the clinical social worker may still view the total situation of the client in his or her environment. The social worker can interpret in that context the specific findings of problem changes selected for work by the clinical social worker and the client.

Many clinicians have argued, though, that it is difficult, and perhaps impossible, to obtain baseline measurements. The social worker may approximate baseline measurements through retrospection or by using available data from other sources when there is insufficient time to obtain measurements before intervention (see Chapter 3). However, the proponents of this argument implicitly are looking at the use of single-subject design methodology to produce causal knowledge. The social worker can obtain descriptive knowledge by studying the trends in measurements within the follow-up phase. Moreover, he or she can derive correlational knowledge from the comparisons of measurements during the intervention and follow-up phases. For example, the clinical social worker may initiate an intervention immediately with a substance-abusing client. During intervention, the client reduces the substance abuse, and the clinical social worker and client believe the client has achieved the treatment goal. The social worker also takes measurements at follow-up to detect the possibility of relapse (a return to a condition of severe substance abuse). If, on the withdrawal of intervention, there is relapse, the clinical social worker can infer that there is a correlation between treatment and the severity of substance abuse. (See Chapters 2, 3, and 4 for procedures for determining correlational relationships.)

ORGANIZATION OF THE BOOK

Chapter 2, on measurement is basic to the other chapters. It presents the process of measurement and criteria for selecting simple, but useful measures. It describes problems that are typical for clients in mental health, industry, and other clinical settings and discusses the measurement of problems such as absenteeism, depression, anxiety, productivity, and stress.

Chapter 3 defines baselines, the first phase of the single-subject design model, and explicates their purposes for assessment and evaluation. Furthermore, the chapter presents arguments for and against the use of baselines. It details the process of constructing baselines, including the plotting and analysis of graphic patterns, statistical analysis, and the illustration of practice decisions. Moreover, it discusses procedures for simultaneous baselining of clients, situations, and problem variables.

Intervention, the second phase of the basic model, is discussed and defined in Chapter

4. The author provides methods for specifying interventions and discusses arguments for and against the use of measurement during this phase. In addition, the chapter illustrates comparisons of patterns of measurement at the intervention phase to the baseline phase and considers different patterns of change or no change with respect to clinical social workers' decisions.

Follow-up, the third phase of the model, is discussed and described in Chapter 5, which presents arguments for and against the use of measurements in this phase. The chapter illustrates the process of measurement during follow-up, shows how to derive patterns that are obtained by comparing follow-up to intervention and to baseline, and discusses those patterns with respect to practice decisions.

Chapter 6 presents three variations of the basic model: (1) multiple baseline design with clients, situations, or problems; (2) graduated intensity designs; and (3) natural withdrawal–reversal designs. The author presents arguments for and against the use of these designs and discusses inferences that the social worker can make about the effectiveness of interventions.

CHAPTER 2

MEASUREMENT

Fundamental to single-subject design is the measurement of practice problems during baseline, intervention, or follow-up. Through measurement, clinical social workers transform problem indicators into variables that have properties of measurement scales (Blythe & Tripodi, 1989; Corcoran & Fischer, 1987a; Hudson & Thyer, 1987). Clinical social workers are well aware of the many important variables pertaining to direct practice. These variables often are tied to treatment goals, for example, the reduction of anxiety, an increase in positive relationships with children, the elimination of child-abusing behavior, compliance with medical regimens to foster positive health, reduction of substance abuse, and increase in attendance at school and on the job.

The clinical social worker begins the transformation process of measurement by locating an indicator or indicators of the problem. Suppose the client has a problem with substance abuse. Potential indicators are the number of substances (alcohol or drugs) the client has taken during a fixed period, identification of drug use in urine analysis, reported use of drugs, and so on. The practitioner then operationally defines the indicators so that anyone following the same procedures will reliably specify each indicator on any one of four measurement scales: (1) nominal, (2) ordinal, (3) interval, or (4) ratio. The operational definition ("recipe") might include the following: The client should indicate his or her weekly severity of drug use on a seven-point scale in which 0 = no drug use, 1 = use of drugs one day a week; 4 = use of drugs four days per week, 7 = use of drugs seven days per week, and so forth. The clinical social worker transforms the problem of substance abuse into a variable of severity of

drug use, which he or she measures on a seven-point ordinal scale. Before intervention, a client may show high severity (7); after intervention, using this same operational definition, the clinical social worker and the client hope to attain the objective of 0 and register it as the measurement for the client.

MEASUREMENT SCALES

Measurement scales, then, are the end products of operational definitions (Table 2). The simplest measurement scale is the nominal scale—the researcher classifies objects into two or more categories that are mutually exclusive and exhaustive. For example, the categories "abused child" and "did not abuse child" are mutually exclusive because assignment of the client to one category precludes assignment to the other. The scale is exhaustive if the practitioner assigns all of the objects (in this case, people) to be classified to either of the two categories. Many variables in clinical social work are nominal, particularly variables related to decisions (for example, place in foster care/not place in foster care); diagnostic classification; characteristics of clients (such as gender, sexual orientation, or religious preference) and presence or absence of specified symptoms. Nominal scales perhaps are qualitative rather than quantitative because the practitioner need not assign numbers to the categories—A and B are just as useful as 1 and 2. However, the practitioner can use nominal scales quantitatively, for example, with the percentage or population of clients classified as schizophrenic in the *Diagnostic and Statistical Manual of Mental Disorders— 4th Edition* (DSM-IV) (American Psychiatric Association, 1994); the proportion of

table 2 *Measurement Scales*

Type of Scale	Properties of Scale	Examples of Variables
Nominal	Mutually exclusive categories	Abused child/Did not abuse child
	Exhaustive categories	Status of child: Remove from home; keep in home
Ordinal	Mutually exclusive categories	Degree of self-reported depression
	Exhaustive categories	Degree of comfort in
	Order among categories	discussing interpersonal conflicts
Interval	Mutually exclusive categories	Number of days in attendance at work
	Exhaustive categories	for the past month
	Order among categories	Number of work tasks
	Distance between adjacent categories	completed within designated period
Ratio	Mutually exclusive categories	Number of positive interactions with
	Exhaustive categories	spouse
	Order among categories	Amount of money
	Distance between adjacent categories	earned in part-time job
	A true zero point	

SOURCE: Blythe, B. J., & Tripodi, T. (1989). *Measurement in direct practice* (p. 30). Newbury Park, CA: Sage Publications. Adapted by permission.

client statements that are positive, neutral, or negative when discussing his or her spouse; and the proportion of interviews devoted to topics that represent interpersonal conflict.

Variables defined so that they satisfy the requirements of ordinal measurement scales contain the properties of nominal scales plus the property of order among categories. A 10-point rating scale to reflect a continuum of depression ranging from 0 = no depression to 10 = the greatest degree of depression possible is an ordinal scale. The numbers 0 through 10 are mutually exclusive and exhaustive, and the numbers between adjacent categories represent increased depression. Hence, 10 represents a category reflecting a greater degree of depression than 8, and so on. Although the practitioner may use numerals to represent categories in an ordinal scale, he or she should not treat them as having properties of numbers, because, for example, the practitioner does not know whether the degree of depression between 10 and 9 equals the differences between 9 and 8, 8 and 7, and so forth. Ordinal scales are useful in representing a particular client's perceptions of moods, feelings, and other subjective states, such as the degree of comfort in discussing interpersonal conflicts, the extent of fear in public speaking, the degree of anger toward significant others, the sense of betrayal by a spouse, and the degree of trust.

Interval scales have all the properties of nominal and ordinal scales plus the property of equidistance between adjacent categories. A clinical social worker in a corporate EAP may have the objective of reducing a client's substance abuse, thereby increasing the number of days the client attends work. The social worker may begin counting at an arbitrary date (hence, there is no true zero point as in ratio scales), represented by zero. Every day thereafter is a numerical category, with the difference between 9 and 8 days ($9 - 8 = 1$) exactly the same as the difference between 8 and 7 days ($8 - 7 = 1$). The social worker uses interval and ratio scales for counting, for example, the number of work tasks or homework assignments completed to reflect productivity at work and performance at school. The clinical social worker also may use interval scales to represent the amount of time (such as number of days) in which a client exhibits an absence (or presence) of symptoms.

Ratio scales contain all of the properties of nominal, ordinal, and interval scales; in addition, they contain an absolute zero point. The number of positive interactions a client has with a significant person over designated periods (for example, in one week) or the amount of money a client gains or loses are examples of ratio scales.

The social worker can use all of the scales in single-subject designs because he or she can obtain repeated measurements over time. These scales can represent a number of problems and needs involved in clinical practice.

TYPES OF VARIABLES

Blythe and Tripodi (1989) classified client variables into the following types: type 1, client characteristics; type 2, moods, feelings, attitudes, beliefs, and values; type 3, knowledge, ability, and achievement; and type 4, observable behavior. Type 1 variables, which the clinical social worker typically obtains from social histories or intake information, reflect physical and mental health statuses and social characteristics. They refer to the presence or absence of symptoms, medical and psychiatric classifications, and social information. The social worker can use those variables that show change, for example, from the presence of symptoms to their absence, in single-subject design. Nominal scales typically represent type 1 variables.

Either nominal or ordinal measurement scales can represent a type 2 variable, for example, a mood such as depression. Whereas a nominal scale would indicate whether depression (as defined by either the social worker or the client) is present or absent in a client, an ordinal scale would represent the degree (or severity) of depression on a specified scale. Practitioners often gear practice interventions toward changing clients' subjective states of moods, attitudes, beliefs, values, and feelings.

In contrast, practitioners gear many interventions toward changing the client's level of knowledge, ability, or achievement. Practitioners typically measure these type 3 variables, which are in the form of interval or ratio scales, as scores on objective tests (that is, the number of questions correctly answered). Whereas type 2 variables refer to subjective states that are neither correct nor incorrect, type 3 variables are objective—the number of correct responses indicates the degree of knowledge, ability, or achievement in selected areas. For example, a medical social worker who attempts to impart knowledge to clients about breast cancer can measure client gains by referring to or developing an objective knowledge test that would provide a score of the degree to which the client has learned.

Observations of behavior are type 4 variables. The client, social worker, or significant others directly observe these variables, which typically are in the form of interval or ratio scales. Hence, for instance, a spouse may observe the number of times her husband uses physical force to control their children, or she might observe the number of times her husband threatens her daily.

RELATIONSHIP OF VARIABLES TO ASSESSMENT AND EVALUATION

Repeated measurements on a variable at baseline can provide information regarding the extent of the problem. Moreover, baseline measurements can serve as a benchmark to evaluate the extent to which the pattern of subsequent measurements during the intervention differs from those at baseline.

Information about problem variables can pertain to existence (Blythe & Tripodi, 1989), magnitude, duration, or frequency (Corcoran & Fischer, 1987b). These categories correspond to measurement scales (Table 3). The existence of a problem refers to its presence or absence. Hence, a psychiatric client may or may not report that he or she is experiencing hallucinations; a medical patient may or may not be ambulatory; and a parent may or may not be physically abusive to her child.

Problem severity or magnitude is an indicator of the extent of the problem. On a scale of perceived client stress ranging from 0 = no stress to 10 = the highest degree of stress possible, a magnitude of 9 indicates a problem, whereas a score of 1 does not. Furthermore, if the severity of the problem continues at a relatively high degree of stress on repeated measurements during baseline, it indicates a persistently high degree of problem severity, which warrants an intervention to alleviate the stress.

Another indicator of problems is the duration: How long has the problem been occurring? A high degree of anxiety for one day is less problematic than a high degree of anxiety every day for two months, which

---

table 3 *Indicators of Problems*

Indicator	Type of Measurement Scale	Example
Existence of problem	Nominal	Presence of clinical symptoms; absence of clinical symptoms
Magnitude of problem (severity)	Ordinal	A high degree of problem severity on a scale ranging from low severity to high severity
Duration of problem	Interval	The length of time that a problem persists from an arbitrarily designated point in time; for example, the persistence of clinical symptoms for two months
Frequency of problem	Ratio	The number of times the problem occurs within a specified time interval, for example, 20 occurrences within two weeks

figure 6

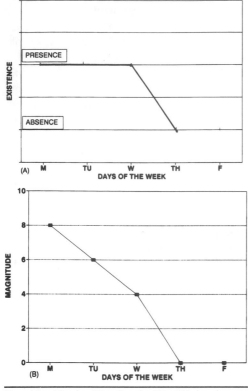

Graphs of Depression for a Five Day Period: Existence (A) and Magnitude (B)

NOTE: M = Monday, TU = Tuesday, W = Wednesday, TH = Thursday, F = Friday.

worker has obtained repeated measurements of depression for a client on five successive days of the week. Figures 6 and 7 are graphs that depict the existence, magnitude, duration, and frequency of depression for the same client. For each graph, the vertical (y) axis represents the indicator of depression and the horizontal (x) axis represents days of the week (Monday through Friday).

As Figure 6A shows, the client was depressed on Monday, Tuesday, and Wednesday, but not on Thursday or Friday. The figure, however, does not show the magnitude or frequency of occurrences. Figure 6B shows a decreasing magnitude from 8 to 6 to 4 from Monday to Tuesday to Wednesday, respectively, followed by 0 and 0 on both Thursday and Friday. Figure 6B shows the perceived daily intensity of depression, whereas Figure 7B indicates the number of depressive occurrences during each day: increases from 4 to 6 on Monday and Tuesday, respectively, and then decreases to 4, 0, and 0 on Wednesday, Thursday, and Friday, respectively. Figure 7A shows a decrease in duration from three of five days to zero per five-day period.

These data are informative during the baseline, intervention, or follow-up phase of single-subject design. Comparisons of patterns between intervention and between follow-up and baseline provide information clinical social workers can use to evaluate the extent to which there are or are not changes in indicators of depression. Methods for determining the extent of these changes are discussed in Chapters 3, 4, and 5.

CHARACTERISTICS OF USEFUL VARIABLES

A useful variable is one that practitioners can measure over time and use in each of the three phases of the single-subject design model. Practitioners can construct variables to uniquely represent a particular client or groups of clients. For particular clients, though, practitioners can only use the variables specific to those clients; they cannot generalize those variables to other

more likely is associated with difficulties in psychosocial functioning than is high anxiety for one day.

The frequency of problem occurrences within a designated period also indicates the nature of client problems. These frequency counts may be relatively trivial or life threatening, for instance, the number of cigarettes smoked, the number of drugs taken, the number of times a patient follows a prescribed medical regimen, the number of times a couple argues, and the number of perceived conflicts in a relationship.

Practitioners can plot on graphs these indicators over time. (Subsequent chapters present more detail on graphic analysis.) In addition, each indicator provides different information. Suppose a clinical social

clients. For example, a practitioner may construct a self-anchored rating scale of depression for a male client who, when he feels depressed, shows symptoms of fatigue and apathy. On a self-anchored rating scale of depression, 0 may represent no feelings of apathy and fatigue and 10 the highest degree of depression possible (extremely intense feelings of apathy and fatigue). Another client may consider thoughts of suicide and unexplained tears as symptomatic of depression; that client's ratings of depression are unique to him or her and cannot be compared with the other client. In contrast, the practitioner might obtain "depression" by using an instrument with the intent to have standardized definitions and response systems represent a generalizable variable of depression. For example, the Costello-Comrey Depression Scale (Corcoran & Fischer, 1987b) consists of 14 items, each of which the client rates on a nine-point scale ranging from 1 = absolutely not or never to 9 = absolutely or always. The sum of the responses represents a variable ranging from possible scores of 14 to 126. Examples of items are "I feel that life is worthwhile"; "I feel that there is more disappointment in life than satisfaction"; "I am a happy person"; and "I feel blue and depressed."

Characteristics of useful variables will vary depending on whether the clinical social worker intends the variable to be unique or generalizable across clientele with similar problems. Variables that produce generalizable information (that is, information produced by available standardized instruments) can provide information about a client compared with others; however, the information may not be specifically geared toward the client's unique needs and problems. Therefore, the following discussion of characteristics of useful variables distinguishes the unique from the generalizable. The five characteristics of useful variables are (1) relevance, (2) reliability, (3) validity, (4) feasibility, and (5) nonreactivity.

Relevance

The variable must be relevant to the problem the practitioner is measuring and to the

goals the social worker and the client have selected for treatment or intervention. The clinical social worker determines the relevance based on the contents of the variable and on his or her judgment. When the variable is unique to the client, relevance is at a maximum, because the definition of the variable is within the client's frame of reference, and both the social worker and the client can understand that definition. Hence, the contents of a rating scale of depression are relevant if the practitioner gears them toward the client's perceptions of depression and the goal of ameliorating that depression. In contrast, an instrument that attempts to measure depression and is standardized across a group of clients may or may not be relevant. The instrument is relevant if the items in the instrument are congruent with clinical usage of the term depression and if the items in the Costello-

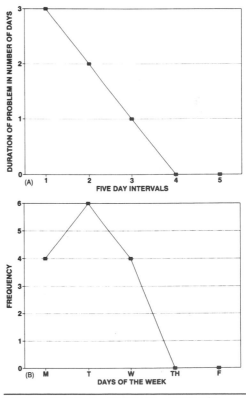

figure 7

Graphs of Depression for a Five Day Period: Duration (A) and Frequency (B)

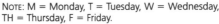

NOTE: M = Monday, T = Tuesday, W = Wednesday, TH = Thursday, F = Friday.

figure 8

Self-Ratings of Depression before Treatment

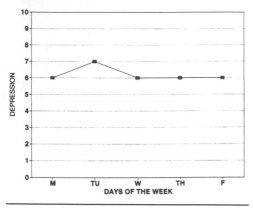

NOTE: M = Monday, TU = Tuesday, W = Wednesday, TH = Thursday, F = Friday.

Comrey Depression Scale (Corcoran & Fischer, 1987b) refer to satisfaction with life and generalized feelings of depression, but not to symptoms of depression such as fatigue, difficulty in sleeping, or withdrawal from interpersonal relationships. The contents are generally relevant depending on the social worker's conception of depression and depending on the fit of those contents with the particular client in treatment. Or, the contents are generally relevant if they appear to fit or be discrepant with items reflecting the client population's culture, economic status, or race.

Reliability

Reliability refers to the consistency of responses in measurement, given the same information on which to base judgments or responses. Corcoran and Fischer (1987a) referred to three approaches for determining the reliability of an instrument: (1) internal consistency, (2) test–retest reliability, and (3) parallel forms. Correlation coefficients that range from 0 to 1.00 assess the degree of reliability for these approaches; 0 represents no reliability and correlations of .8 or higher indicate an adequate degree of reliability.

Internal consistency refers to the extent to which the responses of many subjects on one-half of an instrument are highly corre-lated with their responses to the other half. Two related procedures are coefficient alpha and split half reliability. The practitioner determines coefficient alpha by randomly drawing one-half of the items from an instrument and then correlating it with responses with the other half. For example, responses to seven items randomly drawn from the Costello-Comrey Depression Scale (Corcoran & Fischer, 1987b) will correlate highly with responses to the other seven items if there is a high degree of internal consistency reflected in coefficient alpha. This type of reliability refers to the degree to which responses to the instrument are consistent at one point in time. It indicates whether the items in an instrument refer to the same variable, that is, whether the instrument is unidimensional. Split half reliability is similar, but the social worker obtains the items systematically by comparing responses to odd versus even items. Internal consistency is not relevant when constructing an instrument for one client because there is no variation from other subjects.

Test–retest reliability is the extent to which the same people make responses to an instrument at one point in time; the practitioner then correlates those responses with responses made at a later point in time. It reflects stability. For example, suppose the practitioner obtains the responses for a group of clients from an instrument designed to measure perceptions of anxiety. If the same group responds to the same instrument and if there are no changes in their situations at the two time periods, a high degree of correlation between the two sets of responses reflects test–retest reliability. Test-retest reliability is relevant for the selection of instruments for single-subject designs, because it is based on repeated measurements of variables over time. It is also pertinent for the individual client in that the practitioner may attain it when there is horizontal stability over time. Horizontal stability occurs when a line connecting points on a graph for repeated measurements over time is horizontal to—parallel with—the line representing 0 on the graph. For example, in Figure 8, self-ratings of depression stabilize at point 6 for the client who has had repeated measurements during baseline.

Another approach for determining reliability is parallel forms. The practitioner correlates responses to one instrument with responses to another form of the same instrument (that is, the contents of the items are similar but not identical). This approach is relevant to the measurement of reliability across subjects but is not germane to the measurement of a single client.

Interobserver reliability (Blythe & Tripodi, 1989), another type of reliability, is the extent to which two or more observers independently agree in their observations. The practitioner assesses interobserver reliability by correlation or by percentage agreement, which is calculated as the percentage of the total number of agreements out of the total number of statements. Clinical social workers can use interobserver reliability for single-subject designs or for research with many subjects, and with live observations, process recordings, taped recordings, or videotapes. Suppose a clinical social worker tape-records an interview with a client and is interested in observing the number of times a client makes negative comments about his or her mother during a 15-minute segment of the tape. The social worker and the client can define "negative comments" and discuss when to record them. The social worker tape-records the client's statements about the client's mother and then rates each sentence as positive, negative, or neutral. The social worker and the client rate the sentences separately and then compare them for percentage agreement. For example, they may have identified 20 sentences about the client's mother (Table 4). The social worker calculates percentage agreement as follows:

table 4 *Rating of Negative Comments by Client and Social Worker*

Sentence	Client	Social Worker	Agreement
1	1	1	Yes
2	1	1	Yes
3	1	0	No
4	0	0	Yes
5	0	1	No
6	1	1	Yes
7	1	1	Yes
8	1	1	Yes
9	0	0	Yes
10	1	1	Yes
11	1	1	Yes
12	1	1	Yes
13	1	1	Yes
14	0	0	Yes
15	1	1	Yes
16	1	1	Yes
17	0	0	Yes
18	0	0	Yes
19	0	0	Yes
20	0	0	Yes

NOTE: 0 = positive or neutral; 1 = negative.

$$\text{Percentage} \atop \text{agreement} = 100 \times \frac{\text{Number of agreements}}{\text{Total number of possible agreements}}$$

$$= 100 \times \frac{18}{20}$$

$$= 90 \text{ percent}$$

The social worker and the client agreed on 90 percent of their ratings. An acceptable degree of interobserver reliability is 70 percent to 80 percent agreement.

Validity

The two main types of validity considered in this book are content validity and empirical validity (Blythe & Tripodi, 1989). Content validity deals with the criteria of relevant contents of a conceptual sampling of representative contents in the measuring instrument. Content validity enables the social worker to judge whether the contents of the measuring instrument are measuring what they are supposed to measure. The social worker should base an instrument for measuring anxiety for one client on the client's definition of anxiety and his or her perception of whether he or she is anxious with respect to perceived relevant indicators. On the other hand, an instrument for assessing anxiety for many different clients should contain contents that are pertinent to all clients whom the social worker is measuring for anxiety. Zung's Self-Rating Anxiety Scale (Corcoran & Fischer, 1987a) contains items that indicate bodily symptoms and perceptions of fear, anxiety, and nervousness, for example, "I feel more nervous and anxious than usual"; "I am bothered by headaches, neck and back pains"; and "I am bothered by dizzy spells" (p. 300).

Conceptual sampling of item representativeness refers to whether the items used to indicate anxiety represent the possible situations in which anxiety occurs and the different types of indicators that are manifest. Zung's measure of anxiety represents most physical indicators and does include items referring to generalized feelings of anxiety. However, it does not refer to behaviors such as crying for no apparent reason, nor does it refer to anxiety about specific domains of behavior, such as performance anxiety, anxiety related to anticipated loss of a loved one, or anxiety regarding the failure to exhibit culturally expected behavior. Hence, Zung's measure may not be useful for a client with anxiety related to specific events in his or her family and with cultural expectations that are, for example, based on religious holidays and family interactions.

Empirical validity is a type of validity based on predictions in which the practitioner can use statistical methods. The practitioner uses empirical validity only when using instruments on the same variable for many clients. If the practitioner predicts the correlation of the score for the variable in question with an external criterion that is logically related, then the variable has empirical validity. There is no single criterion of empirical validity. There are as many criteria as there are predictions. Thus, when there is evidence of an expected prediction, the practitioner might use the term partial-validation, or indicate there is evidence of validity. The three basic types of empirical validity are (1) concurrent validity, (2) predictive validity, and (3) construct validity (see Bloom & Fischer, 1982; Blythe & Tripodi, 1989; Corcoran & Fischer, 1987b; Rubin & Babbie, 1993, for similar discussions and related concepts of validity).

With concurrent validity, the clinical social worker predicts that the variable measured by a particular instrument is correlated with the same variable measured by another instrument. For example, the practitioner should correlate subjects' responses to Zung's measure of anxiety with their responses to another measure of anxiety such as the Clinical Anxiety Scale (Corcoran & Fischer, 1987a, pp. 123–124), which contains items such as "I feel tense"; "I have spells of terror or panic"; and "My hands, arms, or legs shake or tremble." Or a diagnosed group of "anxious patients" should score higher on Zung's measure of anxiety than a group diagnosed as non-anxious.

The social worker obtains predictive validity by demonstrating that a correlation exists between the variable measured and the future occurrence of a behavior. For example, a questionnaire pertaining to attitudes toward drug use might produce scores related to positive or negative attitudes about drug use. The practitioner might predict that those subjects with positive attitudes (for instance, "Marijuana increases reaction time" and "The use of cocaine gives me a wider perspective of life's events") will be more likely to report substance abuse in the future. If the prediction is borne out, there is evidence pertaining to predictive validity of the questionnaire.

Construct validity is a prediction based on theoretical expectations between the variable measured and other variables. For example, the practitioner can predict that persons who indicate on self-ratings of depression they are depressed also will rate themselves as under stress and anxious. Hence, if the social worker correlates the responses of those persons to measures of depression, anxiety, and stress, there is evidence of construct validity.

Feasibility

Feasibility refers to the extent to which it is possible to use an instrument to obtain a measure of the variable in the context of clinical social work practice. The clinical social worker should gear the instrument to the language of the respondents and should ensure that the respondents can complete the instrument in a relatively short period. In addition, the clinician should have access to the information he or she will be using to measure the variable. Moreover, if the practitioner uses questionnaires or other paper-and-pencil formats, he or she should ensure that the respondents will understand the contents and be able to respond appropriately.

Feasibility is enhanced if the practitioner fully explains measurement procedures to the client. Furthermore, the clinical social worker who wishes to create instruments, such as questionnaires, forms, or self-rating scales, should develop them in consultation with clients, if possible. On the other hand, if using available instruments, the clinical social worker should explain why he or she is using them, what variables he or she is measuring, and how the social worker will use these variables to assess the degree to which the client is progressing in treatment.

Nonreactivity

Nonreactivity—the opposite of reactivity (Corcoran & Fischer, 1987b)—is a condition in which the process of measurement does not influence changes in behavior. The concern about reactivity is that the practitioner would be unable to attribute desirable changes to his or her intervention if the variable measured reacts to the measurement process. For example, if the social worker asked a client to monitor the number of times he or she had suicidal thoughts in a particular period—say one day—the number of times the client recorded suicidal thoughts daily might decrease over time owing to the influence of the measurement process. This state reactivity is unapparent if measurements over time at baseline are consistent, that is, there is test–retest reliability regarding the number of suicidal thoughts over time.

Contrary to Corcoran and Fischer's (1987b) apparent assumption, reactivity is only one possible explanation for change. Another explanation is that of spontaneous recovery, the reduction of a problem through natural occurrences, not as a result of any interventions. To distinguish a real change from reactivity, the practitioner would need to obtain repeated measurements for an extended period at baseline. Changes in reactivity presumably are short-lived, whereas consistency in the diminution of a problem may indicate spontaneous recovery. Hence, the lack of reactivity is related to the attainment of test–retest reliability in the variable the practitioner is measuring.

ARGUMENTS FOR MEASUREMENT

Measurement involves specifying the procedures for gathering data and classifying them into one of the measurement scales. Once such classification exists, it is possible to use statistical techniques to summarize large amounts of descriptive information and to make inferences to larger populations. With respect to single-subject designs, repeated measurements over time are called time series measurements, which the practitioner can summarize using statistical techniques and graphic analyses. Measurement provides quantitative information related to the achievement of treatment objectives. If the clinical social worker can translate treatment objectives into variables that the social worker can measure repeatedly, then he or she can make systematic comparisons from one period to another. Indeed, this is the basic rationale for using a single-subject design methodology.

The measurement process also is useful when the social worker must adhere to specified standards of practice to maintain a high degree of quality (as in quality assurance, in which the clinical social worker follows the best guidelines available for effective practice). Measurement provides a set of procedures for efficiently matching observed practice against prescribed standards for practice, providing information that the social worker and his or her supervisor can use to discuss the implementation of interventions. However, quantitative information is insufficient for supervision; qualitative information the practitioner obtains from clinical observations and interviews also is necessary to enable the supervisor and social worker to reflect on the barriers and facilitators to the achievement of practice standards.

Four interrelated arguments for incorporating measurement into clinical practice involve (1) precision, (2) objectivity, (3) documentation, and (4) communication (see Blythe & Tripodi, 1989, for a more complete exposition on the uses of measurement in direct practice). Measurement entails the use of relatively specific definitions of phenomena. If the definitions are clinically relevant, the social worker can compare changes in the phenomena to determine whether desired changes have occurred, obtained changes are maintained, relapse is prevented, or no changes are manifest. The social worker who uses graphs to make visual comparisons must specify the treatment or intervention objectives.

Clinical social workers may indicate that they deal with the whole person, rather than with one specific aspect of the client's behavior, attitudes, perceptions, knowledge, or skills, and that measurement is less relevant and possibly mechanistic and overly simplistic. This need not be the case. If the social worker is looking at the complete person, he or she typically will expect changes in the client's state or condition as a result of treatment. This is a situation of nominal scale measurement, in which specificity of the ingredients of the client's current state or condition enables the social worker to more precisely judge whether the client has achieved a desired new condition. For example, a client may exhibit several undesirable behaviors: alcohol abuse, spouse abuse, child abuse, low productivity in work, frequent absences from work, low self-esteem, and depression. All of those behaviors and moods form a complex condition, which the social worker can specify in a nominal scale of measurement, with categories such as "all specified undesirable ingredients are present" and "none of the specified undesirable ingredients is present."

Measurement can enhance objectivity in making judgments about the effectiveness of clinical practice objectives. The practitioner, client, or other persons can determine progress in treatment objectives and effectiveness (that is, the attainment of treatment objectives) by comparing observed changes in reference to a common benchmark measurement at baseline. If a specified point does not serve as an objective frame of reference, perhaps the subjective judgments of the client, clinical social worker, or relevant others will be distorted. The greater the period between intake—when the social worker first sees the client—and the social worker's observation of client progress, the more likely retrospective falsification—distortions—will occur, particularly when there are no observed benchmarks at baseline. The social worker may tend to recreate the past into the framework of present observations.

Measurement also facilitates record keeping—through videotapes, tape recordings, process recordings, and clinical notes, for example—by providing a frame of reference that is specified into observable measurement scales. Graphs, measurement scales, and other instruments provide information social workers can use in decision making at various stages of practice, from assessment to termination. These documents are evidence of the client's state or condition and of the clinical social worker's judgments at critical points in treatment. The social worker also can use the documents for future purposes. For example, through measurement, the social worker may compare his or her relative efficacy with different types of clients. This process can enable the social worker to develop a repertoire of interventions—to determine what intervention works best with what kind of clients, given the same objectives as specified in the measurement scales.

Furthermore, measurement facilitates communication. With a common frame of reference operationalized in observable terms, communication among clients, social workers, and their supervisors can be relatively reliable. The development of common definitions operationalized into concrete references can clarify treatment or intervention objectives. Graphs can demonstrate dramatic changes in clients, or they can clearly show a lack of change for important indicators of the client's problems.

ARGUMENTS AGAINST MEASUREMENT

On the other hand, measurement tends to oversimplify a client's problems, thus distorting them from their true meaning. Measurement enacts the use of rigorous procedures to enable practitioners to make objective comparisons. The practitioner specifies the criteria for measurement, but these criteria are arbitrary—they are relevant for some, but not all clients. However, standardized definitions will enhance communication. All disciplines prioritize the selection of measurement devices for creating variables. As the researcher accumulates information about variables, especially those associated with the presence or absence of well-defined interventions, the measurements become increasingly valid. If the researcher does not gather information about the relationship of other variables to the variable he or she is measuring, then the measurement is indeed mechanical.

Furthermore, measurement ignores qualitative information. Measurement involves the process of translating qualitative information from data such as open-ended interviews, narratives, and participant observation into nominal or ordinal scales. The clinical social worker cannot—and should not—easily convert all qualitative information into quantitative information. Historical information about the perceived dynamics of the client's interactions with friends, family, employer, and the clinical social worker can be quite fruitful in the development of clinical hypotheses, the generation of interventions, and the understanding of facilitators and barriers to practice effectiveness. Obviously, the social worker ignores qualitative information when he or she does not attempt to transform it into a measurement scale; however, qualitative information is not necessarily irrelevant for single-subject designs. Chapters 4, 5, and 6 suggest how clinical social workers can use qualitative information to provide additional knowledge about the relative control of internal validity threats. Hence, qualitative information can supplement quantitative data in single-subject designs by providing descriptive data, suggestive insights, and additional information for verifying causal relationships between interventions and their outcomes.

The clinical social worker can easily incorporate the process of devising measurement scales when he or she uses the measurement primarily with a single client. Such a process does not take much additional time. However, the development of instruments for use with many clients, including the establishment of norms and data regarding reliability and validity, requires a great deal of time; primarily clinical researchers should undertake such development. Clinical social workers should develop measures for single-client systems and use already available measuring devices to measure multiple numbers of clients so that the time required to develop measures does not hinder the conduct of practice.

Another argument against measurement is that the process of measurement distorts practice. The social worker can incorporate the process of measurement into practice. It does not require that practice accommodate to research procedures; rather, practice must be systematic. The types of practice that call for specificity of treatment goals and evaluation of effectiveness no more distort practice than does the incorporation of measurement devices into some aspects of practice. The position in this book is that measurement, like single-subject design methodology, is a tool of practice. Not all practice is measurement, nor is all practice single-subject design methodology. However, measurement as part of single-subject designs can facilitate aspects of practice (such as the provision of feedback to clients, social workers, and supervisors in the form of graphs).

STANDARDIZED INSTRUMENTS

Standardized instruments are forms for gathering data and categorizing them into variables that are operationally defined, have acceptable degrees of reliability and validity, and may have norms or average scores for specified populations. Instruments may be paper-and-pencil tests, questionnaires, interviewing schedules, observation forms, and so forth. To be feasible for use in clinical practice, instruments should be standardized, short, easy to administer and to score, and focused on problems encountered in clinical practice. Such instruments, called rapid assessment instruments, are readily available in *Measures for Clinical Practice: A Sourcebook* (Corcoran & Fischer, 1987b). That book includes 125 rapid assessment instruments that are categorized by populations (for example, adults, children, couples, and families) and by problem areas (for example, anxiety, family functioning, marital–couple relationship, self-efficacy, social support, and stress). Instruments also are available in sourcebooks such as *Family Assessment Inventories for Research and Practice* (McCubbin & Thompson, 1987) and in journals pertaining to social problem areas such as gerontology, public health, and drug and alcohol addictions.

The clinical social worker should use standardized instruments if they are appropriate to and can facilitate his or her practice. For single-subject design methodology incorporated into clinical social work practice, it is preferable that the social worker use rapid assessment instruments because they do not require much time to administer and because the social worker can use them for repeated measurements.

The clinical social worker should appraise available instruments for their content, reliability, validity, and possible norms. To illustrate how a clinical social worker could decide whether or not to use a rapid assessment instrument, refer to Hudson's Index of Self-Esteem (ISE) (Corcoran & Fischer, 1987a, pp. 188–189) in Appendix 1. First, the clinical social worker should look at the ISE items. If the social worker is working with white middle-class adults, the contents of the questionnaires appear to be relevant because of the norms established for this questionnaire (Cocoran & Fischer, 1987a). However, it is unclear whether the contents could be useful for African Americans, and they are not recommended for children.

Reliability is adequate because alpha = .93 (an index of internal consistency) and stability or test–retest reliability is .92. An adequate degree of reliability is .80 or higher (Corcoran & Fischer, 1987a). Validity also is adequate because the contents of the instrument apparently are related to self-esteem and the instrument is measuring what it is supposed to measure.

The section Description (Corcoran & Fischer, 1987a) indicates that the clinical social worker can use ISE scores to identify clinical problems (scores above 30 ± 5, that is, scores ranging from 25 to 35, are indicators of clinical problems). Hence, the social worker can compare a client's score with the norms to determine whether the client has a clinically significant problem.

DEVELOPING MEASURES

The clinical social worker can use standardized instruments to make comparisons among many clients or for a single client. Often it may be impossible to locate standardized instruments relevant to the clinical social worker's tasks and objectives with a particular client. In that case, the social worker can develop an instrument that is unique to the client. Easily developed instruments include self-anchored rating scales, rating scales, systematic observations, and questionnaires.

Self-Anchored Rating Scales

A self-anchored rating scale is a scale in which the client rates a dimension chosen by the client and his or her social worker. The scale represents a continuum ranging from a very low point to a very high point. There could be as few as three points and as many as 100. However, it is recommended that the range of scalar points be as low as five and as high as nine (Bloom & Fischer, 1982). For example, a female client who has difficulty expressing feelings (positive or negative) toward her adult daughter may use a five-point scale in which 1 = "I cannot tell my daughter how I feel about anything concerning her," 3 = "Half of the time I can tell my daughter how I feel about

many things concerning her," and 5 = "I can tell my daughter how I feel about anything concerning her." The client also might use a nine-point scale in which 1 = "I can never tell my daughter how I feel about her," 5 = "Sometimes I can tell my daughter how I feel about her," and 9 = "I can always tell my daughter how I feel about her." The client can use either scale to rate the degree to which she can express her feelings about her daughter to her daughter. Bloom and Fischer (1982, pp. 170–172) have recommended the following procedures for constructing self-anchored rating scales:

Prepare the client. Explain the concept of a continuum representing the lowest and highest points of a problem on which the social worker and the client have agreed. The client should understand the lowest and highest points of the scale; therefore, the client should define the points with the social worker's assistance. If the social worker and the client follow this procedure, the content validity is high because it is relevant to the client's perception of the problem.

Select the number of scale points. Use an odd number of points, with the middle point representing the halfway point on the scale. Scales with five, seven, or nine points are preferable because clients can effectively discriminate among the various points. Discriminating scale points is much more difficult and ambiguous with scales that have more points.

Use equal intervals. The client should regard distances between adjacent numbers, say 5 and 6 on a nine-point scale, as equal to distances between any other adjacent numbers on the scale, that is, 1 and 2, 2 and 3, 8 and 9, and so on.

Use one dimension. Refer to only one attitude, behavior, or mood. Using more than one dimension (for example, intelligent–stupid or rigid–flexible) is less accurate than using only one, and it leads to ambiguity in interpretation.

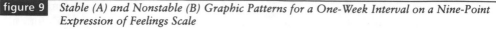

figure 9 *Stable (A) and Nonstable (B) Graphic Patterns for a One-Week Interval on a Nine-Point Expression of Feelings Scale*

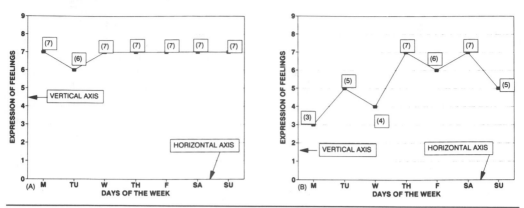

NOTE: M = Monday, TU = Tuesday, W = Wednesday, TH = Thursday, F = Friday, SA = Saturday, SU = Sunday.

Anchor the scale points. As a minimum, the clinical social worker should define through concrete examples the extreme ends (for example, 1 and 9 on a nine-point scale) and the middle value of a scale. The examples should be from the client's point of view, hence the notion of self-anchoring. The clinical social worker should ensure that the client understands how the scale works. Moreover, he or she should refer to the client's specific situation, thinking about how the client might feel if he or she selects any of the scale points.

Decide when, where, and how often. The clinical social worker discusses with the client when to use the scale, where to use it, and how often to use it. When using such an instrument for assessment at baseline, it is important to use standardized procedures. For each measurement, the social worker should follow the same procedures. For example, the client may make a rating once per day at the same time, right after dinner, and at the same place, in the living room. In addition, the practitioner should specify the frequency of measurement, such as once a week for one week. Adhering to the same specific procedures aids in increasing the instrument's reliability.

Use as repeated measures. The clinical social worker can use self-anchored rating scales for repeated measurements. If he or she uses these scales at baseline without in-

troducing an intervention, then he or she can obtain an estimate of reliability. (Chapter 3 presents a statistic that can provide evidence of stability in the baseline pattern.) A consistent pattern that is parallel to the horizontal axis would indicate stability or test–retest reliability. For example, Figure 9 shows the relative differences between reliable and unreliable data over time. Figure 9A is relatively stable and is parallel to the horizontal axis, whereas Figure 9B is relatively unstable and is not parallel to the horizontal axis.

Rating Scales

Rating scales are scales used by persons other than the client, typically the clinical social worker or persons important to the client. The rater uses rating scales as measures during baseline, intervention, and follow-up and for assessment, monitoring progress, and evaluation. Just as in a self-anchored rating scale, a rating scale represents a continuum of ordinal measurement ranging from a low to a high degree on a specified dimension. Many standardized instruments comprise a number of items to which a client responds with the same scale; then the scale's values are added to form a variable. These rating scales differ from self-anchored rating scales in that they use the same reference points with the same ostensive meaning for all persons responding to each item. An example is the Marital Happiness Scale (Corcoran &

Fischer, 1987a, pp. 458–459) used for couples and families. The 10 areas of marriage listed are (1) household responsibilities, (2) child rearing, (3) social activities, (4) money, (5) communication, (6) sex, (7) academic (or occupational) progress, (8) personal independence, (9) spouse independence, and (10) general happiness. For each area, the client rates how happy he or she currently is on a scale ranging from 1 = completely unhappy to 10 = completely happy. The social worker can use a scale for each area or obtain a total score of marital happiness by adding the scores for each item, with a possible range of 10 to 100.

Clinical social workers can devise rating scales to measure changes in clients over the course of an intervention. Tripodi and Epstein (1980, pp. 190–199) have discussed several principles for constructing rating scales when standardized rating scales are unavailable.

Specify treatment objectives. Measures should be relevant to the treatment objectives that the social worker and client have selected as the object of intervention. The social worker should then operationally define the treatment objectives and determine whether change is expected in client attitudes, moods, behaviors, relationships, and so forth. Having specified a mood change—for example, anxiety—the clinical social worker should consider what indicators he or she wants to use. The social worker could define anxiety globally with respect to the client's perception of it or could create various indicators of anxiety, constructing rating scales for each indicator, such as sleep disturbances, loss of appetite, feeling of "butterflies" in the pit of one's stomach, dryness of mouth, and so forth. This process results in the specification of one or more dimensions to be rated on an ordinal measurement scale.

Determine whether the social worker can use existing rating scales. The social worker should use existing rating scales if available. He or she should consult Corcoran and Fischer (1987a), professional journals, compendia of research instruments, research centers, and so forth.

Determine who will do the ratings. The person other than the client who does the rating should be one who is in a position to observe the client, is relatively objective, and has the time and the inclination to make ratings. If the clinical social worker is not making the ratings himself or herself, the social worker should explain the dimensions being rated to the rater, who might be the client's spouse or other significant relative, friend, employer, or teacher. The conditions for rating should be the same from rating to rating, and the social worker should instruct the rater on how often to make ratings. For example, a group worker may make ratings of cooperation for a particular client every group meeting at the end of each session.

Construct stimulus and response systems. In rating scales, the stimulus refers to the question, set of instructions, or statements to which the rater is supposed to respond. Stimuli can take the form of narratives that describe sets of behaviors, single sentences, phrases, words, or questions. Response systems represent the formats within which the ratings are made. They are similar to the response systems in closed-ended questions. In the Severity of Depression Scale (Figure 10) severity of depression is the stimulus, and the numbers 1 through 9 are the response categories. The statements under scale steps 1, 3, 5, 7, and 9 are the anchoring illustrations—they promote the reliability of the ratings.

As with closed-ended items, the response categories are mutually exclusive and exhaustive. The following are six possible stimuli and response systems for rating a client's level of anxiety (Tripodi & Epstein, 1980):

1. **Presence or absence of symptom**
   Appearance of anxiety

   0 = Absent
   1 = Present

2. **Adverbial scales of frequency of symptom**

figure 10 *Severity of Depression Scale*

Severity of Depression

1	2	3	4	5	6	7	8	9
+		+		+		+		+
Not Depressed		Slightly Depressed		Moderately Depressed		Strongly Depressed		Severely Depressed

How often is the client anxious?

1 = Very infrequently
2 = Infrequently
3 = Frequently
4 = Very frequently

3. Adverbial scales of severity of symptom
How anxious is the client?

1 = Not at all anxious
2 = Slightly anxious
3 = Moderately anxious
4 = Strongly anxious
5 = Severely anxious

4. Frequency scales by percentage
About what percentage of the time is the client anxious?

```
 0 =   0%
 1 =   1%– 10%
 2 = 11%– 20%
 3 = 21%– 30%
 4 = 31%– 40%
 5 = 41%– 50%
 6 = 51%– 60%
 7 = 61%– 70%
 8 = 71%– 80%
 9 = 81%– 90%
10 = 91%–100%
```

5. Frequency designated by time intervals
About how often does the client appear anxious?

1 = Once a month or less
2 = Once every two weeks
3 = Once a week
4 = Twice a week
5 = Every other day
6 = Daily

6. Likert scale (with or without neutral category)

The client appears anxious

1 = Strongly agree
2 = Agree
3 = Uncertain
4 = Disagree
5 = Strongly disagree
   or
1 = Strongly agree
2 = Agree
3 = Disagree
4 = Strongly disagree

(pp. 193–194)

The clinical social worker might construct these suggested formats. He or she should use only one dimension (concept) for each scale and avoid having too few or too many response categories; scales from four to nine categories are preferable. Furthermore, the raters should completely understand the dimension and the response system.

Minimize bias in the stimulus and response systems. The social worker should avoid bias in instructions to the rater; instructions must be clear and direct. As much as possible, the social worker should avoid value-laden terms in the stimuli and should instruct raters to be honest and objective in their ratings. The social worker should balance the response systems, with no obvious biases favoring any of the response categories.

Write instructions. The practitioner should provide the rater with clear instructions and examples of how to use the scales. The more specific the instructions (for example, "Circle the response that most clearly reflects your opinion"), the greater the degree of reliability in using the rating scale.

Pretest and implement the rating scales. The social worker should test the rating scales before using them. He or she should look for clarity of instructions, ambiguity in concepts, lack of understanding in their application, and possible biases. The practitioner can use the scales in an actual situation similar to the one for which they are designed or in a role-play situation. After use, the clinical social worker should seek the opinions of the raters on how to make the scales more standardized; if necessary, the social worker should modify the scales. On implementation of the scales, the clinical social worker should ensure that the conditions for rating are as standardized as possible.

Systematic Observations

Clinical social workers are participant observers of the treatment or intervention process. However, it is not recommended that social workers make systematic observations—that is, observations of behaviors during specified time segments that social workers rate on a measurement scale in the form of rating scales, tally sheets, or checklists—so they may measure while simultaneously conducting practice. The reasons are that they may distort the observations and may not adequately implement the intervention. Systematic observations, though, are useful under two conditions: (1) The social worker makes a videotape or an audio-videotape of clinical sessions to later observe behaviors or events that occurred in those sessions; and (2) the clinical social worker teaches a significant person in the client's life (such as a relative, friend, or employer) to systematically observe during specified periods.

Through systematic observations, the clinical social worker might observe the frequency of themes in interviews, the extent to which the client makes eye contact, the degree to which a client's utterances (sentences) about himself or herself or others are positive or negative, the attentiveness of members in group sessions, and so forth. The social worker applies the same principles for developing rating scales when constructing rating scales for systematic observations. For example, a group worker might use a tally sheet—a paper on which observers indicate how many times an event occurs—to record how many times a particular member leaves the group and returns or the amount of time that a client talks or is silent. On a checklist, the social worker indicates whether a behavior occurs. A checklist for observing a client's interactions with other group members and with the group leader might look like the following:

Gazes at leader	X
Talks to leader	
Listens to leader	X
Gazes at a group member	
Talks to a group member	
Listens to a group member	

The pattern indicates that the client gazed and listened to the leader, but did not engage in any other behaviors.

Clinical social workers can use systematic observations in single-subject design to develop measures within sessions. The social worker should apply several principles adapted from Tripodi and Epstein (1980, pp. 54–74 and pp. 103–120) when constructing an instrument for systematic observations.

Determine the object of observation. The clinical social worker and client or supervisor can independently observe their participation in a session that the social worker has tape-recorded or videotaped. Suppose, for instance, that a clinical social worker wishes to observe aspects of family interaction in a segment of a clinical interview with a father, a mother, and their son. What the social worker wishes to observe is how much time each person speaks and how many utterances each person makes within the middle half hour of an hour session.

Specify the source of the information. The source of information in the preceding family interaction example is a tape recording. However, videotape, live observations, or process notes might be other sources. The source the social worker uses should be relevant to what he or she is observing.

Indicate the unit of analysis. The unit of analysis is the segment of information from the source being observed. When the source is a tape recording, the unit is a work unit that could range from single words or sentences to interview segments or the entire interview. In the family interaction example, the unit is a sentence. For example, the social worker could observe the number of sentences each of the family members uttered within a half-hour interview segment, as well as the amount of time each family member spent talking.

Operationally define the variables. The social worker operationally defines variables when he or she observes them on a measurement scale. The clinical social worker can develop a form for this purpose that is simple, easily readable, and readily convertible to measurement. For example:

Number of sentences spoken in a half-hour interview:

Father	_____
Mother	_____
Son	_____
Therapist	_____
Total	_____

Amount of time spent talking in a half-hour interview:

Father	_____
Mother	_____
Son	_____
Therapist	_____
Total	_____

The clinical social worker would listen to the tape recording after the first 15 minutes of the hour interview and count the number of sentences spoken and the time each

family member spent talking. For example, the social worker might note that the father speaks most of the time (50 percent); followed by the mother (45 percent); followed by the son (5 percent). An objective of treatment may be to increase the talk time for the son; the social worker would discern this objective from repeated measurements at baseline and during intervention.

Test for reliability. Because the social worker will use the measures to detect changes over time, the relevant type of reliability is test–retest reliability, which is consistency in observation over time. The clinical social worker can test reliability by listening to the tape recording and by classifying a sample of sentences—say 20— with respect to who (that is, father, mother, or son) is uttering them. The social worker can repeat the same task one week later and then classify the 20 sentences as shown in Table 5. A comparison of time 1 and time 2 reveals agreement on 19 out of 20 sentences. The social worker would then calculate percentage agreement as follows:

$$\text{Percentage agreement} = 100 \times \frac{19}{20}$$
$$= 95 \text{ percent}$$

This is an acceptable degree of reliability.

Gather and analyze the information. The last step in the systematic observation process is to gather and analyze the data. The social worker could show on a bar graph (Figure 11) the amount of time each person spends talking. The figure indicates that the son talked more in interviews 3, 4, and 5 than in interviews 1 and 2. The social worker also can plot on a graph the number of sentences spoken (Figure 12).

Questionnaires

Questionnaires—sets of instructions, questions, and response systems that contain open-ended or forced-choice responses— are useful when the clinical social worker wishes to obtain information from more than one client. The social worker can obtain data from groups of clients at intake,

table 5 *Test–Retest Reliability Information for Classifying Speakers of Sentences as Father, Mother, or Son*

Sentence	Time 1	Time 2
1	F	F
2	M	M
3	F	F
4	M	M
5	F	F
6	M	M
7	S	S
8	F	F
9	F	F
10	F	F
11	M	M
12	F	M
13	M	M
14	F	F
15	M	M
16	F	F
17	M	M
18	F	F
19	M	M
20	M	M

NOTE: F = father; M = mother; S = son.

from a caseload, or from clinical practice with a group. In single-subject design, he or she can create measures for group practice by averaging information for all of the group members.

The social worker should adhere to the following principles when constructing questionnaires for group practice measures (the principles have been adapted from Epstein & Tripodi, 1977, pp. 10–19).

Specify the purpose. The purpose is to obtain information from clients who are members of a group. For example, a clinical social worker may construct a questionnaire to gather information from five clients about their satisfaction with the discussion of their problems in a group devoted to problem solving.

Decide on the information desired. The social worker should know what type of information he or she needs to develop measures. For group practice, as a minimum, the social worker needs identifying information: name of the client, date, and the session number for the group. Other information he or she obtains should pertain to the purpose. For example, the social worker might obtain data about a problem a client wishes to discuss, the amount of time spent on the problem, and the client's satisfaction with the group process in discussing the problem.

Decide on the format. The format of the questionnaire includes a description of the purpose of the questionnaire and how the social worker will use it, directions for answering the questionnaire, and the questions or stimuli and the response system. It is preferable to use mostly forced-choice questions and only a few open-ended questions so that the social worker can tabulate responses more easily. Epstein and Tripodi (1977, pp. 12–13) provided several

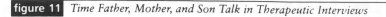

figure 11 *Time Father, Mother, and Son Talk in Therapeutic Interviews*

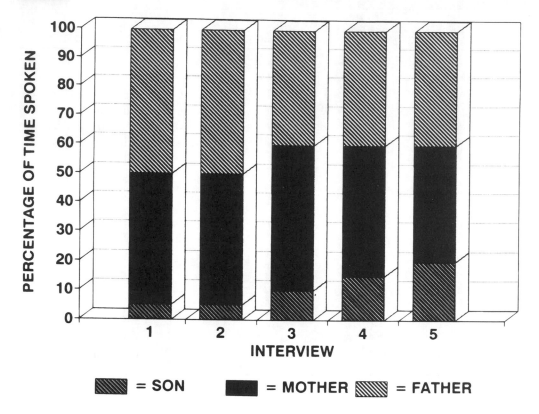

examples of response systems for the same question about a homemaker:

• An open-ended question might be as follows: In what ways would a homemaker be most useful to your family? _____.
• Closed questions might be as follows: (1) Would a homemaker be helpful to you in dealing with your current family problems?
Yes ___ No ___
(2) Indicate how much you agree or disagree with the following statement: A homemaker would be helpful to me in dealing with my current family problems (Check one):

> Strongly agree ___
> Agree ___
> Disagree ___
> Strongly disagree ___

• Frequency of response scales could have (1) adverb modifiers: If a homemaker were available, how frequently would you need that person's services? (Check one)

Frequently ___
Occasionally ___
Never ___

(2) numerical modifiers: If a homemaker were available to you, on how many days of the week would you need that person's services? (Check one):

> Seyen ___ Six ___
> Five ___
> Three or Four ___
> One or Two ___
> None ___

or (3) percentages: If a homemaker were available to you, what percentage of your family problems would be solved? (Check one):

> 75%–100% ___
> 50%–74% ___
> 25%–49% ___
> 0%–25% ___

• Comparative response scales might be: Compared with other services you currently needs, how important are home-maker services? (Check one):

> Very important ___
> Somewhat important ___
> Unimportant ___.

• An identification response question could be stated: Below is a list of ways in which a homemaker could be helpful to you. Please check those areas in which you could most use that person's help. (Check as many as apply):

Help with housecleaning   _____
Help with budgeting   _____
Help with child management   _____
Help with prepared meals   _____

The clinical social worker should only use one or two response systems. Note that the response alternatives should be clear and mutually exclusive (that is, they should not overlap). The format for the questionnaire on group practice might be open-ended responses and a closed (multiple choice) response system such as follows:

> Strongly agree ___
> Agree ___
> Disagree ___
> Strongly disagree ___

Construct the questionnaire. The questions and responses should be unbiased and clear, and each question should contain only one thought. The questionnaire should be geared to the vocabulary of the clients, and it should be understandable and easy to complete in a relatively short period. For example, a questionnaire for group practice might look like the following:

The purpose of this questionnaire is to provide information about the extent to which the group discusses your problems and your satisfaction with the group process. The group leader will use the information only to provide feedback to you and the other group members. Please respond to each of the following questions.

1. Including today's session, how many group meetings have you attended? ___
   _____

2. (a) Describe the problem you wanted to discuss today. _____
   _____

   (b) How much time was spent on your problem in the group session (approximately, in minutes)? _____

   (c) Indicate the extent to which you were satisfied or dissatisfied with the following statements by checking that response that best describes your opinion:

   My problem was thoroughly discussed.
   Strongly agree ___ Agree ___
   Disagree ___ Strongly disagree ___

   I received good ideas from the group leader.
   Strongly agree ___ Agree ___
   Disagree ___ Strongly disagree ___

   The members of the group gave me useful information.
   Strongly agree ___ Agree ___
   Disagree ___ Strongly disagree ___

   I was satisfied with the group process today.
   Strongly agree ___ Agree ___
   Disagree ___ Strongly disagree ___

3. Please fill in your name and the date.
   Name _____
   Date _____

figure 12

Number of Sentences Spoken by Son during Five Interviews

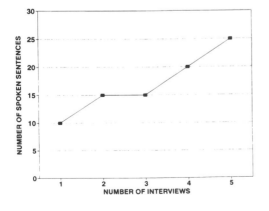

After you have completed this questionnaire, give it to the group leader. Thank you.

Pretest the questionnaire. After constructing the questionnaire, the clinical social worker should pretest it with group members to see whether they understand the instructions and whether the task of completing the questionnaire is reasonable. If necessary, the social worker should modify the questionnaire to facilitate client responses.

Administer the questionnaire and tabulate the results. The social worker should administer the questionnaire in the same way for each group session. For example, he or she could give it at the end of the group session; the group would return the completed questionnaire to the social worker. At the beginning of the next session, the social worker would present responses from group members in terms of satisfaction. For example, the results of the first session might be as follows:

- Two out of five members agreed or strongly agreed that the group thoroughly discussed their problem.

- Four out of five agreed or strongly agreed that they received good ideas from the group leader.

- One out of five agreed or strongly agreed that the members of the group gave them useful information.

- Four out of five agreed or strongly agreed that they were satisfied with the group process today.

For examples of instruments included in the book by Corcoran and Fischer (1987a), refer to Appendixes 1, 2, 7, and 11. Clinical social workers who work in substance abuse programs, EAPS, child and family agencies, and psychiatric and medical social work settings can use these instruments. All of them form variables that social workers can use in single-subject designs.

CHAPTER 3

PHASE 1: BASELINE

DEFINITION OF BASELINE

The first phase of single-subject design is constructing the baseline. In this phase, the clinical social worker takes repeated measurements of variables related to treatment objectives typically at equally spaced intervals over time. The social worker then interconnects and displays the repeated measurements on a graph; the resulting pattern is the baseline, which the social worker uses to make inferences pertinent to assessment and evaluation. Measurements can reflect magnitude (or severity), frequency, duration, or existence of a problem. Baselines can consist of as few as three measurements or can contain as many measurements as necessary to achieve horizontal stability, that is, a line that is parallel to the x axis on a graph (Barlow & Hersen, 1984). This chapter discusses the basic principles clinical social workers can use to construct and read graphs that depict baselines.

Figure 13 provides six examples of baseline graphs—three each for each partner in a married couple seeking counseling. After the first exploratory session, the clinical social worker asked Jack and Jill, the married couple, to each complete three instruments—the Index of Marital Satisfaction (Corcoran & Fischer, 1987a, pp. 443–444); the Index of Self-Esteem (ISE) (Appendix 1); and the Self-Rating Anxiety Scale (SAS) (Corcoran & Fischer, 1987a, pp. 371–379)—every day for one week. The social worker scored each instrument and plotted graphs that reflected the magnitude of the problem.

The social worker observed that both Jack and Jill are dissatisfied with their marriage; both their scores are above the critical score of 30 for all of their measurements, which indicates a clinical problem (Figure 13A). Moreover, their graphic patterns are relatively horizontal, that is, parallel to the x axis, indicating a persistent problem for the seven days of measurements. However, Jack has relatively low self-esteem compared with Jill, who has a high degree of self-esteem (Figure 13B). Yet, Jack does not show he is anxious, whereas Jill's anxiety has been increasing so that it is becoming a clinical problem (Figure 13C). These graphic patterns provide information the clinical social worker can use to probe further in his or her assessment of the clinical situation, formulation of treatment goals, and the evaluation of treatment effectiveness. The social worker, for example, may have goals of reducing the anxiety in Jill, increasing self-esteem in Jack, and increasing marital satisfaction for both Jack and Jill.

PURPOSE OF BASELINE

The two basic functions of baselines are (1) to provide information for assessment and (2) to serve as a frame of reference for evaluation (Bloom & Fischer, 1982). For assessment purposes, baseline graphs can provide information on the magnitude of the problem and its persistence, assuming that the variables the social worker is measuring indicate relevant problems. From Figure 13, it is clear that marital satisfaction inventories are pertinent to marital counseling. However, anxiety and self-esteem may or may not have been relevant. Jack may have complained about his lack of self-esteem in the first interview, and the clinical social worker may have used ISE

figure 13

Baselines of Marital Dissatisfaction (A), Self-Esteem (B), and Anxiety (C) for Jack and Jill over One Week

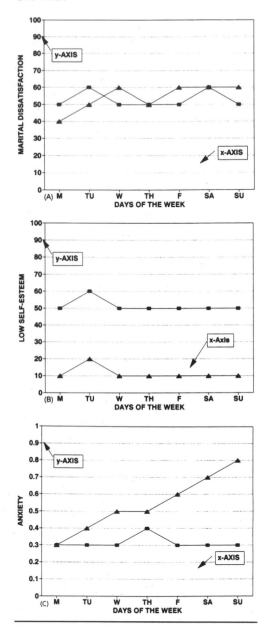

NOTE: M = Monday, TU = Tuesday, W = Wednesday, TH = Thursday, F = Friday, SA = Saturday, SU = Sunday.

couples seeking marital counseling, one partner or both often exhibit signs of anxiety. That anxiety is becoming a problem for Jill is clinically relevant because it is of high magnitude and is becoming worse (Figure 13C). However, the social worker cannot discern from the graphs other possible problems such as depression, spouse abuse, or extramarital affairs. These problems, if they exist, would emerge in the clinical interview when the social worker would notice discrepancies in Jack's and Jill's graphic patterns regarding self-esteem and anxiety. The social worker would explore with them the reasons for their marital dissatisfaction and what they want to do about it.

The second major function of a baseline is to serve as a frame of reference or benchmark against which to appraise the extent to which the clinical social worker's intervention is effective. Hence, the social worker must compare observations he or she made during the second phase—intervention (see Chapter 4)—with those in the first phase. To illustrate, suppose one goal of intervention is to increase marital satisfaction for both Jack and Jill. Suppose further that the social worker provides a brief cognitive–therapeutic intervention three times per week for four weeks' duration. The intervention is apparently effective because marital satisfaction has steadily increased for both Jack and Jill (Figure 14). Moreover, the magnitude of the problem has decreased so that it is relatively stable in the last week of intervention and is below the cut off point of 30 (Corcoran & Fischer, 1987a), indicating that it is not a clinical problem. In contrast, the intervention shown in Figure 15 is ineffective: The magnitude of marital satisfaction is the same or maybe less than it was at baseline for both Jack and Jill.

OBTAINING INFORMATION FOR BASELINES

The clinical social worker obtains information for constructing baselines in four ways:

(see Appendix 1) to verify his complaint. On the other hand, neither Jack nor Jill may have complained about anxiety, but the social worker might have asked Jack and Jill to complete the SAS because, in the social worker's experience with marital

figure 14

Using Baseline as a Frame of Reference to Depict an Effective Intervention for Increasing Marital Satisfaction: ■ = Jack, □ = Jill

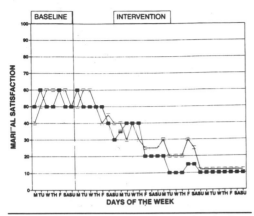

NOTE: M = Monday, T = Tuesday, W = Wednesday, TH = Thursday, F = Friday, SA = Saturday, SU = Sunday.

1. Making observations during assessment before any intervention takes place.
2. Making observations on a specific problem while intervention is being carried out to address a different problem than the one being baselined.
3. By reconstruction based on archival data and available records.
4. By retrospection based on questionnaires with clients and/or significant others. (Blythe & Tripodi, 1989, p. 77)

figure 15

Using Baseline as a Frame of Reference to Depict an Ineffective Intervention for Increasing Marital Satisfaction: ■ = Jack, □ = Jill

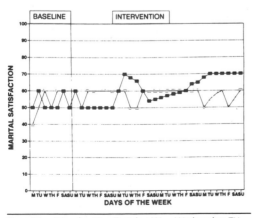

NOTE: M = Monday, T = Tuesday, W = Wednesday, TH = Thursday, F = Friday, SA = Saturday, SU = Sunday.

The first way requires that the social worker withhold intervention until he or she constructs a baseline with stable characteristics. Typically one to two weeks is a minimum period for observing trends in the time series of repeated measurements, assuming the time interval is in days. For moods, attitudes, and behaviors, this period appears feasible. However, this does not mean that the clinical social worker cannot see clients. Rather, if the first interviews are exploratory and devoted to assessment, the social worker can arrange for clients to do homework and rate themselves on standardized scales or self-anchored scales or observe themselves on a daily basis, as the social worker in the previous example instructed Jack and Jill to do. In many situations, however, the clinical social worker may make a relatively quick assessment during the first interview and begin with an intervention. The social worker still can baseline after the first interview, provided the intervention is less intense than it might be in subsequent interviews. The social worker can graph observations on important variables ostensibly related to client problems to show whether there is a problem (magnitude); that the problem is persistent (the baseline graph is horizontal to the x axis); that the problem is getting worse; or that the client solves the problem before more intensive intervention.

Although many proponents of single-subject design would like to believe that the social worker makes observations at baseline without the presence of any intervention because the particular social worker is withholding intervention until he or she makes an assessment, this requires a heroic assumption: that is, that the client has not had any previous interventions or the client has not been exposed to materials and information that are identical, similar, or akin to the planned intervention. For example, many clients have received services from a variety of professional and social agencies. Moreover, the substance of many interventions is present in forms other than the clinical social worker's treatment modality, such as the ministrations of clergy with their parishioners or popular books or newspaper articles on positive thinking—similar to some tenets of cognitive therapy; possible discussions with friends and relatives on topics and feelings similarly encountered in therapeutic sessions; or client involvement in recreational or self-help group situations, such as Parents without Partners or Adult Children of Alcoholics. Hence, the social worker can know whether he or she provides intervention during baseline, but the social worker may not be able to discern whether the client has received intervention similar to the one the social worker is offering. Of course, through clinical interviews, the social worker can estimate current or previous interventions the client has received or is receiving by asking the client.

The second way the social worker gathers information for baseline construction is to obtain the information on a problem other than the one with which he or she is dealing during an intervention. For example, if the clinical social worker is working with Jack and Jill on their marital dissatisfaction, he or she might obtain information on another problem such as attendance at work or school, following prescribed medical regimens, or depression for either spouse. However, the social worker assumes that the intervention for a problem—marital dissatisfaction in this instance—does not also influence the other problem the social worker is baselining. The social worker can infer the independence or dependence of data by observing and comparing graphic patterns. For example, Figure 16A shows a baseline pattern of horizontal stability with a high magnitude of marital dissatisfaction, followed by an increase in marital satisfaction following intervention. Baselining depression during the intervention for reducing marital dissatisfaction can result in a baseline that depends on—is influenced by—the intervention (Figure 16B) or is independent of—

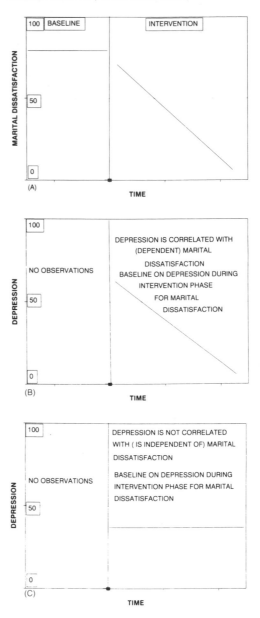

figure 16

Independent (A and C) and Dependent (B) Baseline Patterns for the Same Client

is not influenced by—the intervention (Figure 16C). The social worker can use the baseline for depression in Figure 16C for subsequent analysis and evaluation of an intervention focused on depression. However, the social worker should use only the baseline in Figure 16B for assessment in which it is clear that the problem is being reduced without any further intervention.

A third way to gather data is to use available information that the social worker might have systematically recorded. Such data might include employment records such as absences, school tardiness and attendance records and grades, delinquency records such as arrests or convictions, and hospital records regarding physical and medical characteristics. The social worker should use this information only if it was previously recorded and if the social worker believes that the data were gathered consistently and are reliable and valid. The clinical social worker can use the information, however, only if he or she has the client's permission and the permission of the organization that keeps the records to gain access to the data. Suppose that, in the illustration of Jack and Jill, the clinical social worker was interested in Jack's employment. Jack might have indicated that he had a problem with work and he did not like his job. With his permission, the clinical social worker might gain access to his work records, for example, of his attendance and visits to the company nurse. Such records are available in large nationally run corporations and, once tabulated, can serve as baselines. If the social worker finds that Jack has an attendance problem at work, he or she might use that variable as an objective of treatment. The social worker might hypothesize, for example, that Jack may not regularly attend work for other reasons such as substance abuse, and might further hypothesize that an increase in marital satisfaction might be associated with increased attendance at work.

A fourth way to obtain information for constructing baselines is to ask the client to remember information from the past. The client's recollections generally are more accurate when the client is recalling extreme quantities, such as smoking two packs of cigarettes every day for one year rather than remembering lesser quantities, such as smoking five to 10 cigarettes per day. The clinical social worker might make estimates from the client's recollections. For example, in response to "How often did you drink liquor in the past week?" the client might indicate that he or she drinks at least four shots of whiskey per day and has done so for the past month. The clinical social worker may estimate that the client drank some amount of alcohol every day during the past month, drank more than four shots a day during the past 30 days, and so forth.

Behaviors that clients can easily recall because of their extreme positions include spouse abuse or child abuse, substance abuse, cigarette smoking, and yelling at the dinner table. If a client is unable to recall such data, the social worker may enlist a spouse, a friend, a relative, or other important person to help provide the desired information. The chief danger in this method of obtaining information is that of retrospective falsification, that is, the client alters his or her recollection of the past so that it more likely will coincide with the present. Or, clients may want to please the social worker by telling him or her what they think the social worker wants to hear—there may be a bias of social desirability.

Overall, the social worker obtains the most accurate information by making observations over a designated period before applying the intervention. In contrast, the social worker procures the least accurate information through client retrospection.

TIME-SERIES DATA

Time-series data are the patterns of measurements within specified periods, such as in the baseline, intervention, or follow-up phase of single-subject design. Measurements over time for the same client are useful for determining patterns at baseline as long as there is test–retest reliability—stability—of the measures and content relevance of the measuring instrument.

figure 17

Baseline Graphs of Anxiety over Three Time Points

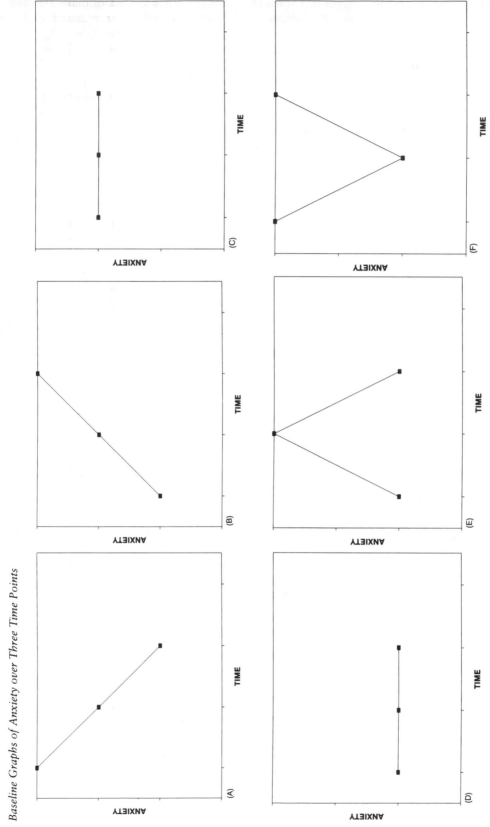

Two critical decisions in creating a baseline concern the selection of time intervals between measurements and the number of measurements to be made. The social worker should base the decision for selecting time intervals on clinical judgment; that is, the time intervals should reflect a sufficient amount of time so that change might reasonably occur. For example, moods such as depression and anxiety can change daily. Furthermore, the social worker may measure attendance at work or at school daily, but weekly attendance may be a more realistic measure. The time interval chosen should make clinical sense in relation to the client's problem. If there is daily spouse abuse in a marital relationship, according to the couple, it makes sense to obtain daily measurements; on the other hand, if the abuse apparently occurs once a week, then weekly measurements are appropriate. Likewise, if the social worker's treatment objective is to reduce the number of family arguments from every day to no arguments, then he or she should measure the arguments daily.

The number of measurements the social worker makes determines when he or she should establish the baseline. Jayaratne and Levy (1979) and Barlow and Hersen (1984) suggested that at least three points determine trends. This criterion is useful for the graphs in Figures 17 A, B, C, and D but not for E and F. Figure 17A shows a steady decline in anxiety at baseline; 17B, a steady increase; 17C, a horizontally stable graph of high anxiety; 17D, a horizontally stable graph of low anxiety; and 17E and 17F, fluctuating patterns with too few data points to characterize a trend. Another criterion is to take measurements continually at baseline until there is a discernible stable trend. Stability means that a straight line will connect all the points at baseline; the more variation there is from a straight line, the less stable the graph. Figure 18 provides examples of relatively stable and relatively unstable graphs when appraised by the eye ("eyeball").

Ideally, for purposes of making clear inferences when comparing patterns of measurements at intervention and follow-up with those at baseline, stability should be horizontal. The clinical social worker can estimate horizontal stability by eyeball; or, when there are at least eight measurements, he or she can assess horizontal stability by using the C statistic (Tryon, 1982). The C statistic is one of two statistical methods used in this book; the other is the binomial (see Chapter 4). These statistics are relatively easy to use and provide a means of assessing graphic patterns. (For a wide array of statistical procedures, see Barlow and Hersen, 1984, and Kazdin, 1992.)

Suppose the social worker makes the following 10 measurements of marital satisfaction (the higher the number, the less the satisfaction) for a client over eight days: 68, 66, 64, 60, 56, 55, 53, 50, 46, and 40. The social worker can construct a graph with these data and discern by eyeball a downward trend in the data. But is there really a trend or is it horizontally stable? The C statistic can inform whether these time-series data are on an upward or a downward trend beyond a five in 100 chance (that is, statistically significant at or beyond the .05 level of probability) or are horizontally stable (that is, nonstatistically significant at the .05 level of probability).

The first step is to put each score (x) in column 1; the sum of these scores is 558, and the mean score (average) is x divided by the number of scores ($n = 10$), or 55.8 (Table 6). In column 2, the mean of 55.8 is subtracted from each score, and in column 3, each value from column 2 is squared, for example, $12.2 \times 12.2 = 148.84$ and $10.2 \times 10.2 = 104.04$. All of the values in column 3 are added to produce the sum of squares (SS) of x [$S(x)$] or $(x - M)^2$. Column 4 consists of adjacent scores (x_i): beginning with the first score of 68 (column 1), the next score—66—is adjacent to 68 and is the first score in column 4; the adjacent score for 66 is 64; for 64, it is 60, and

figure 18 *Stable and Unstable Baseline Patterns: (A) Horizontally stable, (B) Horizontally unstable, (C) Ascending stable, (D) Ascending unstable, (E) Descending stable, (F) Descending unstable*

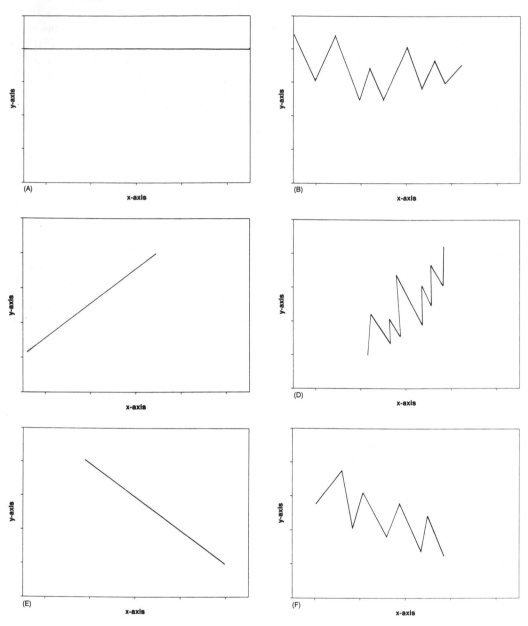

so on. In column 5, the adjacent scores are subtracted from the scores, $x - x_i$, and in column 6, the $x - x_i$ values are squared [$(x - x_i)^2$]. The sum of the $(x - x_i)^2$ values in column 6 produces D^2. The C statistic then is calculated as shown in Table 6. The standard error (SE) of C is

$$Sc = \sqrt{n + 2 / (n + 1)(n - 1)}$$

where n equals the number of scores. The probability of the C statistic is evaluated by Z, which is C divided by Sc. This is the Z statistic for the normal curve, used to evaluate the time series as unstable when Z is greater than 1.64 and as stable when it is 1.64 or less.

The result of these calculations is the determination of whether the time series at baseline is horizontal. In the example shown in Table 6, it is not, meaning that the data are on a downward trend, increasing marital satisfaction.

The social worker follows the same procedures for calculating C, Sc, and Z for other baseline data. For more information on the use of C for agency research in social work, see Blythe, Tripodi, and Briar (in press).

GRAPHING

The following material on graphs is adapted from Blythe and Tripodi (1989, pp. 67–75). Before constructing a graph, it is helpful to know the basic terminology. In Figure 19, the vertical line with units zero through 12 is the y axis; the horizontal line with units zero through eight is the x axis. The variable that indicates problem magnitude, existence, frequency, or duration is the dependent variable; it is subject to change under the possible influence of intervention. During baseline, the social worker constructs a graph to show trends in the dependent variable, which he or she plots on the y axis. The y axis is divided into equal units, and the nature of the units depends on the particular variable chosen. If the dependent variable is the Index of Marital Satisfaction, for example, the units

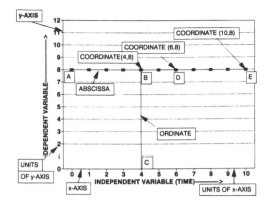

figure 19

Basic Terminology for Constructing Graphs

range from zero to 100 (Corcoran & Fischer, 1987b, pp. 443–444), whereas, the units may range from zero to 10 on a self-anchored scale of marital satisfaction. Correspondingly, the x axis contains equal units of time; the specific units depend on the clinical relevance of the time points, which may be hours, days, weeks, and so forth. The range of units can differ from graph to graph.

To plot a graph, the social worker must know the coordinates for each point. The coordinates for point B in Figure 19 are (4,8): 4 represents the time unit and 8 represents the value of the dependent variable. Count to 4 on the x axis, and then draw line BC, a line perpendicular to the x axis at time unit 4. Extend the line to the intersection of line AB, which is perpendicular to the y axis at the dependent variable value 8. Line AB represents the abscissa and line BC the ordinate. Following the same procedure, coordinates (6,8) form point D and (10,8) point E. A line connecting points B, D, and E is a graph consisting of the coordinates to points B, D, and E.

Graphs may reflect magnitude, the severity or strength of a phenomenon; magnitude shows the intensity of beliefs, feelings, moods, or attitudes, typically on standardized scales. For example, the data obtained from a client's self-ratings of depression (on a scale ranging from 0 = no depression to

figure 20

Depression Scores for 10 Successive Days

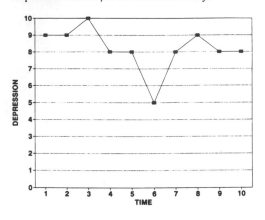

10 = the greatest degree of depression possible) for 10 successive days are as follows: day 1, rating 9; 2,9; 3,10; 4,8; 5,8; 6,5; 7,8; 8,9; 9,8; 10,8. These data are the coordinates for Figure 20. The social worker should construct the graph on a piece of graph paper with equal units and compare it with the graph in Figure 20. Except for the sixth day of measurement, the graph in Figure 20 represents a high intensity of depression for a client, 8 or higher on the 10-point self-anchored scale.

Problem existence refers to the presence or absence of a behavior, symptom, or problem within a particular period such as a day, a week, and so forth. The client may have a symptom of depression, but that differs from the intensity of a feeling of depression. Clinical social workers might observe common behaviors such as feeling of anxiety, indicated by excessive perspiration and heart palpitations; hitting a child; abusing a spouse; skipping school; frequenting a neighborhood bar; complying with a medical regimen—taking medication or monitoring blood pressure; practicing safe sex; abusing substances; or seeking employment. Graphs depicting problem existence typically have two points on the y axis: 0 = the absence of the problem and 1 = the presence of the problem or symptom. A baseline for a client measured daily for one week with respect to whether the

client had symptoms of anxiety is depicted in Figure 21. In that figure, the x axis is in days and the y axis reflects the presence or absence of anxiety, with the following coordinates: (1,1), (2,1), (3,1), (4,0), (5,0), (6,1), and (7,1). With this baseline, it is clear that the client had symptoms of anxiety five out of the seven days during the week. Stability would represent a straight line connecting all the points at either 0 = no problem or 1 = a persistent daily problem. The clinical social worker's objective would be to achieve stability at zero, which he or she would simply evaluate by eyeball; statistical procedures are unnecessary for evaluating this type of baseline because there are only two points on the graph.

Problem frequency refers to the number of times a problem occurs within a specified period. The social worker can transform problem existence into problem frequency when he or she changes the time unit. For example, in Figure 21, days are the time unit. Changing the unit to weeks, the social worker can count the number of times the problem exists within a week. Thus, anxiety occurred five times out of seven possible days during that one week. Figure 22 illustrates a baseline for three weeks. The coordinates for graph ABC are (1,5), (2,5), and (3,4), respectively. It is unnecessary for the divisions or time intervals on the x axis to be equal to the divisions on the y axis.

figure 21

Problem Existence of Anxiety for One Week; 0 = No anxiety, 1 = Anxiety

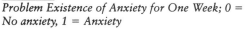
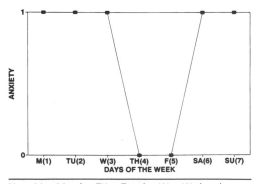

NOTE: M = Monday, TU = Tuesday, W = Wednesday, TH = Thursday, F = Friday, SA = Saturday, SU = Sunday.

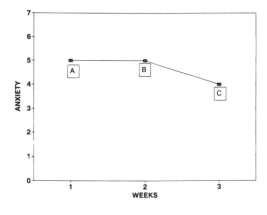

figure 22

Problem Frequency of Anxiety for Three Weeks

GRAPHIC PATTERNS

One forms a graph by connecting all adjacent coordinates by straight lines. The resulting shape is linear, nonlinear, or a combination of both. It is impossible to characterize all possible patterns of graphs, but a rough estimate of possible shapes is depicted in Figure 23. Linear shapes are simple straight lines that are ascending (Figure 23A1), horizontal to the x axis (Figure 23A2), or descending (Figure 23A3). Nonlinear or curvilinear graphs are ascending (Figure 23B1), cyclic (Figure 23B2), and descending (Figure 23B3). Figures 23 C1, C2, and C3 illustrate combinations of linear and nonlinear shapes or patterns.

Shapes or patterns of graphs indicate trends. Hence, Figures 23A1, 23B1, and 23C1 represent an increase or an acceleration of the problem over time, whereas Figures 23A3, 23B3, and 23C3 indicate a declination of the problem. An acceleration of the problem is a cause for concern, because it indicates the problem is getting worse; the clinical social worker would attempt to intervene with the objective of ameliorating the problem. In contrast, a descending or decelerating trend indicates the problem is diminishing. If this is occurring at baseline, intervention may be unnecessary. The patterns in Figures 23A2, 23B2, and 23C2 represent constancy at a particular level horizontal to the x axis; if the magnitude or frequency indicates there is a problem, then the social worker should plan intervention. In contrast, a horizontal pattern with little evidence of a problem may indicate that intervention is not warranted for that particular problem.

TRANSFORMING GRAPHS

Often graphs are not smooth lines—they are full of jagged edges, peaks (maximum points), and valleys (minimum points). When they serve as benchmarks at baseline and the social worker uses them for comparisons with graphs at intervention or at follow-up, they can be transformed. Trans-

Problem duration is the length of time the problem occurs during a designated time interval. To illustrate the relationships among problem existence, frequency, duration, and magnitude, suppose that a client is prone to having attacks of acute anxiety during which time the client feels jittery, with butterflies in his or her stomach, nauseous, and extremely apprehensive. Further suppose that the clinical social worker asks the client to record information about the anxiety attacks each day. If the client has any attacks during a day, there is evidence of problem existence. Problem frequency would refer to the number of attacks during the day; if there is more than one attack, the variable of frequency would differ from that of existence: two versus one. Problem duration would refer to the total length of time for attacks. If the first attack lasted for 15 minutes and the second lasted for 20 minutes, the problem duration for that day would be 35 minutes. Problem magnitude would refer to the intensity of each attack; on an intensity scale ranging from 0 = no anxiety to 10 = high anxiety, the magnitude for the first attack might have been 10 and for the second attack, 9. The clinical social worker might plot on a graph the magnitude of each attack or the average of the magnitudes for the attack (10 + 9/2 = 9.5), depending on what is most related to the objectives of the clinical social worker and the client.

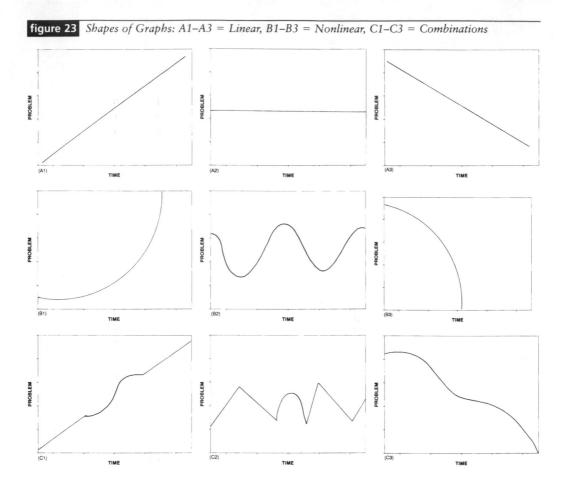

formations serve to smooth the graphs to make the patterns more horizontal, which leads to easier interpretations on comparison. However, if the social worker transforms baseline graphs, he or she must transform the graphs for intervention and follow-up; otherwise, the comparisons would be inaccurate. When transforming the data, the social worker must carefully report the data, noting the transformation that he or she made. In addition to rendering it easier for the clinical social worker to make comparisons, transformations also can lead to a better understanding of feedback in the form of graphs when the social worker presents them to clients.

The social worker can transform graphs in four ways so that they become more horizontal. Graphic analysis for statistics, business, and economics commonly follows the first procedure, which is averaging across adjacent points. For example, in Figure 24 (top), the pattern of a cyclic linear graph is shown by ACFGHIJ, whose coordinates are A (1,1), C (2,3), F (3,1), G (4,3), H (5,1), I (6,3), and J (7,1). To transform the graph, take the average of each adjacent pair of coordinates by taking the midpoint of each pair of coordinates. For example, B is the midpoint of AC; draw lines perpendicular to the midpoint from the y axis (BD) and from the x axis (BE) to obtain the new coordinate (1.5, 2). Following this procedure, the new coordinates are depicted in Figure 24B as A′ (1.5,2), B′ (2.5,2), C′ (3.5,2), D′ (4.5,2), E′ (5.5,2), and F′ (6.5,2). The transformed graph is a horizontal straight line but has one point less than the graph in Figure 24A. Also it is

figure 24

Transforming Graphs by Averaging Adjacent Points: (Top) Cyclic Linear Pattern, (Bottom) Transferred Horizontal Linear Pattern

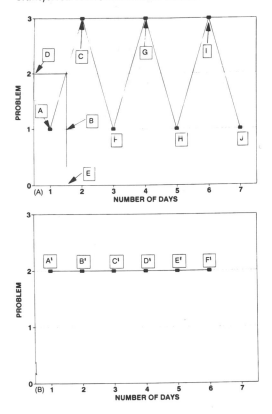

a graph of averages of the first two weeks, the second two weeks, and so on.

A second way to transform a graphic pattern is to change each problem value by a constant amount. One way to flatten or make a linear curve more horizontal is to take the common logarithm of each value; another way is to take the square root of each value. Figure 25A shows three problem values of 1, 3, and 2 over three successive periods. Figures 25 B and C show two transformations of the graph. In the figure, the common logarithms of 0, .30103, and .47712 are taken of 1, 3, and 2, respectively, to produce a graph that is more horizontal than the one shown in Figure 25A. The square roots of each value (1, 3, and 2) yield new points of 1, 1.732, and 1.414

(Figure 25C); this graph is more horizontal than the original graph. These transformations are only for purposes of comparing other patterns at intervention or follow-up to baseline and only if those graphs use the same algorithm for transforming data. For purposes of assessment only, the social worker would use the original graph and not its transformation.

A third way to flatten a graph and make it more horizontal is to shrink the y axis by reducing the size of its units. The original values remain the same but the distance between adjacent time units on the y axis is made shorter. Figure 26B shows a flatter graph than Figure 26A by shrinking the units in the y axis while keeping the units in the x axis constant.

Correspondingly, a fourth way of making a graph more horizontal is to change the units of the x axis. By increasing the length of the units on the x axis and keeping the units of the y axis constant (compare Figures 26C and 26A), the resulting graph in Figure 26C becomes more horizontal.

OBTAINING MULTIPLE BASELINES

Multiple baselines are two or more baselines for the same client or for different clients with the same problem. The social worker can use multiple graphs when two or more problems can be translated into variables and graphed to provide more information at assessment. Multiple graphs also can serve as frames of reference for one of the design variations discussed in Chapter 6: the multiple baseline design. (Multiple baselines in this chapter are not identical to multiple baseline designs as discussed in Chapter 6.)

Multiple baselines for the same client have two or more problem variables or two or more situations with one problem variable. The y axes have equivalent time units, and measurements are taken simultaneously. The social worker should use the same x axis only if the intervals for different prob-

figure 25

Transforming Graphs by Changing Values by Common Logarithms and Square Roots; (A) Original Values, (B) Common Logarithms of Original Values, (C) Square Roots of Original Values

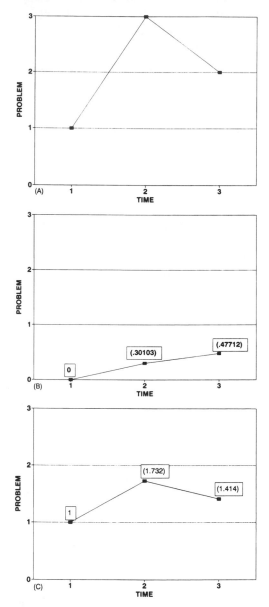

for single baselines also apply to multiple baselines.

For one type of multiple baseline—one with the same client, same situation, and more than one problem variable—suppose that a male client indicates that at home with his family (the situation) he has high anxiety, is frequently depressed, and rarely feels angry at other family members, although he would like to exhibit more anger because he believes he is too passive and his family is taking him for granted. Although the clinical social worker's tentative objectives might be to reduce the client's level of anxiety, reduce his frequency of depression, and increase his expression of anger, the social worker first wishes to verify the extent and nature of the problems. He or she operationally defines each variable. Hence, anxiety is defined on a self-anchored rating scale ranging from 0 = no anxiety to 10 = the highest level of anxiety; the social worker defines depression as a feeling of being very sad and lonely concomitant with a crying episode and defines an expression of anger as the client's raising his voice and speaking negative words to any family member. The client is to report daily on the number of times he feels depressed and the number of times he expresses anger; in addition, he reports the magnitude of intensity of anxiety each day.

The social worker creates three separate graphs, each representing a different problem variable (Figures 27 A, B, and C). The variables do not appear to be highly correlated with each other because the patterns of the graphs are dissimilar. The range of units and the equivalencies for units on the y axis (intensity of anxiety, frequency of depression, and frequency of expressed anger) are dissimilar, whereas the x axes are equivalent in all three graphs. The measurements are obtained at the same time for each variable; for example, the client might write down his ratings and observations for the three variables just before bedtime each night for all seven days. This observation is

lem variables are identical; he or she should use different y axes if the problem variables have nonequivalent time intervals. Multiple problem variables and multiple situations should be independent of each other. Principles for constructing baseline graphs

important because a common mistake is not to conceive of multiple baseline measurements as taken simultaneously (see Chapter 6), which is a primary requisite for multiple baseline designs. Figure 28 shows the same baseline patterns as in Figure 27, except that they are not taken at the same time and are time-lagged baselines.

The clinical social worker cannot use the baselines in Figure 28 for making inferences in multiple baseline designs. Furthermore, he or she cannot use them to talk about those three problem variables during the same week for purposes of assessment, where it is observed that the client has two or more episodes of depression daily, has a moderate-to-strong feeling of anxiety (5–7) but is not at the highest level of anxiety (10), and has expressed anger four out of the seven days at baseline.

If the client had reported feelings of anxiety, depression, and anger on self-rating scales with equivalent time units, then the social worker could have reported all of the problem variables on one graph (Figure 29), in which self-ratings of anxiety, depression, and anger are reported on the same scale of intensity or magnitude from zero to 10. Figure 29 shows that the client's feelings of depression are the most intense, followed closely by anxiety, with very low feelings of anger.

A second type of multiple baseline is one with the same client, different situations, and one problem variable. Often some clients in their clinical work may feel or behave differently in different situations, such as at home, on the job, in school, in recreational activities, in religious functions, and so forth. A clinical social worker's objective might be to assist the client to act differently in one situation and to generalize his or her behavioral changes to other situations. For example, the clinical social worker may work with the client to be more assertive in the workplace, rather than concentrating through role play and discussions about how or when to be as-

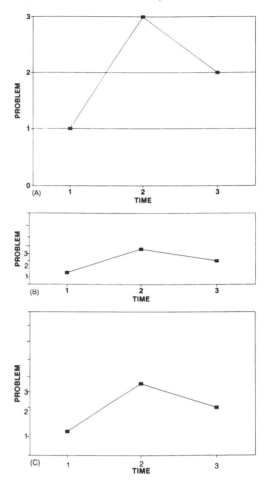

figure 26

Transforming Graphs by Changing Units of the y Axis; (A) Original units, (B) Changing units in the y axis but not in the x axis, (C) Changing units in the x axis but not the y axis

sertive in other situations such as the home. The clinical social worker might simultaneously baseline for the same client the degree to which the client is assertive at the workplace and at home. Suppose the social worker defines assertiveness as any situation in which the client asserts his or her belief and desire for a certain action to occur in which the client might be involved. At home, the client might indicate he or she will not do a particular chore but will do another; at work, the client might indicate he or she would like to be a member of a committee to discuss a union contract. The

figure 27

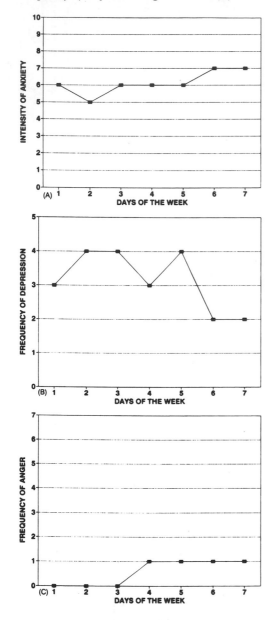

Simultaneous Multiple Baselines of Intensity of Anxiety (A), Frequency of Depression (B), and Frequency of Expressed Anger at Home (C)

one y axis are used because the units are the same for both situations. Although the social worker can use one graph for assessment, he or she can still use two graphs. For comparing interventions with the baselines, it is more manageable to use two graphs. Figure 30 shows that for the same period of seven successive days, the client reported he or she was hardly assertive at home and slightly assertive at work. If the social worker concentrates his or her work with the client on how to be assertive at home, the social worker can observe changes in assertiveness at home; in addition, he or she can observe whether there is generalization to the workplace, ultimately deciding whether interventions should necessarily focus on the workplace as well as on the home.

A third type of multiple baseline involves two or more different clients with the same problem variable and the same situation. This type of baseline technically is not within the single-subject design methodology because more than one subject (that is, client) is involved. The purpose of obtaining multiple baselines on more than one person is to build an understanding of the nature of a problem variable that is the same for many clients. In this way, the clinical social worker can begin to generalize across clients about the nature of the problem variable. This is only possible, however, if the social worker operationally defines the variable in the same way. Still another purpose of multiple baselines with clients is to use them as benchmarks for evaluating the effectiveness of an intervention and to rule out extraneous factors that can increase inferences about causal relations between an intervention and specified outcomes.

For this type of multiple baseline, the social worker follows the same procedures for constructing graphs as previously discussed. Again, it is important to note that the data for the baselines should be gathered simultaneously. For example, Figure

client might rate for seven consecutive days the extent to which he or she has been assertive at home and at the workplace on a scale ranging from 0 = not very assertive at all to 7 = very assertive.

Figure 30 shows multiple baselines for work and for home. Only one x axis and

31 illustrates a multiple baseline for two clients who would like to reduce their alcohol consumption. The baselines represent time series of alcohol consumption for 10 successive days. The social worker defines the measure of alcohol consumption as the number of ounces of alcohol consumed, which the clients report daily. If possible, persons in the clients' lives—close friend, spouse, or relative, for instance—who are in a position to make daily observations of the clients' drinking behavior verify the self-reports. The coordinates for client 1 are (1,4), (2,5), (3,4), (4,6), (5,7), (6,5), (7,4), (8,4), (9,5), and (10,4). For client 2, they are (1,0), (2,0), (3,0), (4,10), (5,10), (6,0), (7,0), (8,0), (9,10), and (10,10). Two distinctive patterns for clients 1 and 2 over the same period of 10 days are clear: Client 1 drinks four or more ounces daily, whereas client 2 appears to go on two-day binges during which he drinks 10 ounces of alcohol daily. The clinical social worker needs more information from each client during the clinical interview to obtain an understanding of when the drinking occurs, what events precipitate the drinking, how the client feels before and after the drinking, and so forth. For client 2, this information is relatively more vital because that client may harm himself or herself and perhaps others with the excessive doses of alcohol. The clinical social worker recognizes that drinking patterns are not necessarily the same for clients. Moreover, it appears that the graph for client 1 is closer to representing horizontal stability than that for client 2.

The social worker can evaluate the stability of the patterns by using the C statistic (see Table 6). Tables 7 and 8 represent the calculations for clients 1 and 2, respectively. Both graphs in Figure 31 represent horizontal stability, and the calculations confirm that the graph for client 2 is relatively more unstable than the graph for client 1, although neither graph displays a statistically significant trend beyond the .05 level of probability. Therefore, the social worker

figure 28

Time-Lagged Baselines of Intensity of Anxiety (A), Frequency of Depression (B), and Frequency of Expressed Anger at Home (C)

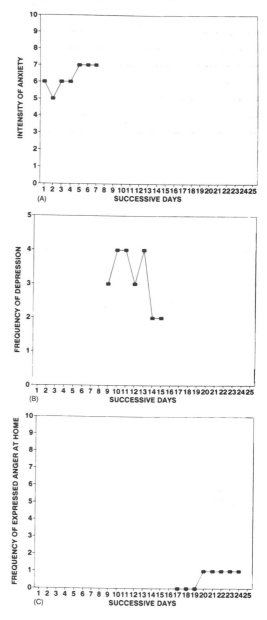

could use both of these graphs as benchmarks to evaluate subsequent trends in drinking behaviors after administering intervention.

There may be a variety of other, more complicated patterns of multiple baselines than

figure 29

Multiple Baselines for Self-Reported Feelings of Anxiety (■), Depression (▲), and Anger at Home (□)

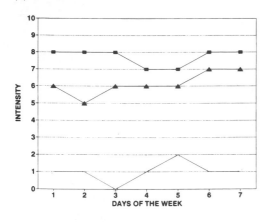

the ones presented. For example, for the same client, there might be two problem variables and two situations leading to four possible baselines. If an adolescent client who appears to be at risk for delinquent behavior indicates he or she often is tardy at school and late for curfew at home, the clinical social worker might baseline tardiness as well as another relevant behavior at home and at school. Through an initial interview, the client may indicate he or she has feelings of hostility toward authority, which the client might rate on a self-anchored scale. The operational definitions of tardiness at home would be late for cur-

figure 30

Multiple Baselines for Degree of Assertiveness at Home (▲) and at Work (■)

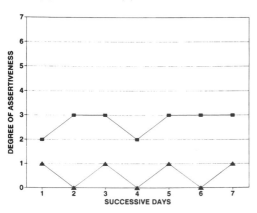

few or not late as monitored by the client's mother; at school, tardiness would represent lateness to the first class of the day as monitored by the client's teacher. The client would rate feelings of hostility toward his or her mother or toward the teacher daily on a self-anchored rating scale ranging from 0 = no hostility to 10 = extreme hostility. Figure 32 illustrates the resultant four baseline graphs for 10 successive weekdays; the social worker eliminated data from weekends so that all the observations would be simultaneously reported at home or at school daily. Clearly, the graphs indicate that the client reported more hostility toward the teacher than the mother; moreover, the client was tardy every day at school (during the 10-day period of measurement) and was late for curfew only two out of 10 days.

READING GRAPHS

Colleagues, supervisees, clients, and other professionals can produce graphs of baselines at meetings, workshops, in the literature, and so forth. When reading baseline graphs pertaining to clinical social work, the social worker should consider several criteria:

• **Determine whether clinical objectives exist.** An implicit objective might be to reduce the symptomatic behavior (such as child abuse) to nonsymptomatic behavior (that is, the behavior no longer occurs). Knowledge of possible objectives will assist in determining whether the baseline data suggest practice intervention. Life-threatening behavior such as child abuse, spouse abuse, or suicide attempts warrant intervention with relatively few occurrences during a baseline period, whereas mild feelings of anxiety during a situation (an examination for a professional license, for instance) that normally provokes anxiety may be insufficient to warrant intervention. On the other hand, no precise clinical objectives may be evident in the baseline period. However, the decision to gather in-

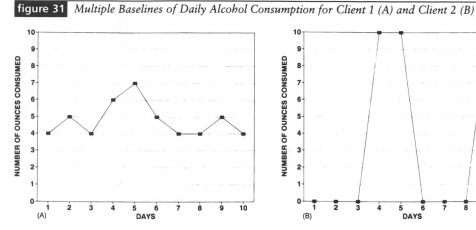
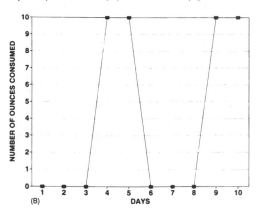

formation that the social worker can baseline suggests that a problem for the client may exist; if it does, then the social worker should reduce or eliminate it through intervention.

• **Determine whether a point on the problem variable is regarded as clinically significant.** Standardized tests such as Hudson's Index of Marital Satisfaction (see Corcoran and Fischer 1987b, pp. 443–444) might have a cut off score above which a score indicates a problem for the client. Or the clinical social worker and the client might have agreed that a rating at or

table 6 *Computing C, Sc, and Z to Evaluate Time-Series Data*

Score (x)	x − M	(x − M)²	x_i	x − x_i	(x − x_i)²
68	12.2	148.84	66	2	4
66	10.2	104.04	64	2	4
64	8.2	67.24	60	4	16
60	4.2	17.64	56	4	16
56	.2	.04	55	1	1
55	−.8	.64	53	2	4
53	−2.8	7.84	50	3	9
50	−5.8	33.64	46	4	16
46	−9.8	96.04	40	6	36
40	−15.8	249.64	—	—	—
558 = Σx		| 725.60 | = SS(x)			106 = D²

$$M = \frac{\Sigma x}{n} = \frac{558}{10} = 55.8$$

$$C = 1 - \frac{D^2}{2SS(x)} = 1 - \frac{106}{2(725.60)} = .927$$

$$Sc = \sqrt{\frac{n + 2}{(n + 1)(n - 1)}} = \sqrt{\frac{10 + 2}{(10 + 1)(10 - 1)}} = .348$$

$$Z = \frac{C}{Sc} = \frac{.927}{.348} = 2.66$$

NOTE: If Z > 1.64, there is a trend in the time series; otherwise, there is horizontal stability. Because Z = 2.66 is greater than 1.64, there is a trend in the time series.

above a point on a self-anchored rating scale indicates a problem. For example, the social worker and client might regard as clinically significant 7 on a 10-point scale of depression ranging from 0 = no depression to 10 = very depressed.

- **Analyze the problem variable and the y axis.** In analyzing the y axis, the social worker should determine if the problem variable is one of magnitude, existence, frequency, or duration. Furthermore, does the problem variable relate to any articulated objectives (for example, to reduce anxiety)? The social worker also needs to determine if the intervals on the y axis are equally spaced. If they are not, the graphic picture will be distorted and will be more difficult to eyeball. In addition, the social worker should examine how the baseline was constructed. Retrospective data are apt to be less reliable and valid than data collected prospectively.
- **Analyze the time dimension and the x axis.** Through an analysis of the x axis, the social worker should determine if the time interval appears to be of sufficient length to allow for baseline stability. He or she also should ensure that time intervals are equally spaced; otherwise, the graphic picture will be distorted. The social worker also should determine how many measurements were made. Eight measures are necessary to determine the statistical significance of a trend at baseline, whereas three measures are sufficient for eyeballing a stable pattern.
- **Read the graphic pattern.** If there is a cutting score or a point on the y axis that is considered clinically significant, count the number of measurements that are clinically significant or problematic out of the total number of measurements taken. For example, if 30 or above represents a clinically significant score, out of 10 measurements over 10 days, the social worker might observe that nine out of 10 have scores of 30 or higher. Furthermore, the clinical social worker needs to describe a point above or

table 7		Computing C, Sc, and Z for Client 1						
	Day	x	x − M	(x − M)²	x_i	x − x_i	(x − x_i)²
	1	4	−.8	.64	5	−1	1
	2	5	.2	.04	4	1	1
	3	4	4	.64	6	−2	4
	4	6	1.2	1.44	7	−1	1
	5	7	2.2	4.84	5	2	4
	6	5	.2	.04	4	1	1
	7	4	−.8	.64	4	0	0
	8	4	−.8	.64	5	−1	1
	9	5	.2	.04	4	1	1
	10	4	−.8	.64	—	—	—
		48 = Σx			9.60	= SS(x)			14	= D²

$$M = \frac{\Sigma x}{n} = \frac{48}{10} = 4.8$$

$$C = 1 - \frac{D^2}{2SS(x)} = 1 - \frac{14}{2(9.60)} = .271$$

$$Sc = \sqrt{\frac{n + 2}{(n + 1)(n - 1)}} = \sqrt{\frac{10 + 2}{(10 + 1)(10 - 1)}} = .348$$

$$Z = \frac{C}{Sc} = \frac{.271}{.348} = .779$$

NOTE: Because $Z < 1.64$, there is horizontal stability.

table 8	*Computing C, Sc, and Z for Client 2*

Day	x	x − M	(x − M)²	x_i	x − x_i	(x − x_i)²
1	0	−4	16	0	0	0
2	0	−4	16	0	0	0
3	0	−4	16	10	−10	100
4	10	6	36	10	0	0
5	10	6	36	0	10	100
6	0	−4	16	0	0	0
7	0	−4	16	0	0	0
8	0	−4	16	10	−10	100
9	10	6	36	10	0	0
10	10	6	36	—	—	—
	40 = Σx			240	= SS(x)		300	= D²

$$M = \frac{\Sigma x}{n} = \frac{40}{10} = 4$$

$$C = 1 - \frac{D^2}{2SS(x)} = 1 - \frac{300}{2(240)} = .375$$

$$Sc = \sqrt{\frac{n + 2}{(n + 1)(n - 1)}} = \sqrt{\frac{10 + 2}{(10 + 1)(10 - 1)}} = .348$$

$$Z = \frac{C}{Sc} = \frac{.375}{.348} = 1.078$$

NOTE: Because $Z < 1.64$, there is horizontal stability.

below which most measurements lie. For example, on a 10-point rating scale, the practitioner might discern that eight out of 10 measurements are above a certain magnitude. If possible, the practitioner also should describe the number of measurements that indicate goal attainment. For example, the goal might be to eradicate the problem, and the client might report that the problem exists only for one day. However, the social worker must consider that information with respect to the nature of the problem occurrence. One alcoholic binge in a baseline of one week is a serious problem and, more than likely, considering other available information, would still warrant intervention.

In reading the graphic pattern, the practitioner should look for trends in the measurements. Is there stability? Is the pattern horizontal, ascending, or descending, or is it indeterminate on the basis of the available information? To assist in eyeballing a

possible trend, the practitioner can draw a straight line that is an estimate of the average of the points and reflects the trend as shown in line AB in Figure 33. Line AB is extended to point A on the y axis; at point A, draw another line—AC—that is parallel to the x axis. The angle, 14 degrees, measured with a protractor, indicates the slope. The higher the number of degrees (up to 90 degrees), the greater the apparent acceleration in the graph.

Computing C, Sc, and Z if There are Eight or More Measurements

Eyeballing can be deceiving. A slight observable trend might be evident, but there might not be a statistically significant trend. The social worker can verify whether there is horizontal stability (no statistical significance) or evidence of an accelerating or decelerating trend in the data (statistical significance). In Table 9, there is no statistical evidence of a trend for the graph in Figure 33.

figure 32 *Multiple Baselines of Feelings of Hostility toward Authority (A) and Tardiness (B) at Home (▲) and at School (■) for One Client*

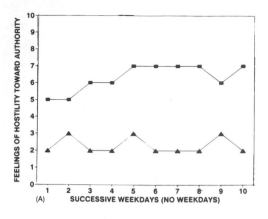

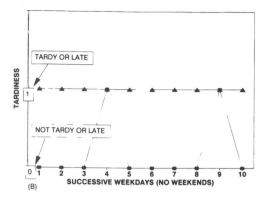

Reading the Graph for Additional Baselines if More than One Baseline Is Used

Compare the patterns from the two baselines to estimate whether the data are independent or correlated—that is, appear to have the same related pattern. If the patterns are highly related, it is possible that intervention focused on one of the problem variables might lead to changes in the other related problem variables.

For each of the following graphs and their accompanying tables, the reader should apply principles learned in this chapter for describing baseline data. The reader should then compare the reading of the graphs with comments made in the text.

| table 9 | Computing C, Sc, and Z for Figure 33 |

x	x − M	(x − M)²	x_i	x − x_i	(x − x_i)²
40	−3.75	14.06	30	10	100
30	−13.75	189.06	40	−10	100
40	−3.75	14.06	40	0	0
40	−3.75	14.06	50	−10	100
50	6.25	39.06	40	10	100
40	−3.75	14.06	50	−10	100
50	6.25	39.06	60	−10	100
60	16.25	264.06	—	—	—
|350| = Σx		587.48 = SS(x)			|600| = D²

$$M = \frac{\Sigma x}{n} = \frac{350}{8} = 43.75$$

$$C = 1 - \frac{D^2}{2SS(x)} = 1 - \frac{600}{2(587.48)} = .489$$

$$Sc = \sqrt{\frac{n+2}{(n+1)(n-1)}} = \sqrt{\frac{10}{(8+1)(8-1)}} = .398$$

$$Z = \frac{C}{Sc} = \frac{.489}{.398} = 1.229$$

NOTE: Because Z < 1.64, there is no statistical evidence of a trend.

figure 33

*Baseline of Marital Dissatisfaction; a = 14; Line
AC is Parallel to x-axis; Line AB is the
Estimated Straight Line that is the Average of the
Eight Points*

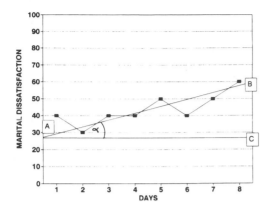

Figure 33 represents a graph constructed
on the basis of eight daily measurements on
Hudson's Index of Marital Satisfaction
(Corcoran & Fischer, 1987b, pp. 443–
444), in which a score above 30 indicates a
clinical problem of marital dissatisfaction.
The index ranges from zero to 100; the
higher the score, the greater the degree of
marital dissatisfaction. Assume that a clinical objective would be to increase marital

figure 34

*Multiple Baseline of Self-Anchored Depression
(▲) and Anxiety (■)*

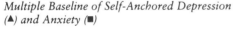

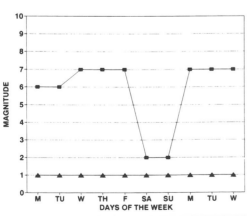

NOTE: M = Monday, TU = Tuesday, W = Wednesday,
TH = Thursday, F = Friday, SA = Saturday, SU = Sunday

satisfaction (that is, reduce the score) per
the client's expressed wish. (Obviously,
other clients may need to focus on an objective of separation or divorce as opposed
to the objective to increase marital satisfaction while still being married to the same
person.) In Figure 33, clearly all eight of the
measurements are at the cutoff score of 30
or higher, which is strong evidence of a
clinically significant problem. The coordinates of the eight measurements are (1,40),
(2,30), (3,40), (4,40), (5,50), (6,40), (7,50),
and (8,60). Line AB shows a slight ascending curve; however, the calculations in
Table 9 indicate that there are no statistical
trends in the data. On the basis of the information presented in the graph, intervention
is warranted.

Figure 34 displays two baselines for one client over 10 successive days of the week,
from Monday through Wednesday. The intervals on both the x and y axes are equally
spaced. The two problem variables, anxiety
and depression, have the same possible
range of magnitudes from 0 = absence of
the phenomenon to 10 = the highest degree
of anxiety or depression. The client, a male
adolescent, records his ratings of anxiety
and depression at the same time each day,
just before bedtime. The client and the clinical social worker should have thoroughly
discussed the operational definition of anxiety before the client makes his ratings.

The graph of depression has the same rating of 1 for each of the 10 days (Figure 34).
It is a horizontal straight line; if the magnitude of 6 is regarded as problematic, clearly
depression is not problematic for the client
during the baseline period. The graph representing anxiety also appears to be relatively horizontal. Except for Saturday and
Sunday, for which the magnitude of anxiety
is 2 each day, the other eight measurements
are at a magnitude of 6 or higher, which,
assuming that the social worker and the client agreed on this number, is clinically significant. The graph indicates that the client's anxiety is high during the week while

table 10 *Computing C, Sc, and Z for Figure 34*

x	x − M	(x − M)²	x_i	x − x_i	(x − x_i)²
6	.2	.04	6	0	0
6	.2	.04	7	−1	1
7	1.2	1.44	7	0	0
7	1.2	1.44	7	0	0
7	1.2	1.44	2	5	25
2	−3.8	14.44	2	0	0
2	−3.8	14.44	7	−5	25
7	1.2	1.44	7	0	0
7	1.2	1.44	7	0	0
7	1.2	1.44	—	—	—
	58	= Σx		37.60	= SS(x)		51	= D²

$$M = \frac{\Sigma x}{n} = \frac{58}{10} = 5.8$$

$$C = 1 - \frac{D^2}{2SS(x)} = 1 - \frac{51}{2(37.60)} = .322$$

$$Sc = \sqrt{\frac{n + 2}{(n + 1)(n - 1)}} = \sqrt{\frac{12}{(10 + 1)(10 - 1)}} = .348$$

$$Z = \frac{C}{Sc} = \frac{.322}{.348} = .925$$

NOTE: Because $Z < 1.64$, there is no statistical evidence of a trend.

table 11 *Computing C, Sc, and Z for Figure 35*

x	x − M	(x − M)²	x_i	x − x_i	(x − x_i)²
5	1.88	3.53	5	0	0
5	1.88	3.53	5	0	0
5	1.88	3.53	4	1	1
4	0.88	0.77	3	1	1
3	−0.12	0.016	2	1	1
2	−1.12	1.25	1	1	1
1	−2.12	4.49	0	1	1
0	−3.12	9.73	—	—	—
	25	= Σx		26.84	= SS(x)		5	= D²

$$M = \frac{\Sigma x}{n} = \frac{25}{8} = 3.125$$

$$C = 1 - \frac{D^2}{2SS(x)} = 1 - \frac{5}{2(26.84)} = .886$$

$$Sc = \sqrt{\frac{n + 2}{(n + 1)(n - 1)}} = \sqrt{\frac{10}{(8 + 1)(8 - 1)}} = .159$$

$$Z = \frac{C}{Sc} = \frac{.886}{.159} = 5.572$$

NOTE: Because $Z > 1.64$, there is evidence of a trend.

he is at school, but not during the weekend, presumably while he is at home. Obviously, the clinical social worker needs to further explore with the client this possible relationship of school, home, and anxiety. Intervention to reduce anxiety appears to be warranted. Calculations indicate that the baseline of anxiety is horizontally stable because the calculated Z of .925 is less than the Z of 1.64 (Table 10). The calculated Z can be considered statistically significant only if Z is equal to or greater than 1.64.

Figure 35 shows the baseline of an adult child abuser who, in his interview with a clinical social worker in private practice, indicated that he spanked his child too often and believed the spankings were abusive to his child. The social worker asked for him to obtain a baseline of abuse generated by his daily observation of abuse for eight successive days. Any abusive incident is considered clinically significant. The intervals on the frequency of abuse scale are equally spaced (Figure 35). The time intervals for the x axis also are equally spaced. The first three measurements are recorded as five abuses daily; then there is a rapid deceleration, with one less abuse in each suc-

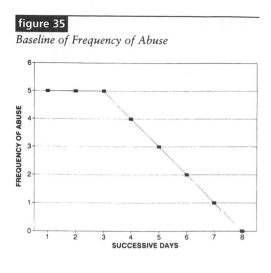

figure 35

Baseline of Frequency of Abuse

cessive day until there is no abuse on the eighth day. The statistics in Table 11 verify that there is a decelerating trend in the data because the calculated Z of 5.704 is greater than 1.64, indicating a statistically significant shift in the time series. Because child abuse is a serious problem and there was only one day without abuse, the clinical social worker may decide to extend the baseline period, still noting whether child abuse recurs.

CHAPTER 4

PHASE 2: INTERVENTION

DEFINITION OF THE INTERVENTION PHASE

The intervention phase is the second phase in the basic model of single-subject design methodology. Following the establishment of a baseline, the clinical social worker introduces an intervention, a set of actions, behaviors, or activities the clinical social worker arranges or exhibits to achieve one or more prescribed objectives. He or she takes repeated measurements, ideally in the same periods as at baseline and of the same problem variables that the social worker measured during baseline.

The purpose of the intervention is to achieve change or, in the case of prevention or maintenance, absence of change. For example, a clinical objective with a client who is an alcoholic may be to change the amount of his or her daily intake of alcohol; on achievement of the change objective, a further clinical objective might be to prevent the recurrence of alcoholic consumption at the same rate as at baseline—another way of indicating prevention of relapse. Correspondingly, an objective with a child of the alcoholic client might be to prevent the occurrence of alcoholic consumption.

An intervention may be as simple as a direct verbal communication to make a telephone call or as complex as an interactive mode of psychotherapy. Thus, interventions are broadly conceived and can represent the full range of approaches, principles, and techniques clinical social workers use, such as group psychotherapy, reinforcement schedules, task-centered treatment, cognitive therapy, advice giving, insight development, social support, and communication. Interventions are described in and derived from social work theories and assumptions about human behavior and the conditions and factors that can change interventions.

Social workers learn interventions in schools of social work, continuing education classes, seminars and workshops on particular problems and techniques; from the literature; and from their own and shared experiences with colleagues and supervisors. In an analysis of the direct practice literature pertaining to the use and generalization of principles that guide practice, Nurius, Wedenoja, and Tripodi (1987) reported that authors who used practice prescriptions or proscriptions were most likely to base them on their own experiences or others' experiences. They defined prescriptions and proscriptions as follows:

> A prescription mandates a specific action, intervention or treatment structure to be performed or implemented by a social work practitioner in the context of interpersonal practice when working with a specific client or defined client population. This may involve direct practitioner and client interaction in a clinical setting or interventions carried out by the practitioner on behalf of the client (for example, case management, advocacy, and so forth). Prescriptions are identified by statements directed toward the practitioner's actions by means of words such as "should," "must," "need to," "is mandatory," "is required," "essential," or "vital" and sentence structures describing what practitioners are "to do."

> Proscriptions follow the same definitional guidelines as prescriptions except that they mandate what actions, interventions, or treatment structures the practitioners should not perform or implement. (pp. 590–591)

CLINICAL INTERVENTION OBJECTIVES

Intervention objectives for clinical social workers can be roughly classified as those that deal with change, maintenance, prevention, or care (Blythe & Tripodi, 1989; Ivanoff, Blythe, & Tripodi, 1994; Tripodi & Epstein, 1980). Change refers to an increase, a decrease, or a qualitative difference in problem variables measured at intervention and compared with baseline. Hence, shifts in the time-series data indicate change. Of course, the objective is that change be clinically desirable. Thus, a reduction in anxiety, an increase in problem-solving behavior, and a change from living in a situation that discourages social interaction to one that encourages social interaction are examples of clinically desirable change objectives. Changes are registered in knowledge, attitudes, beliefs, skills, living situations, places of residence or employment, clinical symptomatology, and so forth. For example, a teenager may learn about safer sex practices, parents may change their attitudes about the use of punishment in child rearing, the introverted person might learn social skills for developing and nurturing social relationships, the abused child may function better in a foster home environment than in the home where he or she is abused by the natural parents, and the person with bipolar depression may not exhibit symptoms with persistent use of appropriate medication.

Maintenance and prevention are both change objectives as long as there is no change within a specified period. For example, if the objective is to prevent the incidence of substance abuse, baseline measurements should indicate no substance abuse. To accomplish the clinical objective, there should be no change in substance abuse after the social worker has initiated an intervention. Undesirable changes possibly may occur during a person's lifetime, but that is typically too long a period for evaluation. The social worker should specify the clinical time frame for objectives more precisely. The clinical social worker, for example, may seek no change in substance-abuse behavior for a particular year that a teenage client is enrolled in school. The problem of relapse among alcoholics, child abusers, schizophrenics, and so forth is severe. The purpose of maintenance intervention is to maintain such clients (who previously had the undesirable symptomatology) in a symptom-free state, showing no reversion to their previous problems.

Another area that represents clinical objectives is difficult to define in terms of change: care. Care refers to the humaneness in showing care for the welfare and humanity of clients; its intent is to show the client that people do care—they will listen to the client's opinions and beliefs. Care overlaps with the maintenance and prevention intervention objectives and may lead to measurable objectives in specific situations. For example, the elderly person in a hospice may feel lonely; the social worker's intervention might help meet that need. The social worker can measure change in loneliness if the practitioner and the client can define the change to produce, for example, self-anchored rating scales.

CHOOSING INTERVENTIONS

The clinical social worker chooses interventions that are relevant to the accomplishment of clinical objectives, consonant with the clinical social worker's experience, feasible, ethical, effective, and efficient (Blythe & Tripodi, 1989; Ivanoff et al., 1994; Tripodi & Epstein, 1980). Relevance is based on the clinical social worker's knowledge and perception of the utility of interventions for accomplishing clinical objectives. Although the social worker chooses interventions that are consistent with his or her experience in working with a variety of clients or are based on the experience of seasoned consultants and supervisors, the clinician also needs to choose realistic interventions. The social worker might use such interventions, depending on the specific clinical situation, within a specified time with a limited number of interviews. Interventions designed for long-term therapy, for example, to induce insight about the relationship of past relationships to present social interactions, would be inappropriate for emergency, short-term, crisis interventions (Ivanoff et al., 1994). Correspondingly, a short-term intervention would be inappropriate for sustaining supportive psychotherapy and medication for a chronic schizophrenic client living in a group home.

Furthermore, a clinician should use interventions only if the social worker, the client, and the community perceive them as ethical. Using negative reinforcement or punishment in the form of electroshock in a therapy based on theories of classical conditioning is unethical. Chief guidelines for the ethical use of interventions are promulgated in the *NASW Code of Ethics* (National Association of Social Workers, 1994).

When choosing interventions that are based on research or the social worker's experiences, the social worker needs to meet the criteria of effectiveness and efficiency. Empirically based practice is based on research knowledge about effectiveness and efficiency (Siegel, 1984) and also on experiential knowledge gained through cumulative practice experiences (which also are empirical, that is, amenable to the senses). Basically, the social worker requires the knowledge that the intervention will lead to or has led to the accomplishment of clinical objectives with clients like the client with which the clinical social worker is engaged. When choosing among competing interventions, the social worker can meet the criterion of efficiency, that is, the relationship of effectiveness to the cost of implementing an intervention (Tripodi, 1983). For example, a discussion group designed to reduce preoperative anxiety in patients would be more efficient than individual interviews with each group member if the practitioner can achieve the same reduction in anxiety using either method.

SPECIFYING INTERVENTIONS

Specifying interventions will clarify when an intervention is or is not occurring. In this way, the clinician can more appropriately apply the logic of single-subject design methodology for evaluating the effectiveness of an intervention. Furthermore, the clinical social worker can accumulate a repertoire of interventions and their relative successes and failures for individual practice and can communicate this knowledge to colleagues and other professionals.

The practitioner should first specify clinical objectives with respect to their emphases on change, maintenance, prevention, or care, or a combination of these. The social worker can then further delineate the objectives by considering parameters related to the clinical objectives and factors that describe the intervention. Parameters that further specify the clinical objectives are the variables related to the problem: an indication of when the social worker expects change (or no change) to occur and an estimate of how long the change will last if it occurs. These parameters involve measuring problem indicators as discussed in Chapters 2 and 3. For example, the clinical objective may be to reduce symptomatology about depression; the variable may be a 10-point self-anchored rating scale ranging from 0 = no depression to 10 = severe depression. The clinical social worker bases his or her expectations on an assessment of the client and on whatever knowledge the social worker has of client anxiety and the intervention. For example, the practitioner may expect change as defined in the clinical objective, from an average rating of 8 to an average rating of 2, within two months after six to eight interviews. If change occurs, the social worker may expect it to endure for a minimum of three months. The specificity of these objectives guides the social worker in evaluating the effectiveness of the intervention. If no change occurs after two months of intervention, the social worker would need to determine, if possible, the reasons and then decide whether to continue or modify the intervention or substitute intervention alternatives. Assuming change occurs after two months, the social worker would want to build in plans for follow-up (see Chapter 5) to determine whether changes persist after three months.

To make decisions about intervention modifications, the social worker must have detailed descriptions of intervention. He or she can specify in advance factors that might characterize the essence of simple interventions such as straightforward verbal communications, behaviors, and actions, for example, a directive to complete an activity, contact a person, or initiate a discussion or a verbal positive reinforcement and a smile for positive interactions in a family interview. However, it is impossible to specify in advance the contents of interactive psychotherapeutic interventions. With more complex forms of intervention, it is possible to specify a few factors, but the practitioner can determine the contents only after the interventions occur; thus, interview notes, process and summary recordings, and tape-recorded interviews are mechanisms for obtaining more complete descriptions of the interventions.

General factors the practitioner can specify in advance include the intervenors, location of the intervention, frequency of the intervention, duration of the intervention, and information about the contents of the intervention (Tripodi, 1983). The clinical social worker typically is the intervenor, but he or she also may work with colleagues or enlist the services of significant persons. For example, intervention may require "homework assignments" the clinical social worker gives to the client that the client's spouse monitors daily. Or, the clinical social worker may engage in the contents of the intervention during interviews, while the client's spouse ensures that the client takes prescribed dosages of medication, another aspect of the intervention.

The location of the intervention is another factor that defines general characteristics of the intervention. The clinical social worker's office, the client's home, a waiting room, and so forth are possible sites. The frequency of the intervention refers to the number of different contacts the clinical social worker makes with the client. Contacts may be in the form of interviews, telephone calls, or group meetings, among others. Contacts may range from complete 24-hour-per-day availability for six weeks, as in the Homebuilders model of family preservation (Ivanoff et al., 1994), to routine once-per-month maintenance contacts.

The duration of the intervention indicates the length of time the social worker has planned for the intervention. An intervention may be for an indefinite period, for example, with parolees or with severely mentally disturbed children in residential care. Or the intervention may be for a prescribed duration such as one month while a client is in an observational setting such as juvenile court or for the time necessary to include a prescribed set of interviews, as in the conveyance of instructional materials regarding health-promoting behavior.

These factors, though, do not describe the essence of interventions, which is contained in its contents. Information about the contents of intervention might include as much detail as possible about the behaviors, statements, and protocols the clinical social worker uses to implement the intervention. Ideally, the clinician should present enough information so that any other clinical social worker could replicate the intervention. The social worker can easily articulate contents that are didactic or instructional. Furthermore, he or she can only specify contents for interactions by referring to guidelines, that is, principles that inform the social worker but do not bind him or her to act in specific ways. These guidelines might include procedures such as the following: directives on when to probe, to gather information, to listen, to allow the client to vent feelings, and so forth; directions for developing role-play situations with the client; and identification of themes to discuss in individual interviews or group discussions.

Examples of simple to more complex forms of interventions are as follows:

- a daily telephone call to a client to take medication

- an instruction to follow up on referral to a particular agency

- advice to a parent to meet his or her child after school every evening

- five educational sessions over a three-week period, including didactic presentations and discussions about specific areas

- use of role-play situations in four group meetings with eight clients over a one-month period; clients select interpersonal conflict situations; they carry out role plays under the guidance of the group leader, and group members discuss ways to deal with the conflict situations

- a prescribed series of interviews of a short-term psychotherapy (such as cognitive therapy or task-oriented social work) as prescribed by proponents of the therapy and illustrated in the literature and in case vignettes and videotapes.

IMPLEMENTING THE INTERVENTIONS

After establishing a baseline and indicating a need to ameliorate the existing problem, the clinical social worker should introduce the intervention in accordance with his or her plan. The experience of the client who receives the intervention should be discernibly different from the client's experience before the intervention. Distinguishing the presence of an intervention from other possible interventions, however, may be difficult, especially in complex settings in which the client may interact with professionals from a variety of related disciplines, such as psychiatry, psychology, social work, nursing, education, and occupational therapy. The following questions,

though, may help the social worker make the distinction:

- Who provides the intervention? Is the provider similar or different from the client's other intervention providers?

- Where is the intervention provided? Is the location of intervention similar to or different from the location of other interventions?

- What are the contents of the interventions? Are they similar to or different from the contents of other interventions?

- What are the frequency and duration of the interventions? Are they similar to or different from the frequency or duration of other interventions?

- What is the client unit (for example, individual, family, or group)? Is it similar to or different from the client unit in other interventions?

The more differences between the new intervention and other interventions currently in operation, the more likely the clinician can analyze the additional impact of the new intervention. If more similarities than differences among the interventions exist, then the social worker can analyze the joint effectiveness of all the interventions only as a package. To apply single-subject design methodology for evaluating interventions, it is imperative that the clinical social worker and the client can distinguish the presence or absence of the intervention. For example, a VA neuropsychiatric hospital may refer a client to the clinical social worker who will plan the client's departure from the hospital as well as make the necessary arrangements to enable the client to adjust to his or her community. Posthospital planning is one of many interventions, but the social worker and the client can clearly distinguish it from many other hospital interventions that focus on hospital adjustment, diagnoses, and symptom reduction rather than on adjustment in the family and the community. The client unit is the family in posthospital planning in contrast to the individual as client unit in interventions concerned with hospital adjustment. Moreover, the focus of the contents is on behaviors and attitudes pertaining to family and community adjustment.

Monitoring Intervention Implementation

The social worker determines whether an intervention has been implemented by monitoring the implementation. An intervention is valid if implemented as planned and reliable if implemented consistently for the clients in question (Blythe & Tripodi, 1989). The clinical social worker can construct a checklist to monitor the extent to which he or she has followed certain guidelines, prescriptions, and behaviors for implementing the intervention (Blythe & Tripodi, 1989). Also, the clinical social worker can devise a questionnaire whereby he or she asks the client whether the social worker followed the guidelines. The check-

list in Figure 36 and questionnaire (see Appendix 3), for example, indicates whether the social worker has implemented the intervention of posthospital planning in a VA neuropsychiatric hospital.

The items in Figure 36 and Appendix 3 are illustrative rather than exhaustive. The more that the social worker or the client checks "yes," the more likely it is that the social worker has implemented the intervention. Furthermore, social worker and client agreement on specific items provides evidence of the validity of the intervention. If the social worker were to use the same intervention for a caseload of clients, then consistency in responses across clients would indicate that the social worker is reliably implementing the intervention.

In addition, the clinical social worker can create forms that are specific to interviews or that refer to the ingredients of the intervention, which may cover several contacts between the clinical social worker and the client. The more specific the items in terms

---

figure 36 *Checklist for Clinical Social Worker to Monitor Posthospital Planning Intervention*

Item	Implemented or Not
Filled out all necessary insurance and discharge forms	Yes _____ No _____
Discussed medication regimen	
• With client	Yes _____ No _____
• With family	Yes _____ No _____
Considered whether client can live with family	
• With client	Yes _____ No _____
• With family	Yes _____ No _____
Considered alternative living arrangements in community	Yes _____ No _____
Made contacts with family	
• Face to face	Yes _____ No _____
• Telephone	Yes _____ No _____
Planned contact with community social worker	Yes _____ No _____
Discussed employment	Yes _____ No _____
Discussed educational possibilities	Yes _____ No _____
Arranged for follow-up contact	Yes _____ No _____

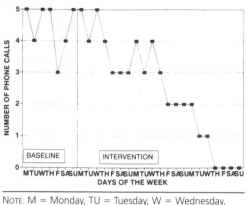

figure 37

*Number of Client Phone Calls per Day
for Four Weeks*

NOTE: M = Monday, TU = Tuesday, W = Wednesday,
TH = Thursday, F = Friday, SA = Saturday, SU = Sunday.

of observable behaviors, the more useful the form for distinguishing between the presence or absence of an intervention. Such forms serve as useful reminders of functions that the clinical social worker needs to carry out. More important, they can indicate whether the client is aware of the social worker's efforts in delivering the intervention.

Measuring during the Intervention Phase

Suppose that a clinical social worker in private practice is beginning to work with a young female client who is disturbed by her obsessive behavior. The client wanted to marry her boyfriend, but he did not want to make that commitment. Their relationship ended, but the client continued to phone her former boyfriend and hang up the phone, without leaving any messages or identification. She also knew how to access his answering machine and would listen to his phone messages at least once per day when she knew he was not home. The social worker asked the client to construct a baseline of calls she made each day to her former boyfriend. The social worker then engaged in short-term cognitive therapy with the client, focusing on the reasons for the phone calls, the client's anger, the possi-

bility of police intervention, realistic alternatives, and so forth.

A daily measurement of the number of phone calls during baseline and three weeks of intervention, two interviews per week, is depicted in Figure 37. Measurement, obtained by the client's self-reports of daily phone calls during intervention, shows a decline in phone calls; hence, the social worker achieved the clinical objective of no phone calls after three weeks of intervention. The clinician also might have constructed a graph to show the number of times the client accessed her former boyfriend's answering machine during baseline and intervention.

Advantages. As shown in Figure 37, measurement during intervention allows the clinical social worker to compare the magnitude of variables at intervention with baseline when there is no intervention. The social worker can use the results of this comparison to evaluate the effectiveness of the intervention in terms of achieving client–social worker clinical objectives. Without measurements at baseline, though, there will not be any comparisons. However, the clinician can use the graphs (Figure 37) to assist in assessment, for example, as determined by high magnitudes on the problem variable such as 5, 4, 5, and 4 telephone calls on the first four days of intervention.

Furthermore, the clinical social worker can observe whether he or she is making progress toward achieving the clinical objectives. A reduction in the number of phone calls over time (Figure 37) indicates progress. In contrast, there might not have been any change in the first three weeks of intervention, and the therapeutic interactions might even have led to an increased number of phone calls. If the social worker has not made progress within a designated period, then he or she would have to rely on his or her clinical experience and knowledge to decide whether to continue the intervention, modify it, discard it for a substitute intervention, seek consultation for assistance in the decision-making process, refer the client elsewhere, or terminate the intervention.

The clinical social worker also can use measurements at intervention to provide feedback to the client and as stimuli for further therapeutic discussion. For example, after the first week of intervention (Figure 37), there is a decline in the number of phone calls, with a plateau of three phone calls per day on Friday, Saturday, and Sunday. Suppose the client and the social worker had an interview on Tuesday of the second week of intervention. The social worker might point out the pattern to the client, reinforcing verbally the progress the client has made and asking about the reasons for the plateau of three calls per day. Overall, measurements at intervention can serve as brief summaries of progress on specified problem variables. The practitioner can use graphs and therapy notes when he or she gives case presentations for consultation, professional workshops, and community presentations to interested groups.

Disadvantages. One disadvantage of obtaining measurements during intervention is that such a process can detract from the intervention, especially when complicated measurements require a great deal of time for data collection. For example, the completion of a long personality inventory during every social worker–client contact would be excessive. Contrariwise, the client's daily recording of measurements outside of the intervention contact with the social worker would not seriously reduce the time devoted to intervention. However, the social worker would require a brief moment to construct the graphs.

Another disadvantage involves incorporating into the intervention the discussion of progress as depicted by graphic trends. If the clinical social worker sees little use for graphic portrayals of progress, then the time he or she devotes to measurements during the intervention might be wasteful. On the other hand, such information can

be useful in decision making about progress in achieving clinical objectives with respect to problem variables.

That the clinical social worker could view the results of measurements mechanically, not attending to important features of the client's life and the client–social worker interactions, is another disadvantage. During intervention, unanticipated events occur; the clinical social worker makes himself or herself aware of these events by observing qualitative differences in the transactions. For example, the client's progress shown in Figure 37 might not have resulted from the intervention; rather, it might have been the result of the client's positive interactions with another person and the fact that she had become more active socially compared with her relatively sedentary life in the past. Hence, the social worker's observations of other events in the client's life can provide a context for interpreting the measurements on one problem variable.

Characteristics. The measurement process during intervention must be consistent with that during the baseline phase. The operational definitions are identical and the procedures for gathering data are equivalent. Moreover, standards of feasibility, reliability, and validity continually apply. Two especially important characteristics are space between successive measurements and the number of measurements that the social worker should obtain. The distance or space between measurements, for example, days (Figure 37), should be identical at baseline and at intervention so that comparisons between intervention and baseline measurements are of the same units of analysis. If the time units in measurements are not equivalent (for example, comparing days versus weeks), distortions among the graphs are possible and may lead to erroneous conclusions about clinical progress.

The number of measurements the clinician makes during intervention depend on the clinical objective with respect to when the social worker expects changes to occur (or for how long changes are not expected to occur, as in maintenance or prevention). If the social worker predicts changes after a designated period and they do not occur, then the clinical social worker has to decide whether he or she will modify the objective regarding when change will occur. Otherwise, the criterion for the number of measurements is the number obtainable during the designated period. As shown in Figure 37, if the practitioner expects changes during three weeks of intervention, then 21 measurements is the required number.

The number of measurements made also depends on the extent to which there is deterioration in the magnitude of problem variables during intervention. An intervention possibly might exacerbate the problem, resulting in an undesirable higher magnitude of problem variables. For example, the client might not have made progress (Figure 37) if she felt the social worker thought she was "crazy" or "pathological." Instead, after the first week, the number of calls might have increased to 10 or more calls, indicating a strong aversive reaction to the therapist. Of course, the social worker might have considered an initial exacerbation of the behavior as part of the clinical plan. Then the social worker's decision making about the number of measurements—given ethical constraints involved in clinical practice— would depend on the length of time the clinical social worker's theory would allow for an increase in undesirable deteriorative behaviors. Many practitioners would seriously consider modifying or changing the intervention if the number of phone calls increased immediately.

The number of measurements a practitioner makes also depends on the attainment of clinical objectives. If, in the example of the female client with obsessive behavior, the number of phone calls decreased to zero after the first week of intervention and she did not make any phone calls during the second week of intervention, then the social worker could suspend measurements for that problem variable during intervention and simultaneously stop the intervention.

Generally, as indicated by Barlow and Hersen (1984), a criterion for the number of measurements during intervention is to attain a horizontally stable baseline showing persistent achievement of the clinical objective regarding the magnitude of the problem variable. For example, in Figure 37, a horizontally stable baseline exists with the last four measurements from Thursday through Sunday on the third week of intervention.

GRAPHING THE MEASURES

Intervention without a Baseline

Even when a baseline is unattainable, there is utility in graphing the problem variables (measures) during the intervention phase. The measurements can verify the clinical social worker's initial assessment and indicate the extent to which the magnitude of the problem variable (or existence, frequency, or duration) is changing (or not changing) in a desirable direction.

Suppose a male client of a clinical social worker at a community mental health center has just returned to the community after a three-month psychiatric hospitalization for an acute depression. Suppose also that the hospital refers the client to intervention immediately on release to the community. Before hospitalization, the client had difficulty attending his job and the clinical social worker decided to use supportive therapy in addition to the client's prescribed medication for depression. One clinical objective was to increase weekly job attendance to 100 percent attendance. The social worker made 12 measurements, each recording the percentage of attendance on the job (Figure 38). Using the same principles for graphic construction and analysis as used for baseline, the social worker plotted the problem variable on the y axis, and time (in number of weeks) on the x axis. During the first five weeks, the client's job attendance oscillated between 10 percent and 20 percent, measurements that verify the assessment of an attendance problem at work. The social worker arranged to obtain, with the client's consent, attendance information from the client's employer. If

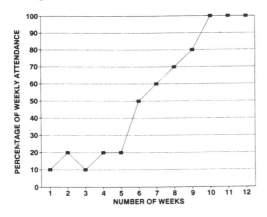

figure 38

Percentage of Weekly Attendance in Client's Job during Clinical Intervention

the client was supposed to be at work 20 hours per week, and he attended only for four hours, his weekly percentage of attendance would be 100 percent times (4/20) = 20 percent. From the sixth week to the 10th week, attendance increased steadily from

50 percent to 100 percent. In addition, the client achieved the clinical objective of 100 percent attendance, which stabilized during the last three weeks; hence, the graph indicates progress during intervention.

It is apparent visually that change occurred during the intervention. However, it is unclear whether change is linked to the intervention or if it would have occurred without the intervention because a baseline was unavailable. What the clinical social worker can infer is whether there is a change in the time series of measurements during intervention, using the same principles of visual analysis and statistical analysis (see Chapter 3). There is a statistically significant shift in the time series of measurements, as indicated by the C statistic (Table 12). Hence, the data, which show there is not horizontal stability but rather an acceleration over time, support the visual perception. No statistical significance indicates a horizontally stable graph, as is

table 12 *Computing C, Sc, and Z for Data in Figure 38*

x	$x - M$	$(x - M)^2$	x_i	$x - x_i$	$(x - x_i)^2$
10	−43.33	1,877.49	20	−10	100
20	−33.33	1,110.89	10	10	100
10	−43.33	1,877.49	20	−10	100
20	−33.33	1,110.89	20	0	0
20	−33.33	1,110.89	50	−30	900
50	−3.33	11.09	60	−10	100
60	6.67	44.49	70	−10	100
70	16.67	277.89	80	−10	100
80	26.67	711.29	100	−20	400
100	46.67	2,178.09	100	0	0
100	46.67	2,178.09	100	0	0
100	46.67	2,178.09	—	—	—
640 = Σx		14,666.68 = SS(x)			| 1,900 | = D^2

$$M = \frac{\Sigma x}{n} = \frac{640}{12} = 53.33$$

$$C = 1 - \frac{D^2}{2SS(x)} = 1 - \frac{1,900}{2(14,666.68)} = .94$$

$$Sc = \sqrt{\frac{n + 2}{(n + 1)(n - 1)}} = \sqrt{\frac{12 + 2}{(12 + 1)(12 - 1)}} = .31$$

$$Z = \frac{C}{Sc} = \frac{.94}{.31} = 3.03$$

NOTE: Because $Z > 1.64$, there is a change in the time series.

desired at baseline. However, in the intervention phase, it is desirable to show statistical significance in the preferred direction of change, as shown in Table 12. No statistically significant change during intervention would indicate no clinical progress when the clinical objective is to achieve change.

Comparing Intervention to Baseline

To construct graphs that contain measurements plotted for both baseline and intervention, the clinical social worker should follow the same principles for constructing baseline graphs, as well as the following suggestions for extending the time series to interventions.

The social worker should use the same measurement processes for gathering data during intervention. As is evident from Fig-

Baseline and Intervention Measurements of Daily Anxiety over 16 Days

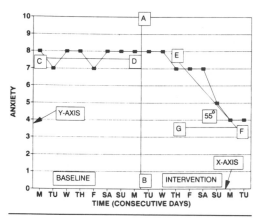

NOTE: M = Monday, TU = Tuesday, W = Wednesday, TH = Thursday, F = Friday, SA = Saturday, SU = Sunday.

ure 39, vertical line AB separates measurements at baseline from those at intervention. The social worker has plotted the first eight measurements of anxiety on a 10-point scale ranging from 0 = no anxiety to 10 = high anxiety during baseline when there was no intervention; he or she plotted the next eight measurements during intervention. The practitioner has plotted measurements for intervention using the same range of possible magnitudes as at baseline. The ordinate of each point can range from

0 to 10 (y axis) for both baseline and intervention. The practitioner plotted measurements for each point on the x axis, which has the same time intervals for intervention and for baseline (each interval is one day).

The number of measurements during intervention should be at least the same number as at baseline. Typically, there are many more measurements at intervention. In Figure 39, the number of measurements at baseline and at intervention is identical. However, the social worker could have extended the measurement to include more measurements so they would be consonant with clinical objectives.

Furthermore, the clinician should know the clinical objectives with respect to when he or she expects the intervention to have an impact. For example, the social worker might not expect anxiety to be reduced until there are five or more clinical sessions over a two-week period; if that is the case, he or she would extend the graph to cover that period. If the clinical social worker did not expect change until five months, he or she would continually take measurements for more than five months, without expecting change until five months had elapsed. Then, the social worker could graph the baseline and compare it with intervention after five months, determining whether the expected change occurred at the expected time. That is, if no change had occurred during the five-month period, the clinician could compare baseline with intervention after five months, omitting the graph for the first five months of intervention. The social worker also should know the clinical objectives with respect to the degree of change expected. For example, the client and clinical social worker might have agreed that a change in magnitude of four points on a self-anchored anxiety scale would be clinically significant.

In reading the graphs comparing intervention with baseline, the clinical social worker must keep the following points in mind. For one, he or she should look for a change in degree from the baseline series of measurements to the intervention series of measurements. In Figure 39 at baseline, anxiety ranges from 7 to 8, but during intervention, the magnitude of anxiety decreases from 8 to 4.

In addition, the practitioner should look for a change in slope in the time series. At baseline, the slope is virtually 0 degrees as shown by line CD, which is an estimated average line of the measurements (Figure 39). During intervention, line EF shows an average estimated slope of 55 degrees (formed by drawing a line parallel to the x axis and intersecting it with point F). These average estimate lines are not completely accurate; instead, they help indicate whether there is a change in the time series. (A section later in this chapter discusses how statistical methods can more precisely indicate change.) The series of measurements at baseline are relatively stable horizontally; the series of measurements during intervention are decelerating downward, with the last two measurements stable at a magnitude of 4.

In reading graphs, the clinician should look for achievement of clinical objectives. If the objective is to reduce anxiety by four points, then the last two measurements in Figure 39 are clinically significant—the social worker has achieved the objective. The clinician also should look for stability after change. For example, in Figure 39, the third, fourth, and fifth measurements during intervention are stable at a magnitude of 7, but all the other measurements are below that point. The apparent stability of the last two measurements at a magnitude of 4 also may change with subsequent measurements that also might decelerate downward. Finally, the social worker should describe the highest and lowest points. In Figure 39, the range of magnitude is 8 to 7 at baseline and 8 to 4 during intervention. The drop of four points in magnitude during intervention represents a change in a desirable direction, that is, in relation to the clinical objective of reducing anxiety.

Examples of Change and No Change

Suppose that a clinical social worker is engaged in short-term cognitive therapy with a female client who is having a great deal of difficulty in her marital relationship. Although both she and her husband have indicated that the husband has not had nor is having an extramarital relationship, the client complained of obsessive thoughts about his infidelity. According to the client, she has these thoughts several times per day. The social worker asks the client to record on a daily basis the number of obsessive thoughts for eight consecutive days to form a baseline.

Figure 40 shows the baseline measurements and eight measurements during intervention in which there was only one treatment session, with no change expected. The magnitude of measurement is roughly the same at baseline and during intervention. At baseline, there are six 5s and two 4s; at intervention, there are five 5s and three 4s. Both intervention and baseline have slopes near 0 degrees without evident change. If a clinical objective were to reduce the number of obsessive thoughts to 1 or 0 per day, then it is evident in the figure that the social worker did not achieve the clinical objective. However, no change is a clinical objective when there is an intervention to stabilize maintenance, thus preventing relapse. If the client achieved the objective of having no obsessive thoughts, a maintenance objective might be to continue to show no obsessive thoughts or to register no change.

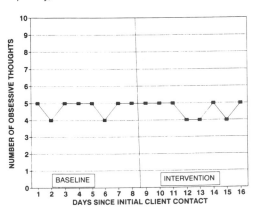

figure 40

Daily Number of Obsessive Thoughts about Infidelity, at Baseline and at Intervention

Negative change or deterioration occurs when the client shows change from baseline to a greater degree of the problem following the introduction of intervention. Deterioration is unplanned; rather, it is an unexpected consequence the clinical social worker must be prepared to confront. To illustrate this type of change, Figure 41 shows that the client with obsessive thoughts about infidelity increased her obsessive thoughts during the first week of intervention, nine days after initial contact with the clinical social worker. The magnitude of the number of obsessive thoughts increased from 5 on the eighth day of baseline to 7 on the first day of intervention, nine days after initial contact with the client at intake. Moreover, the number of obsessive thoughts during intervention increased at a slope of approximately 30 degrees (the angle BAC is formed by intersecting the estimated average line of the measurements, AB, with line AC, parallel to the x axis) to 10 obsessive thoughts per day.

figure 41

Deterioration in the Daily Number of Obsessive Thoughts about Infidelity, from Baseline to Intervention

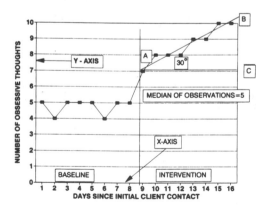

Positive change is a change in the desired direction with respect to clinical objectives. In Figure 42, positive change is evident because there is a decelerating slope, which indicates a decrease in the number of obsessive thoughts. Line AB represents the

median (the point below which 50 percent of the observations fall) of the baseline observations. The social worker calculates the median by rank ordering all of the observations at baseline and selecting the point that is halfway as follows:

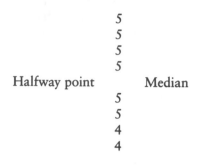

5	
5	
5	
5	
Halfway point	Median
5	
5	
4	
4	

The halfway point in the observation is the average of the fourth and fifth ranked observations; the median is 5.

In Figure 42, all of the observations in the fourth week of intervention, beginning with 22 days since initial contact with the client at intake, are below the baseline median, assuming there are no changes from baseline to the first three weeks of intervention. During the fourth week, the number of obsessive thoughts decreased from 2 to 0 per day. The slope, shown by angle CDE is 26 degrees, which indicates a decelerating trend. The social worker has attained the clinical objective of no obsessive thoughts on day 27 of measurement and has maintained the objective on days 28 and 29.

Calculating Statistical Significance

The clinical social worker can follow two procedures for calculating statistical significance: (1) the C statistic and (2) the binomial test for horizontal baseline. Other procedures are available in Kazdin (1992), Bloom, Fischer, and Orme (1993), and Blythe, Tripodi, and Briar (1994). Using the data in Figures 41 and 42, the social worker calculates the C statistic for comparing the time series at baseline and intervention in the same way as for C baseline only. The social worker uses all of the observations from baseline and intervention, as long as there are eight or more observa-

figure 42

Positive Change in the Daily Number of Obsessive Thoughts about Infidelity, from Baseline to Three Weeks after Intervention

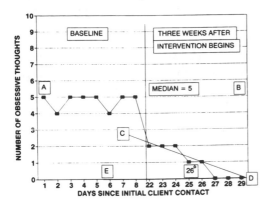

tions, to make the calculations. In Table 13, $C = .88$, $Sc = .26$, and $Z = 3.38$. Because Z is greater than 1.64, the probability of this occurrence is less than five times out of 100, a statistical criterion indicating a shift in the time series of observations from baseline to intervention during the fourth week. If Z were less than 1.64, it would indicate no change from baseline to intervention.

To evaluate whether there are any statistically significant shifts from baseline to intervention, the social worker can use the binomial test for horizontal baseline (Blythe & Tripodi, 1989, pp. 127–130). The social worker can only use this procedure when there is no evidence of change in the baseline series of observations, which he or she can determine by using C as described in Chapter 3.

First, the social worker calculates the median of the baseline observations (which is 5; see Figure 42). Then, he or she draws a dotted line through point 5 on the y axis parallel to the x axis (line AB). The social worker subsequently determines what is a success and what is a failure. Successes should be on that side of the line that is consonant with the clinical objective. In Figure 42, any observation below line AB is considered a success, and observations

above the line are failures. If an observation fell exactly on the median, then the social worker would not use it. The next step is to count the number of successes and the number of observations during intervention. Because all eight observations (Figure 42) are below the median, there are eight successes out of eight observations. Table 14 indicates the minimum number of successes required out of specified observations ranging from 5 to 25 to indicate a statistically significant shift from baseline to intervention beyond the .05 level of probability. For eight observations, the minimum number of successes is seven; this means that there are statistically significant changes with seven or eight successes out of eight observations. Hence, this method also shows statistically significant differences for the data in Figure 42.

The calculations of C for the data in Figure 41 are shown in Table 15. The statistics $C = .93$, $Sc = .26$, and $Z = 3.58$ indicate a statistically significant shift in the time series from baseline to intervention because Z is greater than the criterion of 1.96. Because the observations are not in the predicted direction, the criterion shifts from a one-tailed test with Z is greater than 1.64 to a two-tailed probability test, in which Z at or beyond the .05 level of probability is 1.96. Refer to any standard statistics text for a discussion of one-tailed and two-tailed probability tests. That the criterion value is 1.96 instead of 1.64 reflects that deterioration is not predicted whereas positive change is. Hence, the social worker should use $Z = 1.64$ when predicting positive change and $Z = 1.96$ when testing for negative change. These data indicate that deterioration (or negative change) is associated with the intervention.

The binomial test also indicates negative change. In Figure 41, the median is 5. During intervention, eight out of eight observations are failures because the observations are in an opposite direction from the clinical objective of reducing the number of obsessive thoughts.

Judging Change

The clinical social worker determines whether there is change from baseline to intervention by using clinical judgment or statistical significance. Clinical judgment is based on the clinical social worker's observations of whether there is a significant shift in the client's behaviors, attitudes, or moods. A reasonable criterion is one the client and social worker have agreed on after the social worker has assessed the problems for that particular client. The social worker might make a judgment with respect to a general objective such as an unspecified reduction or increase in the problem variable, for example, a decrease in the number of obsessive thoughts, a decrease in the number of drinks, or an increase in the number of positive interactions. A more specific objective would indicate the ex-

pected magnitude for the problem variable, for example, a decrease to zero obsessive thoughts, a decrease to two drinks per day, or an increase to four positive interactions per day. When the expectation is close to baseline, it is difficult to determine whether change is meaningful or whether it occurs on a chance basis. Suppose there is a baseline of five obsessive thoughts per day. An objective of four thoughts per day could result from an error in the data collection or might occur on a chance basis. In that event, the criterion of statistical significance can help to solidify the conclusion of clinical significance if the result is both clinically significant as specified by an a priori judgment and statistically significant.

Statistical significance may or may not indicate clinical significance. To illustrate, the

---

table 13 *Computing C, Sc, and Z for Data in Figure 42*

x	$x - M$	$(x - M)^2$	x_i	$x - x_i$	$(x - x_i)^2$
5	2.12	4.49	4	1	1
4	1.12	1.25	5	−1	1
5	2.12	4.49	5	0	0
5	2.12	4.49	5	0	0
5	2.12	4.49	4	1	1
4	1.12	1.25	5	−1	1
5	2.12	4.49	5	0	0
5	2.12	4.49	2	3	9
2	−.88	.77	2	0	0
2	−.88	.77	2	0	0
2	−.88	.77	1	1	1
1	−1.88	3.53	1	0	0
1	−1.88	3.53	0	1	1
0	−2.88	8.29	0	0	0
0	−2.88	8.29	0	0	0
0	−2.88	8.29	—	—	—
$|46| = \Sigma x$		$63.68 = SS(x)$			$|15| = D^2$

$$M = \frac{\Sigma x}{n} = \frac{46}{16} = 2.88$$

$$C = 1 - \frac{D^2}{2SS(x)} = 1 - \frac{15}{2(63.68)} = .88$$

$$Sc = \sqrt{\frac{n + 2}{(n + 1)(n - 1)}} = \sqrt{\frac{16 + 2}{(16 + 1)(16 - 1)}} = .26$$

$$Z = \frac{C}{Sc} = \frac{.88}{.26} = 3.38$$

NOTE: Because $Z > 1.64$ and $p < .05$, there is a statistically significant change in the time series.

---

binomial test might indicate statistical significance with all observations below a median of 5 as in the example about obsessive thoughts; however, all of the observations may be at a magnitude of 4, and the reduction of 5 to 4 may not be sufficiently clinically significant to represent progress to the clinical social worker and the client. Hence, to be certain whether or not change has occurred, it is strongly recommended that, along with graphic analysis, the social worker use clinical significance in relation to the clinical objectives for the client.

Making Inferences about Correlational and Causal Knowledge

Correlational knowledge. Graphs and statistical techniques along with clinical objectives can serve as tools that assist the clinical social worker in making inferences about correlational knowledge. Correlational knowledge of interest describes the relationship between an intervention and observed change in a problem variable. Hypotheses about correlational knowledge include clinical examples such as follows: Group cognitive therapy reduces animal phobias in children or short-term psychotherapy increases the number of positive comments that family members make about each other. Evidence to substantiate hypotheses about correlational knowledge includes accurate, reliable, and valid measurements of the problem variable (see Chapter 2) and a significant shift in the time series of measurements from baseline to intervention.

Inferences about correlational knowledge are essentially judgments that there is sufficient evidence to support the correlational hypotheses. A statistically significant change in time series at baseline with no intervention to time series of measurements during intervention provides evidence of a correlation. If the time series shows an in-

table 14 *Minimum Number of Successes for Statistical Significance at* p ≤ .05

Number of Observations during Intervention	Minimum Number of Successes Required
5	5
6	6
7	7
8	7
9	8
10	9
11	9
12	10
13	11
14	11
15	12
16	12
17	13
18	14
19	14
20	15
21	16
22	16
23	17
24	17
25	18

crease with the introduction of the intervention, then the correlation is positive; correspondingly, a decrease in the time series indicates a negative correlation. The social worker may evaluate either negative or positive correlations as positive change (improvement) or negative change (deterioration). The evaluation depends on whether the direction of change is consistent with clinical objectives of intervention. Hence, a positive correlation between short-term psychotherapy and an increase in confidence about a decision to divorce indicates positive change, whereas a positive correlation between group cognitive therapy and an increase in animal phobias is evidence of deterioration or negative change.

Graphs that provide evidence of correlations should show a stable horizontal baseline, followed by an acceleration (positive correlation) or a deceleration (negative correlation) during intervention. Specific clinical objectives such as reducing alcoholic consumption from five drinks to zero drinks per day provide evidence of correlational knowledge if, without intervention, the client consumes five drinks daily and, during intervention, consumes zero drinks.

Causal knowledge. Causal knowledge provides substantiating evidence that an intervention is solely responsible for changes in a problem variable. Not only must there be a verified correlation between intervention and changes in the problem variable,

table 15 *Computing C, Sc, and Z for Data in Figure 41*

x	$x - M$	$(x - M)^2$	x_i	$x - x_i$	$(x - x_i)^2$
5	−1.69	2.86	4	1	1
4	−2.69	7.24	5	−1	1
5	−1.69	2.86	5	0	0
5	−1.69	2.86	5	0	0
5	−1.69	2.86	5	0	0
4	−2.69	7.24	5	−1	1
5	−1.69	2.86	5	0	0
5	−1.69	2.86	7	−2	4
7	.31	.10	8	−1	1
8	1.31	1.72	8	0	0
8	1.31	1.72	8	0	0
8	1.31	1.72	9	−1	1
9	2.31	5.34	9	0	0
9	2.31	5.34	10	−1	1
10	3.31	10.96	10	0	0
10	3.31	10.96	—	—	—
$\mid 107 \mid = \Sigma x$		$69.50 = SS(x)$			$\mid 10 \mid = D^2$

$$M = \frac{\Sigma x}{n} = \frac{107}{16} = 6.69$$

$$C = 1 - \frac{D^2}{2SS(x)} = 1 - \frac{10}{2(69.50)} = .93$$

$$Sc = \sqrt{\frac{n + 2}{(n + 1)(n - 1)}} = \sqrt{\frac{16 + 2}{(16 + 1)(16 - 1)}} = .26$$

$$Z = \frac{C}{Sc} = \frac{.93}{.26} = 3.58$$

NOTE: Because $Z > 1.96$ and $p < .05$, there is a statistically significant difference.

but there also must be evidence that the intervention has preceded (in time) changes in the problem variable and that no other variables are responsible for the changes.

The structure of single-subject designs provides evidence of correlational knowledge and the occurrence of the intervention before the problem variable has changed. The social worker accomplishes the correlation by achieving a horizontally stable baseline on the time series of measurements on the problem variable, followed by introducing the intervention and significant change in the problem variable during intervention.

Single-subject design methodology also can provide evidence of the control of variables other than the intervention that might be responsible for change. These other variables are internal validity threats (Campbell & Stanley, 1963; Cook & Campbell, 1979). According to Blythe and Tripodi (1989, p. 142), the social worker needs to control or minimize the following relevant internal validity threats so he or she can make inferences of causality between an intervention and problem variable changes for a single client: history, maturation, initial measurement effects, instrumentation, statistical regression, multiple treatment interference, expectancy effects, interactions, and other unknown factors.

History refers to any variables or events outside of the intervention that occur between the first measurement of the problem variable at baseline and the last measurement during intervention. It does not include events usually considered "history" that have preceded the measurements. Factors such as natural disasters, changes in employment and occupational status, changes in family income, and health are variables subsumed under history. Suppose a male client reduces the number of negative comments to his spouse during one week of intervention. This change may result from a historical factor between measurements, such as the illness of his spouse. He may have made his negative comments during dinner, but his wife's illness may

have reduced the opportunities for this negative exchange. The clinical social worker would want to know whether he will continue to reduce his negative comments in situations in which he and his wife have dinner together.

The basic single-subject design phases of baseline, intervention, and follow-up do not control historical factors. When applicable, the social worker can achieve control of historical factors by using design variations such as multiple baseline, graduated intensity, and withdrawal–reversal designs (see Chapter 6). In addition, the clinical social worker can use qualitative data obtained from clinical interviews to make inferences about the extent to which events that could affect changes in the problem variables have occurred. For example, the clinical social worker, through interviews, may know whether family composition, economic status, or jobs have changed. If there are no qualitative changes in these apparent factors that could influence change, the clinical social worker can make an inference that, although historical factors are not controlled, their effects on the observed changes appear to be minimal with respect to those historical factors observed.

Maturation refers to events that occur within the client; such events result from changes in growth, physiological mechanisms, illness, and so forth. Design variations also can control these factors (see Chapter 6); however, the basic single-subject design model cannot control these factors. As with historical factors, the social worker can make inferences about the potential influence or lack of influence of maturation effects on problem variable changes by using information gained during clinical interviews and from other available sources such as family members, medical charts for patients in a hospital, or school records of health. Of course, the social worker needs easy access to such data. Assumably, the social worker would use his or her knowledge from clinical interviews but would not actively seek other data simply to minimize the threat of maturation.

However, if changes occur quickly, for example, within several weeks, and there apparently are not any changes in health, growth, medication, or fatigue, then it is plausible for the social worker to assume that maturational effects are minimal.

Initial measurement effects refer to the influence of the first measurements on subsequent measurements of a problem variable. These effects are controlled if there is a horizontally stable baseline. *Instrumentation* refers to the possibility that the process of measurement is nonstandardized and observed changes result from nonstandardization rather than the intervention. For example, changes observed in the problem variable may not result from intervention but from measurement at different times of day and by different observers. Standardized measurement controls possible effects of instrumentation in terms of consistent observers and measurement times and places and by achieving a horizontally stable baseline before intervention. *Statistical regression* refers to the tendency of either positive or negative extreme scores to move toward the average. It also signifies an accelerating or a decelerating trend over time at baseline. Statistical regression, too, is controlled by achieving a horizontally stable baseline.

Multiple treatment interference indicates that other interventions may occur between initial measurements at baseline and subsequent measurements during intervention. The clinical social worker can observe by means of clinical interviews whether the client is receiving interventions other than the one being tested. If there are no apparent competing treatments, then this internal validity threat is minimized. It is essentially a subcomponent of history; hence, by using variations of the basic model of single-subject design—multiple baseline, graduated intensity, and withdrawal–reversal designs—the social worker can control its effects.

Expectancy effects indicate changes in the problem variable that result from client ex-pectations about interventions, prognoses, and so forth. As with history and maturation, the social worker can control these factors by using design variations (see Chapter 6).

Interactions refer to the combined effects of history, maturation, initial measurement effects, instrumentation, statistical regression, multiple treatment interference, and expectancy effects. By using design variations (see Chapter 6), but not the basic model of single-subject design, the social worker can potentially control these factors. Other unknown factors may be responsible for changes in the problem variable. The social worker also can control these factors using design variations. In addition, through interviews, the clinical social worker can gain information about the extent to which it appears that other factors are not responsible for observed changes.

The basic single-subject design model of baseline, intervention, and follow-up can provide a substantial amount of evidence of a causal relationship between an intervention and problem variables. Evidence may be of the intervention occurring before changes in the problem variable; a positive correlation; the control of initial measurement effects, instrumentation, and statistical regression; and additional information gained through clinical interviews that other factors such as history, maturation, and multiple treatment interference are inoperative between initial measurements of the problem variable at baseline and subsequent measurements during intervention. Hence, the social worker can obtain an approximation to causal knowledge using single-subject design methodology.

Making Decisions about Interventions

The clinical social worker can use information based on the attainment of clinical objectives and a comparison of time-series data at intervention to baseline to make decisions about when to change the intervention for a particular client. Changing the intervention involves the social worker's clinical judgment in deciding whether to continue or discontinue the intervention. Berlin and Marsh (1993), for example, have offered intervention guidelines based on the social worker's understanding and use of theoretical perspectives for changing clients' cognitions, emotions, interpersonal interactions, and situations. Although their guidelines provide useful dimensions to consider in planning and implementing interventions, they apparently do not indicate when and how social workers should, if at all, change interventions during the course of treatment. The specific actions ultimately depend on the clinical social worker's judgment, based on the social worker's experience and work with similar clients.

TYPOLOGY FOR CONSIDERING INTERVENTION CHANGES

The clinical social worker can use a topology based on information from single-subject designs to describe conditions under which he or she considers making changes during the intervention phase. The information consists of change (or no change), determined by comparing the intervention phase to baseline, and the judgment as to whether the social worker has attained clinical objectives.

A typology produces six types (Table 16). Type 1 is one of no change but in which the social worker has attained the clinical objective of no change. Type 1 may occur when the objective is to maintain a state that the client already has achieved, for ex-

ample, preventing the occurrence of relapse in an alcoholic client who has quit drinking. Furthermore, a type 1 phenomenon may occur when prevention is the objective, such as a group intervention with adolescent girls to prevent teenage pregnancy.

If the clinical social worker has attained the objectives within the desired period, say one year, then he or she could discontinue the intervention and prepare for follow-up, or the social worker could continue the intervention, but with fewer contacts to determine whether he or she has maintained the objectives before ultimately discontinuing services. The social worker also could simply continue the intervention; such a decision would imply that the social worker had shifted the clinical objective of time, for example, believing that maintenance of an alcoholic's nondrinking behavior is a long-term investment that should warrant intervention for more than one year.

Type 2 consists of positive change and the attainment of the clinical objective. For example, family therapy with a family may have resulted in increased positive family interactions among family members. Assuming there are no other clinical objectives and that the social worker has achieved the objective within a desired period, the social worker needs to decide whether to discontinue or to continue the intervention but with reduced contact. The social worker also could continue to provide intervention to determine whether the observed changes persist.

table 16 *Typology Based on Attainment of Clinical Objectives and Comparisons of Intervention to Baseline*

Change Determined by Comparing Intervention Phase to Baseline	Attainment of Clinical Objectives	
	Attained	Not Attained
No change	Type 1	Type 4
Positive change	Type 2	Type 5
Negative change	Type 3	Type 6

Type 3 is controversial. It occurs when the social worker has attained an objective but the change is negative. Some clinicians would say it is unethical to have an objective of negative change. However, other clinicians might believe that it may be necessary to obtain an instrumental objective of negative change for a particular client before attaining a positive desirable change. For example, in psychotherapy with a male client who desires a constructive relationship with his father, an instrumental clinical objective might be that the client is first able to express hostile feelings to his father. For this type, the clinical social worker must monitor carefully changes that occur if he or she decides to continue the intervention. Discontinuance of the intervention is necessary if the social worker believes there is no relationship between the instrumental goal and the ultimate goal, or if the social worker accepts that he or she has achieved the objective in the specified time. However, the focus of intervention would shift from the promotion of hostile expressed feelings to the consideration of a constructive relationship. The social worker would discontinue the intervention for that particular objective (to express hostile feelings) and modify it to include the ultimate objective (to provide a constructive relationship). Subsequently, there should be a reduction in the magnitude of hostile feelings.

Type 4 consists of no change and nonattainment of the clinical objective. It occurs when the social worker has not achieved an objective of positive change within a specified period. For example, through cognitive therapy coupled with behavior modification, the social worker may have been unable to reduce a 10-year-old child's fear of animals. In this instance, the clinical social worker may continue the same intervention, giving it a longer time to take effect. Or he or she may continue with a modified intervention, adding or subtracting a component, such as adding a token economy system in which the social worker awards points that the client accumulates for a reward as the client increasingly gets closer to petting a tame animal. The clinical social worker also may continue with a substitute intervention, such as group therapy focused on a discussion of animal fears and methods for coping with those fears. If the social worker believes he or she is unable to help the client, then the social worker should consider discontinuing the intervention, consulting with her or his supervisor or other knowledgeable professionals, or perhaps referring the client to another source.

Type 5 is one of positive change, but without achieving the clinical objective. For example, the social worker might have used behavioral therapy to enable a teenage client to adhere to his or her home curfew. Graphic analysis may have indicated positive change as did the statistically significant shifts in the number of times the client missed curfew at intervention compared with baseline. However, the clinical objective may have been to not miss any curfews for one week; the social worker did not attain this objective. Because the data indicate progress, the clinical social worker should continue the intervention, either with no change or with modification. For example, he or she might modify the intervention by increasing the frequency and duration of contacts with the client.

Type 6 is the most serious type because it indicates that the problem variable is becoming increasingly severe as the social worker provides intervention, even though the clinical objective might have been one of positive change, maintenance, or prevention. The clinical social worker should discontinue the intervention, carefully reconsider the assessment, and try to discern what went wrong through clinical interviews. Then he or she should consider using a different intervention or referring the client to another source.

The six types are not pure types; that is, they depend on the a priori clinical objectives of the social worker and the client and on the evidence from single-subject designs of change. Although the decisions suggested assumed there were no other clinical objectives, the processing of information is obviously more complex given multiple objectives. The social worker could prioritize the objectives (see Blythe & Tripodi, 1989, for a discussion of prioritization of objectives).

Single-subject designs can provide information about whether the clinical social worker should make a decision about intervention. Moreover, the six types suggest decisions that the clinical social worker might make. Ultimately, the social worker makes decisions based on the best available information about the client's situation; the assessment of the problem; indications of progress (obtainable from single-subject designs); his or her experience and theoretical orientation; a good sense of timing; practicalities affecting the client's life; and sound clinical judgment.

PHASE 3: FOLLOW-UP

DEFINITION OF FOLLOW-UP

Follow-up is the final phase in the basic model of baseline, intervention, and follow-up for single-subject design methodology. The social worker measures the same problem variables at follow-up as at baseline and intervention; for comparative purposes, the social worker uses the same time intervals between measurements. The purposes of follow-up are to determine whether the positive changes during intervention persist on removal of intervention, the problem recurs or relapses, new problems appear, and the social worker should reinstitute intervention. The discussion in this chapter is based on information from Tripodi and Epstein (1980), Epstein and Tripodi (1977), Blythe and Tripodi (1989), Rubin and Babbie (1993), Corcoran and Fischer (1987a, 1987b), and Fowler (1988).

The two basic types of follow-up are as follows. The first occurs after the social worker has terminated intervention with the client; the second, after the social worker has terminated intervention for a particular objective for a client while another intervention with the same client is occurring (Blythe & Tripodi, 1989). The first type represents a more typical usage of the term follow-up; for example, a clinical social worker in private practice may terminate his or her work with a phobic teenager after accomplishing the objective of reducing the phobia and when there are no other objectives to pursue. The second type of follow-up can occur when there are multiple objectives and the social worker uses multiple interventions. For example, the social worker and the client may have agreed on two clinical objectives: (1) to reduce cigarette smoking and (2) to reduce anxiety when meeting new people. The clinical social worker might use behavioral

modification techniques based on reinforcement theory to reduce cigarette smoking and cognitive therapy and role-playing techniques to reduce anxiety. If the social worker accomplishes the objective of reducing cigarette smoking, then he or she terminates the behavioral modification intervention; however, the social worker still uses cognitive therapy and role-playing techniques to reduce anxiety. Follow-up occurs as the social worker continues to measure the number of cigarettes smoked while using an intervention to reduce anxiety.

Follow-up is planned or unplanned. When planned, it can be cost-effective in that the client is engaged in the therapeutic process. After accomplishing the clinical objectives, the social worker can make plans such as the following to ease the transition from intervention to no intervention. First, the practitioner could reduce the intensity and duration of the intervention to determine whether, on termination of intervention, the client could maintain the positive results he or she achieved with full intervention. For example, the social worker might have two client contacts per week for one-hour duration at each contact for full intervention; a reduced intervention might consist of one contact per three weeks. Second, the social worker could specify clinical objectives for when to measure the problem variables. For example, he or she might anticipate that there will be no differences in the occurrence of problem variables between full intervention and reduced intervention one month later. Third, the social worker can plan termination with the client with an objective to enlist the client's participation in measurement of the problem variables one month after termination and to obtain other follow-up information from the client in a scheduled appointment.

figure 43

Baseline, Intervention, and Follow-up
Measurements of Client's Thoughts
of Inadequacy

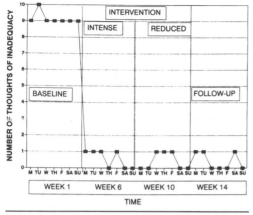

NOTE: M = Monday, TU = Tuesday, W = Wednesday,
TH = Thursday, F = Friday, SA = Saturday, SU = Sunday.

The social worker decides the time of the appointment based on what he or she considers to be a reasonable amount of time to discern whether the problem has recurred. Fourth, the practitioner gathers follow-up data and analyzes them in relation to the clinical objectives for the client. The social worker then decides whether to continue termination or to invite the client to participate anew in the therapeutic process.

Unplanned follow-up refers to the task of obtaining follow-up data when the social worker has not made any previous arrangements with the client or the client's friends or family to engage in follow-up activities. This follow-up procedure is not recommended for single-subject designs because it is difficult to use given potential ambiguities and lack of standardization of measurement. However, the social worker can secure useful information from unplanned follow-up that is based on data gathered at one point in time, such as in a survey.

EXAMPLE OF FOLLOW-UP

Suppose that a male client has low self-esteem and believes that he is inadequate for dealing with most activities and relationships in his everyday life. He is an un-

married adult who works as an insurance underwriter, and throughout each day he thinks about his inadequacy. Taking advantage of an EAP, the client engages in a therapeutic process with a clinical social worker. One clinical objective on which both social worker and client agree is that the client should significantly reduce the number of inadequate thoughts on a daily basis by the sixth week of intervention. The social worker asks the client to count the number of times he has inadequate thoughts about himself daily before intervention at baseline and during intense intervention, which consists of two 45-minute appointments per week.

Results indicate that the client had nine inadequate thoughts daily at baseline, except on Tuesday, when he had 10 inadequate thoughts (Figure 43). The clinical social worker, while assessing the problem, took baseline measurements in the first week of contact. The intervention was cognitive therapy, emphasizing strategies to overcome self-defeating beliefs and cognitive distortions (Burns & deJong, 1980). The social worker instructed the client to continue counting the number of inadequate thoughts just before going to bed each day. Because the clinical objective was to significantly reduce the number of inadequate thoughts by week 6 of intense intervention, the social worker did not record weeks 2 to 5 on the graph; nevertheless, the trend was downward. At week 6, there were three days of no thoughts of inadequacy and four days with only one thought of inadequacy. A visual comparison of the time series of intense intervention to baseline clearly shows a significant shift in a clinically desirable direction (readers can verify this shift by computing C, Sc, and Z using the seven observations at baseline—9, 10, 9, 9, 9, 9, 9—and the seven observations at week 6—1, 1, 1, 0, 1, 0, 0). Having achieved the clinical objective of no more than one inadequate thought per day at week 6 of contact, the social worker decides to reduce the intervention to one 45-minute session every two weeks. This reduced intervention assumes, for purposes of illustration, that there are no other objectives for the client; for example, another objective might have been to increase the client's self-esteem. Furthermore, the social worker would not have reduced the intervention if the clinical objective had been to have no thoughts of inadequacy for at least five out of seven days.

The client continues to count the number of inadequate thoughts on a daily basis and presents his measurements to the clinical social worker. The agreed-on objective was that reduced intervention at week 10 would produce the same results as with intervention at week 6. Results indicate four days with one inadequate thought and three days with no inadequate thoughts during intense intervention, and three days with one inadequate thought and four days with

no inadequate thoughts during reduced intervention (Figure 43). Moreover, Table 17 shows no significant change in the time series of the number of inadequate thoughts. Hence, the results are virtually identical with those at reduced intervention. At this point, the clinical social worker and the client may decide to terminate intervention, but the client will still continue to monitor the number of inadequate thoughts daily. The objective for follow-up is that the results should be the same one month later. Hence, the social worker schedules an appointment for that time and asks the client to complete a follow-up questionnaire. The observations at follow-up—1, 1, 0, 0, 0, 1, 0—are similar to the observations at reduced intervention—0, 0, 1, 1, 1, 0, 0 (Figure 43). In addition, there are no statistically significant changes between reduced

table 17	Computing C, Sc, and Z for Intense Intervention and Reduced Intervention in Figure 43					
x	$x - M$	$(x - M)^2$	x_i	$x - x_i$	$(x - x_i)^2$
1	.5	.25	1	0	0
1	.5	.25	1	0	0
1	.5	.25	0	1	1
0	−.5	.25	1	−1	1
1	.5	.25	0	1	1
0	−.5	.25	0	0	0
0	−.5	.25	0	0	0
0	−.5	.25	0	0	0
0	−.5	.25	1	−1	1
1	.5	.25	1	0	0
1	.5	.25	1	0	0
1	.5	.25	0	1	1
0	−.5	.25	0	0	0
0	−.5	.25	—	—	—
$7 = \Sigma x$		$3.5 = SS(x)$			$5 = D^2$

$$M = \frac{\Sigma x}{n} = \frac{7}{14} = .50$$

$$C = 1 - \frac{D^2}{2SS(x)} = 1 - \frac{5}{2(3.5)} = .29$$

$$Sc = \sqrt{\frac{n + 2}{(n + 1)(n - 1)}} = \sqrt{\frac{14 + 2}{(14 + 1)(14 - 1)}} = .29$$

$$Z = \frac{C}{Sc} = \frac{.29}{.29} = 1.00$$

NOTE: Because $Z < 1.64$, there is no change.

intervention and follow-up (Table 18), which indicates that the results achieved by intervention have persisted in follow-up.

To further verify that the results at follow-up are dramatically different from baseline, the clinical social worker visually compares the observations at baseline—9, 10, 9, 9, 9, 9, 9—with those at follow-up—1, 1, 0, 0, 0, 1, 0 (Figure 43). Furthermore, calculating C, Sc, and Z, the clinical social worker verifies that the time series of the number of inadequate thoughts differ from baseline to follow-up, indicating a statistically significant reduction in the number of inadequate thoughts (Table 19). Hence, the results of the time series show a correlation between the intervention and a shift in the number of thoughts of inadequacy. Moreover, the analysis of data at follow-up indi-cates that the results persist when there is no intervention. Because the baseline measurements indicated horizontal stability, the internal validity threats of statistical regression, instrumentation, and the influence of previous measurements are controlled. Furthermore, there is evidence that the intervention occurred before the changes in the problem variable of thoughts of inadequacy.

An additional procedure at follow-up is to gather data through a questionnaire or interview; the clinical social worker gathers data at the same time the client sees the social worker for a scheduled interview. The data serve to assist the social worker in deciding whether to continue the termination of intervention or reintroduce intervention. The data also provide evidence regarding

| table 18 | Computing C, Sc, and Z for Reduced Intervention and Follow-up in Figure 43 |

x	$x - M$	$(x - M)^2$	x_i	$x - x_i$	$(x - x_i)^2$
0	−.43	.18	0	0	0
0	−.43	.18	1	−1	1
1	.57	.32	1	0	0
1	.57	.32	1	0	0
1	.57	.32	0	1	1
0	−.43	.18	0	0	0
0	−.43	.18	1	−1	1
1	.57	.32	1	0	0
1	.57	.32	0	1	1
0	−.43	.18	0	0	0
0	−.43	.18	0	0	0
0	−.43	.18	1	−1	1
1	.57	.32	0	1	1
0	−.43	.18	—	—	—
$6 = \Sigma x$		$3.36 = SS(x)$			$6 = D^2$

$$M = \frac{\Sigma x}{n} = \frac{6}{14} = .43$$

$$C = 1 - \frac{D^2}{2SS(x)} = 1 - \frac{6}{2(3.36)} = .11$$

$$Sc = \sqrt{\frac{n + 2}{(n + 1)(n - 1)}} = \sqrt{\frac{14 + 2}{(14 + 1)(14 - 1)}} = .29$$

$$Z = \frac{C}{Sc} = \frac{.11}{.29} = 0.38$$

NOTE: Because $Z < 1.64$, there is no change.

the control of historical and maturational factors as well as multiple treatment interference. At the last regularly scheduled meeting, the social worker might ask questions to help him or her uncover whether any other factors could be responsible for the persistence of results and to discern new client needs (Appendix 4). As the responses in Appendix 5 indicate, the client received no help from other sources or persons, increased numbers of thoughts of inadequacy did not recur, he did not change his daily living habits or living circumstances, neither he nor his family members were sick, no other major problems occurred, the client felt more energetic and outgoing, and he was dating women more frequently. Probably no factors of history, maturation, or other forms of intervention were responsible for the consistent positive

changes, although there is partial evidence for a causal relationship between the cognitive intervention and the changes in the problem variable. The evidence suggests that the social worker should terminate services for the client because the client accomplished clinical objectives and no new problems emerged. On the other hand, the clinical social worker might. arrange for one more follow-up interview one to two months later if he or she is not completely convinced that the results will continue to persist.

ADVANTAGES AND DISADVANTAGES OF OBTAINING FOLLOW-UP DATA

In considering the pros and cons of gathering follow-up data, it is helpful to separate follow-up into planned and unplanned

---

table 19 *Computing C, Sc, and Z for Follow-up and Baseline in Figure 43*

x	x − M	(x − M)²	x_i	x − x_i	(x − x_i)²
9	4.22	17.81	10	−1	1
10	5.22	27.25	9	1	1
9	4.22	17.81	9	0	0
9	4.22	17.81	9	0	0
9	4.22	17.81	9	0	0
9	4.22	17.81	9	0	0
9	4.22	17.81	1	8	64
1	−3.78	14.29	1	0	0
1	−3.78	14.29	0	1	1
0	−4.78	22.85	0	0	0
0	−4.78	22.85	0	0	0
0	−4.78	22.85	1	−1	1
1	−3.78	14.29	0	0	0
0	−4.78	22.85	—	—	—
67 = Σx		268.38 = SS(x)			68 = D²

$$M = \frac{\Sigma x}{n} = \frac{67}{14} = 4.78$$

$$C = 1 - \frac{D^2}{2SS(x)} = 1 - \frac{68}{2(268.38)} = .87$$

$$Sc = \sqrt{\frac{n + 2}{(n + 1)(n - 1)}} = \sqrt{\frac{14 + 2}{(14 + 1)(14 - 1)}} = .29$$

$$Z = \frac{C}{Sc} = \frac{.87}{.29} = 3.00$$

NOTE: Because Z > 1.64, there are significant changes.

follow-up and into termination of an objective as opposed to termination of all work with the client.

Condition 1: Planned Follow-up with Termination of Intervention for an Objective

In planned termination, the client is aware of and cooperates in data collection after withdrawal of the intervention. After terminating intervention for an objective, the clinical social worker continues to work with the client to attain other objectives using other interventions. Follow-up data in this circumstance have several advantages. For one, the social worker can easily obtain systematic measurements on the problem variable because the client continues to have contact with the social worker. For example, the client may have reported the number of times he or she shoplifted daily at baseline and at intervention, during which time the client reported no shoplifting. The social worker may terminate intervention for reducing shoplifting and might use another intervention for increasing positive relationships with the client's friends, a second clinical objective. The practitioner can obtain systematic measurements (a log of daily self-reports on the number of times the client shoplifts daily). However, so that the information gathered will be treated as follow-up data, the social worker must provide a different intervention to attain the second objective. Otherwise, the data would reflect an extension of the intervention—the same intervention would be operative.

Other advantages of follow-up data are that the response rate for follow-up would be virtually 100 percent, and the costs would be minimal, reflecting only the social worker's time needed to gather and process the data. Furthermore, accountability would be high. The clinical social worker could use the follow-up data to detect any movement from goal attainment. The identification of undesirable trends or complete relapse would enable the social worker to decide whether to reinstitute the intervention or to seek consultation or make referrals.

One of the disadvantages for gathering planned follow-up data when terminating intervention for an objective is that the social worker may not be able to easily withdraw the intervention while he or she still has contact with the client. The client may discuss the intervention with the social worker and may continue to focus on that intervention or other interventions for the same problem. For example, although the social worker withdraws an intervention based on cognitive theory for dealing with shoplifting, the client continues to discuss ways of dealing with shoplifting, in effect, extending the intervention into follow-up.

Furthermore, if the client is involved in data collection, for example, produces a log of the number of times he shoplifted daily, the client may pursue data collection less rigorously after he knows he and the practitioner have accomplished the objective and that he and the clinical social worker are focusing on other objectives. Another disadvantage is that costs could be excessive if there is an extensive amount of data collection requiring a great deal of the social worker's time.

Condition 2: Planned Follow-up with Termination of Client

This condition has all the advantages of planned follow-up with the termination of an intervention for an objective. In addition, the clinical social worker can obtain additional follow-up information, using a questionnaire, telephone interview schedule, or face-to-face interview schedule for two purposes. One is to assess whether new problems will arise for the client; the second is to obtain data to determine if the social worker can reduce the internal validity threats so that the practitioner may increase inferences about causal relationships between the intervention and changes in the problem variable. One disadvantage of this type of follow-up is that the response rate would be lower than in condition 1 because the social worker would have less frequent contact with the client. Furthermore, the costs for obtaining data and the chance for errors in data collection would be greater than in condition 1.

Condition 3: Unplanned Follow-up with Termination of Intervention for an Objective

In this condition, the social worker does not plan the gathering of follow-up data with the client. However, because the clinical social worker still has access to the client, he or she can obtain data about the client's potential relapse and about new problems with all of the advantages and disadvantages for condition 1. The chief problem is that if the social worker does not plan measurement in follow-up with the client, or considers such measurement only as an afterthought, the data collection might not be standardized across the baseline, intervention, and follow-up phases of the basic model for single-subject design. With unstandardized data, the social worker could not legitimately compare intervention with follow-up and baseline with follow-up.

Condition 4: Unplanned Follow-up with Termination of Client

In this condition, the clinical social worker terminates work with the client and does not involve the client in planning for follow-up data collection. This condition is most costly, has the lowest response rate, and is less useful for making systematic comparisons among baseline, intervention, and follow-up because different conditions of measurement occur in follow-up compared with baseline and intervention—that is, the process of instrumentation is likely to be different.

Hence, the relative advantages and disadvantages for obtaining follow-up information depend on whether the social worker plans or does not plan the follow-up with the client and whether the clinician terminates intervention for an objective or for the client. The most favorable conditions for gathering follow-up data are when the social worker plans the process with the client and systematically implements data-gathering procedures for baseline, intervention, and follow-up. Moreover, follow-up is more likely to be cost-effective when the data collection involves the client's time in recording data and when the type of data obtained are not too extensive. Planned follow-up with client termination is more likely to produce unambiguous data that the practitioner can interpret easily when making comparisons among baseline, intervention, and follow-up. When data collection is unplanned, the client is more likely to use recall in describing events that transpired; therefore, retrospective falsification or distortion of the data can occur with client self-reports. Data not obtained from client self-reports are potentially less subject to measurement error but are more costly to gather.

INFORMATION DURING FOLLOW-UP

The clinical social worker can obtain three types of information during follow-up: (1) time-series on the problem variable measured at baseline and at intervention, (2) qualitative and quantitative information about new problems and factors that might influence the problem variable, and (3) qualitative and quantitative information about the client's perceptions of the clinical social worker and the intervention. The social worker obtains time-series measurements of the problem variable so that he or she can compare intervention with follow-up and baseline with follow-up. He or she follows the same procedures for data collection that he or she followed for the baseline and intervention phases. Data collection should involve the same variables, the same person or persons should conduct measurements systematically in the same places, and the distance between measurements should be identical to the distances for baseline and intervention. If the social worker takes measurements weekly during intervention, he or she also should obtain them weekly during follow-up. The distances between measurements should make

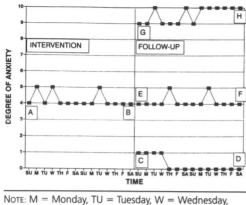

figure 44

Comparisons of Follow-up to Intervention on Self-Reported Daily Anxiety for Two-Week Intervals

NOTE: M = Monday, TU = Tuesday, W = Wednesday, TH = Thursday, F = Friday, SA = Saturday, SU = Sunday.

sense clinically and be realistic in relation to the client's problem. The number of measurements during follow-up is contingent on the clinical objectives developed by the social worker and the client. For example, if the clinician expects that the results (assuming he or she has attained positive results) should persist for three months, then he or she should take measurements up to three months. The clinician can easily implement such a procedure if the client is involved in the measurement process, for example, the client keeps a record of daily measurements that he or she communicates to the clinical social worker by mail, telephone, or face-to-face interview during a scheduled follow-up appointment.

Moreover, the social worker should collect time-series measurements at follow-up in a manner that is consistent with clinical objectives. If no explicit clinical objectives exist, then the practitioner should collect follow-up data until there is horizontal stability in the data pattern, that is, with no accelerating or decelerating trends. The practitioner can show horizontal stability by calculating C, Sc, and Z for the time series at follow-up after a minimum of eight observations—the number that is sufficient for detecting trends.

The clinical social worker compares time-series data at follow-up with time-series data at intervention to determine whether there is a shift from intervention to follow-up and whether the shift is desirable. Suppose that the last two weeks of intervention for a client showed a relatively stable pattern of moderate anxiety: 11 fours and three fives on a scale of 0 = no anxiety to 10 = the highest degree of anxiety (Figure 44). At least three kinds of patterns at follow-up might occur. Line EF shows a similar pattern as line AB at intervention, reflecting a consistency in results from intervention to follow-up. Line GH shows an elevated stable pattern of high anxiety, which is undesirable, whereas line CD shows a reduced pattern of low anxiety, which is desirable.

The clinical social worker also can compare time-series data at follow-up with baseline to show whether there have been desirable changes in the time series of problem variables since intervention. Figure 45 shows the same follow-up data as depicted in Figure 44 compared with baseline data. Line AB shows high anxiety at baseline. At follow-up, line GH, which also represents high anxiety, depicts no change; lines EF and CD show change in a desirable direction: the reduction of anxiety; and line CD indicates the greatest amount of desirable change.

Using a follow-up questionnaire, the clinical social worker can obtain qualitative and quantitative information about new problems and factors influencing problem variables (see Tripodi & Epstein, 1980, for a more comprehensive discussion on collecting follow-up data). Appendix 4 is a generalized form that provides information on what has happened to the client after the clinical social worker has terminated contact with the client. The client's explanations about questions to which she or he answers yes provide the qualitative data. The question pertaining to the receipt of help from other sources or persons aims to obtain information on the extent to which other interventions might be responsible for the results. The client's response to the question regarding recurrences of the major problem should be consistent with the time-series data; the response to that question validates the data obtained from the measurement of the problem variable. If there are undesirable changes in the time-series data, the client should indicate that the major problem has recurred. On the other hand, there may be no undesirable changes reflected in the time-series data, but the client may still believe the problem has recurred. The qualitative data obtained in the client's explanation would clarify this belief. The client may have changed criteria for measurement, the client may have referred to another problem, or the measurement device may have been insufficiently sensitive to detect the problem. Other problems should be obtainable by responses to the question, "Have any other major problems occurred?" Questions regarding daily habits, living circumstances, illnesses, and relationships are designed to elicit information about historical and maturational factors that might serve as stressors that could influence the problem variable. Furthermore, the question about unexpected positive or negative changes provides information about other influences of the intervention.

The social worker can present these general questions through face-to-face contact, by telephone interview, or by mailed questionnaire. Face-to-face contact or telephone interviews are preferred because they are likely to result in higher response rates and more valid information. Telephone interviewing is apt to be more efficient, saving the client travel or scheduled appointment costs.

The clinical social worker can make follow-up questionnaires more specific and personal for clients by designing questionnaires so they are geared to a client's specific circumstances. In constructing such questionnaires, the clinical social worker should aim to obtain unambiguous

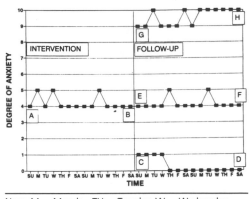

figure 45

Comparisons of Follow-up to Baseline on Self-Reported Daily Anxiety for Two Weeks

NOTE: M = Monday, TU = Tuesday, W = Wednesday, TH = Thursday, F = Friday, SA = Saturday, SU = Sunday.

answers to clear, straightforward questions. For example, the follow-up questionnaire in Appendix 5 is intended to show aspects of the relationship between Tom, the client, and Jerry, Tom's brother. Tom, age 15, and Jerry, age 14, fought a great deal before intervention. Their white, middle-class parents, both of whom are employed as professional workers, singled out Tom as one who should receive help. The social worker's assessment was that Tom did initiate fights and that he was an appropriate target of intervention. Jerry appeared to respond positively or negatively depending on whether Tom behaved in a positive or negative fashion. The questions in Appendix 5 enable the social worker to assess the degree to which Tom and Jerry fight and whether any changes are apparent in their relationship. Furthermore, responses to these questions indicate the degree to which Tom believes the problem in his relationship is changing and is solvable. The social worker has phrased the questions to give Tom the opportunity to consider himself or his brother responsible for their fights and arguments. In addition, questions about the extent to which they like each other and their parents like them are asked. Moreover, specific questions ask about the nature of the relationship between Tom and Jerry, whether it has been improved, and how it could be improved.

Hence, the questions provided data about the clinical objective of reducing fights and arguments as well as including information that is pertinent to a reassessment of the problem.

Another kind of data the social worker can gather during follow-up is qualitative and quantitative information about the client's perceptions of the clinical social worker. The clinical social worker can use these data to analyze specific social work behaviors and attitudes that are important for effective implementation of the intervention; they can furnish clues regarding modifications the social worker might make with the client or for other clients who have yet to receive the intervention.

The social worker derives guidelines for forming follow-up questionnaires by considering questions and responses to dimensions that are relevant to implementation of an intervention and to the social worker's behaviors. Such dimensions include the social worker's sensitivity to client needs; the social worker's adherence to his or her obligations in the therapeutic relationship—keeping appointment times, reviewing progress for the client, explaining measurement procedures and client obligations, providing feedback to the client; specificity of the problems on which the social worker and the client are working; clarity of clinical objectives for the client; provision of sound advice for everyday practical problems; development of client understanding about his or her problems; comfort in discussing personal problems with the social worker; and specific behaviors and tasks associated with the intervention. The follow-up questionnaire in Appendix 6 is designed to elicit information about these dimensions. It is geared to a client who is receiving a cognitive therapy intervention to help him or her reduce anxiety. The clinical objectives are to reduce anxiety and to prevent depression. For example, because the client becomes anxious in interpersonal relationships, the social worker focuses intervention on using role

plays about interpersonal conflicts and on how to deal with those conflicts. In addition, the social worker discusses factors leading to anxiety and how the client might prevent anxiety-provoking situations. The clinical social worker also uses single-subject design methodology to produce graphs of time series during baseline, intervention, and follow-up as well as a standardized instrument for measuring depression. The client makes daily self-ratings of anxiety on a 10-point anxiety scale ranging from 1 = no anxiety to 10 = a great deal of anxiety.

Responses to the questions in Appendix 7 will indicate which social worker's behaviors are necessary for implementing the intervention and for helping the client to reduce anxiety. A general form for assessing client satisfaction from a client who is receiving mental health services is Attkisson's Client Satisfaction Questionnaire (Corcoran & Fischer, 1987a, pp. 120–122). Although it is geared to programs, clinical social workers could use it to refer to their services.

GUIDELINES FOR CONDUCTING FOLLOW-UP

The following guidelines will enable the clinical social worker to obtain data and make inferences so that he or she may make effective decisions about the services offered to clients. For illustrative purposes here, it is assumed that the social worker has realized intervention objectives compared with baseline data before follow-up.

Specify Clinical Objectives

The most common objective is to maintain consistent progress on the problem variable. For example, if a client has stopped smoking—a clinical objective during intervention—the social worker expects that the client will continue to not smoke after termination of the intervention. An objective that varies given the nature of the problem and the intervention specifics for a particular client concerns the length of time desired changes should continue. For example, the practitioner might expect that a client who learns to be assertive will continue to be assertive for an unspecified amount of time, whereas a follow-up clinical objective might be that a father and his son will continue a positive relationship for at least six months and possibly longer.

The social worker should conceive the expected length of time for which observed changes during interventions persist in follow-up in terms of minimum and maximum expectations. A minimum expectation might be one to three months; a maximum expectation can be indefinite. The minimum expectation informs the social worker when to set up a follow-up appointment and for how long to obtain measurements during follow-up. It is simply impractical to follow up every client for a maximum (indefinite) period. The clinical social worker sets his or her objective regarding the minimum expectation for follow-up on the basis of clinical judgment about the individual client, the nature of the problem, and the degree to which the agency is mandated to provide follow-up information. For example, a felon who has served his or her time and is placed on parole has a follow-up period that is mandatory—perhaps one year or more.

Specify Data Collection Strategy

The clinical social worker collects two types of data by questionnaire or interview: (1) time series and (2) follow-up information. The time-series data are the same measurements on the problem variable that the practitioner took at baseline and at intervention. The minimum time expectation for persistence of change at follow-up indicates the period during which the social worker should gather follow-up data on the problem variable. As part of the strategy for data collection, the social worker plans for the measurement (whether by the client or the social worker); for the frequency of measurement (for example, daily); and for the time of measurement (for example, by the client before bedtime).

The client completes the follow-up questionnaire (mailed questionnaire) or the social worker administers the questionnaire by telephone or in a face-to-face interview at the specified minimum time expectation for follow-up.

Plan Follow-up Data Collection with Client

Before terminating intervention, the clinical social worker plans with the client an appointment (by phone or in a face-to-face interview) or a time to mail in data (such as the questionnaire or time series). The appointment time is based on the clinical objectives for follow-up. If the client is to provide daily self-report data on a log or record, the social worker must emphasize to the client consistency in the data collection process. Moreover, the practitioner should stress that follow-up time is a further check on the client's progress and an opportunity for the client to continue with intervention, if needed.

Develop Follow-up Questionnaire

The social worker constructs the questionnaire so that the client can provide relatively simple quantitative and qualitative information. The data should be specific to the client's problem and to factors other than intervention that may assist in easing or exacerbating the problem. In addition, the questionnaire should elicit information that will identify for the social worker possible problems, hence enabling him or her to be helpful and responsive to the client.

Collect Data

The clinical social worker can assist the client who provides self-reported data by reminding the client, in a positive manner, to collect the data. For example, the practitioner may thank the client in a brief telephone exchange or through a brief note for taking the time to provide data. The social worker gathers data at follow-up and graphs the time-series data along with the data from baseline and intervention. He or she may extract data from follow-up as well as from intervention from the time series and graph them for comparison. For example, the social worker might collect data daily for one month but will graph the last week of the month because it is the week targeted for achievement of the clinical objective. The social worker also separately analyzes the data for the first three weeks to determine whether the trend is consistent in follow-up (for example, all of the data for the month may indicate consistency with the time series at intervention).

Compare Phases in Graphs and Conduct Statistical Tests

The clinical social worker should compare the time series at follow-up with the time series at intervention to determine whether the data are consistent. In addition, he or she should compare the follow-up measurements with the time-series measurements to ascertain whether there are desirable positive changes. In addition, the practitioner should conduct statistical tests to verify the observations from the graphic patterns.

Evaluate Data and Decide Whether to Terminate Intervention or Continue Follow-up

The social worker evaluates data to locate other possible facilitators and barriers to the effectiveness of intervention, as well as to provide information about the client's perception of whether he or she has received help for the problem. In addition, the social worker gathers data about potential new problems and the client's willingness to participate in further intervention, if necessary.

The social worker also evaluates and analyzes the data with respect to the accomplishment of clinical objectives for the client. If relapse occurs (for example, return to baseline indicating a reemergence of the problem), the social worker offers to reintroduce intervention to the client. New problems may have developed; thus, the social worker will offer the same or another intervention to the client. If the client continues to show progress, registering a low magnitude on the problem variable and no other problems, the clinical social worker may decide to terminate work with the client.

APPLYING THE GUIDELINES: THREE CLINICAL EXAMPLES

The following clinical examples—consistency in assertive behavior, relapse in coffee drinking, and further progress in the reduction of negative remarks—illustrate how the social worker may apply the guidelines for obtaining and analyzing follow-up information.

Consistency in Assertive Behavior

Specify clinical objectives. The client is a young woman enrolled in college liberal arts courses. She felt that she was unable to handle her interpersonal relationships effectively. In most encounters, she was submissive, doing things she did not want to do but feeling resentful. She rarely expressed her wants and desires and felt that "people were picking on me." She read about a counseling center on campus that dealt with problems such as difficulties in interpersonal relationships, academic difficulties, and speech anxieties. A major problem became evident in discussions with a clinical social worker: the client's lack of assertiveness in interpersonal encounters in the classroom, in the recreation hall, at meals, and so forth.

The clinical objective during intervention was to increase significantly the client's number of daily assertive behaviors at least by the sixth week following the first meeting with the social worker at the counseling center. During week 1, the client fully discussed the meaning of assertive behaviors and contexts in which she may exhibit those behaviors. The social worker taught the client that she should count these behaviors each night after dinner and daily for one week. As the baseline indicates (Figure 46), the client showed no assertive behaviors. The social worker introduced cognitive therapy intervention, including

figure 46

Number of Daily Assertive Behaviors at Baseline, Intervention, and Follow-up

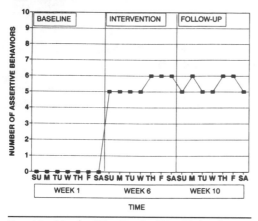

NOTE: M = Monday, TU = Tuesday, W = Wednesday, TH = Thursday, F = Friday, SA = Saturday, SU = Sunday.

exercises on how to be assertive, role-play situations with the social worker, and discussions of how the client felt in a variety of interpersonal situations in college work and with her friends and family.

Assertive behaviors significantly increased from week 1 at baseline to week 6 during intervention (Figure 46). The social worker planned to terminate the intervention and to obtain follow-up information for four weeks. The clinical objectives for follow-up were for the client to show consistent, assertive behavior at week 10 of follow-up (one month after intervention—the minimum objective) to demonstrate that assertive behavior at follow-up was significantly different from baseline and to provide information showing the absence of other problems.

Specify data collection strategy. The client would provide the data by keeping a log of measurements of assertiveness, as well as mailing in the data at the end of each week in stamped envelopes addressed to the clinical social worker at the counseling center. In addition, the social worker would mail a follow-up questionnaire to the client one week before an appointment scheduled in week 10 of follow-up. In the follow-up ap-

pointment, the social worker would ask the client to provide the desired information.

Plan follow-up data collection with client. The practitioner instructed the client to obtain time-series measurements at follow-up in the same way she gathered them at baseline and intervention. Furthermore, the social worker told the client that she would receive a questionnaire in the mail one week before a scheduled appointment during week 10 after initial contact; the client would complete the questionnaire in a face-to-face interview with the social worker.

Develop follow-up questionnaire. The social worker developed the follow-up questionnaire (Appendix 8) to reflect information about the help the client received from the social worker, progress in expressing assertiveness, the location of other problems, and the extent to which other factors influenced the client's assertiveness.

Collect data. The client gathered data on the time series of assertive behaviors at follow-up; they are reflected in the follow-up phase in Figure 46. The responses to the questionnaire are in Appendix 8.

Compare phases in graphs and conduct statistical tests. During four days at follow-up, the client exhibited five assertive behaviors, and during three days the client exhibited six assertive behaviors (Figure 46). This pattern is consistent with week 6 of intervention, which indicates persistence in the achievement of the clinical objectives for intervention and follow-up. Compared with baseline—seven days of no assertive behavior registered—the time-series data at follow-up are radically different in a desirable direction, indicating that the intervention has been effective.

The calculations of C, Sc, and Z for baseline and follow-up indicate significant differences between baseline and follow-up (Table 20). Furthermore, the calculations of C, Sc, and Z in Table 21 show no significant change from intervention to

| table 20 | *Computing C, Sc, and Z for Baseline and Follow-up Data from Figure 46* |

x	x − M	(x − M)²	x_i	x − x_i	(x − x_i)²
0	−2.71	7.34	0	0	0
0	−2.71	7.34	0	0	0
0	−2.71	7.34	0	0	0
0	−2.71	7.34	0	0	0
0	−2.71	7.34	0	0	0
0	−2.71	7.34	0	0	0
0	−2.71	7.34	5	−5	25
5	2.29	5.24	6	−1	1
6	3.29	10.82	5	1	1
5	2.29	5.24	5	0	0
5	2.29	5.24	6	−1	1
6	3.29	10.82	6	0	0
6	3.29	10.82	5	1	1
5	2.29	5.24	—	—	—
38 = Σx		104.80 = SS(x)			29 = D²

$$M = \frac{\Sigma x}{n} = \frac{38}{14} = 2.71$$

$$C = 1 - \frac{D^2}{2SS(x)} = 1 - \frac{29}{2(104.80)} = .86$$

$$Sc = \sqrt{\frac{n + 2}{(n + 1)(n - 1)}} = \sqrt{\frac{14 + 2}{(14 + 1)(14 - 1)}} = .29$$

$$Z = \frac{C}{Sc} = \frac{.86}{.29} = 2.96$$

NOTE: Because $Z > 1.64$, there are significant changes in the time series.

follow-up, verifying the graphic observations and indicating similar patterns for intervention and follow-up. This is evidence that the social worker has achieved the clinical objective at follow-up because no change exists in week 10 of follow-up.

Evaluate data and decide whether to terminate intervention or continue follow-up. As indicated by the data in Appendix 8, the client reported that she had not failed to be assertive when appropriate, no other problems occurred during follow-up, the social worker helped her to understand when to be assertive, she discussed when she should be assertive in interpersonal situations, she has made progress in being assertive by overcoming her reluctance to be assertive, she has not received professional help from other persons, she does not believe she needs to continue seeing the social worker, other events have not influenced her assertive behaviors, and she obtained consistent measures of assertiveness. Therefore, the data indicate a strong relationship between the intervention and assertive behavior and the accomplishment of clinical objectives. The client changed her behavior in a positive manner and she has no other problems for which she needs help.

Furthermore, because the social worker has achieved the objectives and the client does not feel a need to continue to see the social worker, the practitioner should terminate the case. However, the social worker should tell the client that she can contact the social worker again should a relapse occur in assertiveness or if other problems should develop.

Relapse in Coffee Drinking

Specify clinical objectives. The client, a veteran of World War II, is an outpatient at a VA medical center. He has gallbladder and other intestinal problems, which are exacerbated by his excessive coffee drinking. The relationship between him and his spouse is positive and caring. He wants to reduce his coffee drinking, but he has become addicted since his days in the U.S. Navy, when he drank coffee continuously. He was referred to a clinical social worker who interviewed his wife and him, asking them to report the number of cups of coffee he consumed each day for one week. The clinical objective was to reduce the number of cups of coffee consumed to no more than one or two cups per day; the social worker expected to attain this objective during week 5 of client contact.

The clinical social worker met with the client twice a week after the first week of contact and used techniques from behavioral therapy, including the provision of rewards for drinking less coffee. The rewards were the client's small excursions with his wife to nearby cities and museums, an activity that he loved but in which he and his wife had not engaged for years. In addition, the social worker asked the client to substitute decaffeinated coffee for regular coffee. The clinical objective for follow-up was that he would continue to drink no more than one or two cups of coffee per day after week 8 of client contact.

The client consumed 15 cups of coffee per day at baseline, and by week 5 of intervention, he drank one cup of coffee for six out of seven days and two cups on one day (Figure 47). The social worker terminated in-

---

table 21 *Computing C, Sc, and Z for Intervention and Follow-up Data from Figure 46*

x	$x - M$	$(x - M)^2$	x_i	$x - x_i$	$(x - x_i)^2$
5	−.43	.18	5	0	0
5	−.43	.18	5	0	0
5	−.43	.18	5	0	0
5	−.43	.18	6	−1	1
6	.57	.32	6	0	0
6	.57	.32	6	0	0
6	.57	.32	5	1	1
5	−.43	.18	6	−1	1
6	.57	.32	5	1	1
5	−.43	.18	5	0	0
5	−.43	.18	6	−1	1
6	.57	.32	6	0	0
6	.57	.32	5	1	1
5	−.43	.18	—	—	—
$76 = \Sigma x$		$3.36 = SS(x)$			$6 = D^2$

$$M = \frac{\Sigma x}{n} = \frac{76}{14} = 5.43$$

$$C = 1 - \frac{D^2}{2SS(x)} = 1 - \frac{6}{2(3.36)} = .11$$

$$Sc = \sqrt{\frac{n + 2}{(n + 1)(n - 1)}} = \sqrt{\frac{14 + 2}{(14 + 1)(14 - 1)}} = .29$$

$$Z = \frac{C}{Sc} = \frac{.11}{.29} = .38$$

NOTE: Because $Z < 1.64$, there is no significant change.

figure 47

*Number of Cups of Coffee Consumed at
Baseline, Intervention, and Follow-up*

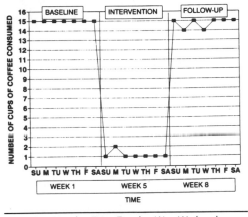

NOTE: M = Monday, TU = Tuesday, W = Wednesday,
TH = Thursday, F = Friday, SA = Saturday, SU = Sunday.

tervention, and the client and his wife co-operated in collecting data on his coffee drinking. The social worker scheduled an appointment for a telephone interview with the client after three weeks of follow-up. The social worker expected that coffee drinking would be consistent with that at intervention and that the interview would yield information indicating that conditions were favorable for the client's reduced coffee drinking.

Specify data collection strategy. The client and his wife were to continue to monitor his daily coffee consumption, writing down each night at 10 p.m. the number of cups consumed during that day. They were to tally on a chart each cup consumed daily. The social worker would devise a follow-up questionnaire for a telephone interview and would mail the questionnaire to the client after one week of follow-up.

Plan follow-up data collection with client. The client was to report the data on coffee drinking to the clinical social worker by telephone each week. The social worker and the client scheduled an appointment for a follow-up telephone interview after three weeks of follow-up.

Develop follow-up questionnaire. The practitioner designed a follow-up question-naire (Appendix 9) to provide information about the continued attainment of the clinical objective and to include information, in the event relapse occurred, on the conditions that might have led to relapse and how the social worker might be able to help.

Collect data. The data on daily coffee consumption the client gathered and reported to the social worker are shown in the follow-up phase of Figure 47. Responses to the questionnaire are in Appendix 9.

Compare phases in graphs and make statistical tests. The follow-up period was not consistent with intervention; rather, coffee consumption increased dramatically, indicating a relapse to the original condition at baseline (Figure 47). Although during intervention, the client drank no more than two cups of coffee per day (and there were two cups for only one day), follow-up showed consumption of 15 cups for five days and 14 cups for two days. The follow-up period is similar to the baseline period, during which the client consumed 15 cups of coffee each day for seven days. Hence, the effectiveness of the intervention was not maintained during follow-up.

The calculations of C, Sc, and Z for baseline follow-up show no statistically significant differences between baseline and follow-up (Table 22)—that is, coffee consumption before and after the intervention was virtually identical. Furthermore, there was a statistically significant shift in the time series from intervention to follow-up (Table 23), further verifying that relapse occurred and that positive changes of reduced consumption were not maintained.

Evaluate data and decide whether to terminate intervention or continue follow-up. The client indicated that he has been drinking more than two cups of coffee per day because he has been upset (Appendix 9). An additional problem weighing heavily on the client is his wife's illness. He felt the social worker was able to help him by using the rewards of excursions with his wife. He drank more when his wife was tired and less available for making excursions. He has received no other professional help and he feels a need to continue to see the social worker to help him deal with his wife's illness and to control his coffee drinking. He also reported that he has had headaches and nausea and that he does not like decaffeinated coffee.

The data indicate that the rewards for drinking less coffee could no longer be effective when the client's wife was ill—that reinforcer is insufficient for behavioral therapy. The data also indicate that the client needs to understand and deal with his wife's illness, and that other therapeutic techniques such as listening, discussing the problem, and providing good advice might be necessary.

In addition, the client himself may need medical intervention. The clinical social worker arranges for a medical appointment for the client and makes an appointment to visit with the client and his wife. The social worker decides to obtain further information in the interview and is considering using more than one therapeutic intervention. In particular, the practitioner believes it is necessary for the client to understand and cope with his wife's illness. If the social worker is to reintroduce behavioral therapy to reduce coffee consumption, he or she must modify the reward system because the client's wife does not appear strong enough to make excursions. However, the social worker first needs to obtain a better understanding of both the wife's and the client's illnesses to provide a more accurate context in which he or she delivers intervention.

table 22 *Computing C, Sc, and Z for Baseline and Follow-up Data from Figure 47*

x	$x - M$	$(x - M)^2$	x_i	$x - x_i$	$(x - x_i)^2$
15	.14	.02	15	0	0
15	.14	.02	15	0	0
15	.14	.02	15	0	0
15	.14	.02	15	0	0
15	.14	.02	15	0	0
15	.14	.02	15	0	0
15	.14	.02	15	0	0
15	.14	.02	14	1	1
14	−.86	.74	15	−1	1
15	.14	.02	14	1	1
14	−.86	.74	15	−1	1
15	.14	.02	15	0	0
15	.14	.02	15	0	0
15	.14	.02	—	—	—
208 = Σx		1.72 = SS(x)			4 = D²

$$M = \frac{\Sigma x}{n} = \frac{208}{14} = 14.86$$

$$C = 1 - \frac{D^2}{2SS(x)} = 1 - \frac{4}{2(1.72)} = -.16$$

$$Sc = \sqrt{\frac{n + 2}{(n + 1)(n - 1)}} = \sqrt{\frac{14 + 2}{(14 + 1)(14 - 1)}} = .29$$

$$Z = \frac{C}{Sc} = \frac{-.16}{.29} = -.55$$

NOTE: Because $Z < 1.64$, there is no statistical difference in the time series.

| table 23 | Computing C, Sc, and Z for Intervention and Follow-up Data from Figure 47 | | | | | |

x	$x - M$	$(x - M)^2$	x_i	$x - x_i$	$(x - x_i)^2$
1	−6.93	48.02	2	−1	1
2	−5.93	35.16	1	1	1
1	−6.93	48.02	1	0	0
1	−6.93	48.02	1	0	0
1	−6.93	48.02	1	0	0
1	−6.93	48.02	1	0	0
1	−6.93	48.02	15	−14	196
15	7.07	49.98	14	1	1
14	6.07	36.84	15	−1	1
15	7.07	49.98	14	1	1
14	6.07	36.84	15	−1	1
15	7.07	49.98	15	0	0
15	7.07	49.98	15	0	0
15	7.07	49.98	—	—	—
111 = Σx		646.86 = SS(x)			202 = D²

$$M = \frac{\Sigma x}{n} = \frac{111}{14} = 7.93$$

$$C = 1 - \frac{D^2}{2SS(x)} = 1 - \frac{202}{2(646.86)} = .84$$

$$Sc = \sqrt{\frac{n + 2}{(n + 1)(n - 1)}} = \sqrt{\frac{14 + 2}{(14 + 1)(14 - 1)}} = .29$$

$$Z = \frac{C}{Sc} = \frac{.84}{.29} = 2.90$$

NOTE: Because $Z > 1.64$, there are significant differences in the time series.

Progress in Reduction of Negative Remarks

Specify clinical objectives. The client is a male adolescent, Jack, who lives in an upper middle-class area in a large midwestern city. He lives with his father, a corporate executive, and his mother, a civil rights lawyer. Since his father took a new job, Jack has been verbally abusive to him and has begun acting up at school. The father in turn has responded in an even-tempered manner but has been preoccupied with his new job. Jack becomes irritable after he is verbally abusive to his father; the mother has tried to calm Jack down during incidents of verbal abuse, which usually occur at meals and in the evening before bedtime. The mother persuaded the family to seek family counseling at a family services agency. The family was involved in family therapy in which the major objective was that each family member would understand the needs of the others. The father spent little time at home; consequently, a further goal was for him to become more involved in family life. A subobjective was to reduce the number of negative comments Jack makes to his father by rewarding Jack with activities of his choice (such as watching a baseball game with his father).

During the first week after initial contact, the mother took a baseline of Jack's negative remarks toward his father each day. The social worker decided to involve the family in a session once per week to achieve the major goals. To attain the subobjective, the clinical social worker also met Jack

figure 48

Number of Negative Remarks Made to Father at Baseline, Intervention, and Follow-up

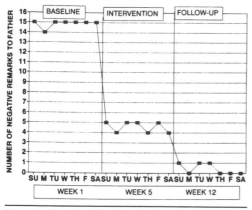

NOTE: M = Monday, TU = Tuesday, W = Wednesday, TH = Thursday, F = Friday, SA = Saturday, SU = Sunday.

alone for 30 minutes each week, discussing events that led up to negative remarks and Jack's reasons for making them as well as his feelings about them. In addition, the social worker described a system of rewards. The social worker expected the number of negative remarks would be significantly reduced by week 8 of intervention with the boy alone.

The number of negative remarks decreased dramatically from 14 to 15 at baseline to four to five during intervention (Figure 48). The social worker decided to terminate the individual work with Jack and to concentrate solely on the family members' being understanding and sensitive to each other's needs. The social worker terminated inter-

---

table 24 *Computing C, Sc, and Z for Intervention and Follow-up Data from Figure 48*

x	$x - M$	$(x - M)^2$	x_i	$x - x_i$	$(x - x_i)^2$
5	2.5	6.25	4	1	1
4	1.5	2.25	5	−1	1
5	2.5	6.25	5	0	0
5	2.5	6.25	4	1	1
4	1.5	2.25	5	−1	1
5	2.5	6.25	4	1	1
4	1.5	2.25	1	3	9
1	−1.5	2.25	0	1	1
0	−2.5	6.25	1	−1	1
1	−1.5	2.25	1	0	0
1	−1.5	2.25	0	1	1
0	−2.5	6.25	0	0	0
0	−2.5	6.25	0	0	0
0	−2.5	6.25	—	—	—
35 = Σx		63.50 = $SS(x)$			17 = D^2

$$M = \frac{\Sigma x}{n} = \frac{35}{14} = 2.5$$

$$C = 1 - \frac{D^2}{2SS(x)} = 1 - \frac{17}{2(63.50)} = .87$$

$$Sc = \sqrt{\frac{n + 2}{(n + 1)(n - 1)}} = \sqrt{\frac{14 + 2}{(14 + 1)(14 - 1)}} = .29$$

$$Z = \frac{C}{Sc} = \frac{.87}{.29} = 3.00$$

NOTE: Because $Z > 1.64$, there is a statistically significant change in the time series.

vention for reducing negative remarks. The objective for follow-up was that the number of negative remarks at 12 weeks should be consistent with the data for intervention at eight weeks since client contact.

Specify data collection strategy. The mother would obtain data on the number of negative remarks; she would tabulate them each day, focusing on breakfast, dinner, and early evening hours when all the family was together. She would bring the data to the social worker during the regular family interviews each week. The social worker would give the follow-up questionnaire to the mother three weeks after termination of individual work with Jack; The mother would discuss the questionnaire with Jack. In the last family counseling session in the 12th week after initial contact with the client, the social worker would ask Jack to complete the responses.

Plan follow-up data collection with client. In addition to the scheduled activities, the social worker made sure the mother, the father, and Jack understood the meaning of negative remarks. Moreover, as a form of understanding the family equilibrium in discussions, the social worker used negative remarks as an assessment tool in family counseling.

Develop follow-up questionnaire. Because the family was to continue in family counseling, the follow-up questionnaire was relatively brief (Appendix 10). It focused on factors affecting Jack's negative comments and the progress he had made since termination of work with the clinical social worker on an individual basis.

Collect data. Jack and his mother were cooperative in systematically collecting the time-series data and in considering the questions for the follow-up questionnaire. Jack completed the follow-up questionnaire and gave it to the social worker before a family counseling session in the 12th week after initial contact. The time-series data for follow-up are shown in Figure 48

and the responses to the questionnaire in Appendix 10.

Compare phases in graphs and conduct statistical tests. At follow-up, there were four days with no negative comments and three days with one negative comment in the 12th week after initial contact (Figure 48). This finding represents further desirable progress compared with termination during week 8, when there were four days with five negative comments and three days with four negative comments. Hence, the intervention (coupled with continued family counseling) appears to have been effective.

Statistical calculations indicate that the time series at follow-up are statistically significantly different from the time series at intervention (Table 24), indicating continued progress. Also, there is a statistically significant difference in the time series from baseline to follow-up in the desired direction of reducing negative comments (Table 25).

Evaluate data and decide whether to terminate intervention or continue follow-up. Jack indicated that he made a few negative comments but that he believed he had made progress (Appendix 10). No other problems had occurred. He said he understood what leads him to make negative comments to his father, and the social worker helped him in this regard by discussing interpersonal situations that would lead to those comments. Jack noted that his father spent more time with him in activities and this, as well as the social worker's intervention, helped him to reduce negative comments. Because the father spent more time with Jack as a reward for his reducing negative comments, the social worker could infer that the intervention was instrumental in helping Jack. Therefore, the questionnaire data verified the clinical subobjective of reducing negative remarks.

Furthermore, the data indicate that the individual objective for Jack was maintained,

table 25 *Computing C, Sc, and Z for Baseline and Follow-up Data for Figure 48*

x	$x - M$	$(x - M)^2$	x_i	$x - x_i$	$(x - x_i)^2$
15	7.36	54.17	14	1	1
14	6.36	40.45	15	−1	1
15	7.36	54.17	15	0	0
15	7.36	54.17	15	0	0
15	7.36	54.17	15	0	0
15	7.36	54.17	15	0	0
15	7.36	54.17	1	14	196
1	−6.64	44.09	0	1	1
0	−7.64	58.37	1	−1	1
1	−6.64	44.09	1	0	0
1	−6.64	44.09	0	1	1
0	−7.64	58.37	0	0	0
0	−7.64	58.37	0	0	0
0	−7.64	58.37	—	—	—
$107 = \Sigma x$		$731.22 = SS(x)$			$201 = D^2$

$$M = \frac{\Sigma x}{n} = \frac{107}{14} = 7.64$$

$$C = 1 - \frac{D^2}{2SS(x)} = 1 - \frac{201}{2(731.22)} = .86$$

$$Sc = \sqrt{\frac{n + 2}{(n + 1)(n - 1)}} = \sqrt{\frac{14 + 2}{(14 + 1)(14 - 1)}} = .29$$

$$Z = \frac{C}{Sc} = \frac{.86}{.29} = 2.96$$

NOTE: Because $Z > 1.64$, there is a statistically significant shift in the time series.

with further progress indicated. Hence, the social worker decided to terminate the individual work for this particular objective. However, Jack will continue to see the social worker as a member of his family unit until the social worker believes he or she and the client have attained the objectives for the family.

DESIGN VARIATIONS

Three variations of the basic model of baseline, intervention, and follow-up are (1) multiple baseline design, (2) graduated intensity design, and (3) withdrawal–reversal design. Although potentially useful in clinical social work, the clinical social worker cannot use them in all cases, and they involve much more planning than does the basic model presented in previous chapters. Descriptions of these designs also appear in Blythe, Tripodi, and Briar (1994), Bloom, Fischer, and Orme (1993), Barlow and Hersen (1984), Tripodi and Epstein (1980), and Jayaratne and Levy (1979).

The major advantage of these designs is that they can control to some extent the internal validity threats of history, maturation, and multiple treatment interference—factors that the basic single-subject design model does not control. Recall that history refers to external events other than the intervention that might influence changes in successive measurements on the problem variable; maturation includes all those internal changes in the client, such as illness, that might influence the problem variable, and multiple-treatment interference is the extent to which other interventions are responsible for observable changes (Cook & Campbell, 1979). Hence, these designs can provide more evidence than the basic model regarding a causal link between intervention and changes in the problem variables. In addition, the multiple baseline design can provide some information regarding generalizability of the results.

The chief disadvantage of these designs is that they are complicated, requiring more procedures for their successful implementation and analysis. To implement them, the clinical social worker must follow procedures systematically. Furthermore, the resulting data must conform with the idealized data patterns required by the particular design variation. Hence, the designs require more time and effort by the clinical social worker. In general, they are more useful with simple interventions such as advice, didactic instruction, and reinforcement schedules. The designs are much more impractical for long-term psychodynamic and gestalt therapies that do not necessarily focus on particular symptoms or behaviors. In this chapter, each of the designs is defined and guidelines for their implementation are presented. Moreover, clinical examples including graphic and statistical analyses are provided so readers can gain a more comprehensive understanding of the procedures involved.

MULTIPLE BASELINE DESIGN

According to Rubin and Babbie (1993),

multiple-baseline designs also attempt to control for extraneous variables by having more than one baseline and intervention phase. . . . This is done by measuring different target behaviors in each baseline or by measuring the same target behavior in two different settings or across two different individuals. Although each baseline starts simultaneously, the intervention is introduced at a different point for each one. Thus, as the intervention is introduced for the first behavior, setting, or individual, the others are still in their baseline phases. Likewise when the intervention is introduced for the second behavior, setting, or individual, the third (if there are more than two) is still in its baseline phase.

The main logical principle here is that if some extraneous event, such as a significant improvement in the environment, coincides with the onset of intervention and causes the client's improved functioning, then that improvement will show up in the graph of each

figure 49

*Idealized Data Patterns for Multiple
Baseline Designs*

	BASELINE	INTERVENTION FOR I OR II OR III	
PROBLEM VARIABLE FOR CLIENT 1(I) OR	A———B		
PROBLEM VARIABLE 1(II) OR		C———D	
PROBLEM VARIABLE FOR SITUATION 1(III)			

	BASELINE	CONTINUED BASELINE	INTERVENTION FOR IV OR V OR VI
PROBLEM VARIABLE FOR CLIENT 2(IV) OR	A'———B'	C'———D'	E₁———F₁
PROBLEM VARIABLE 2(V) OR			
PROBLEM VARIABLE FOR SITUATION 2(VI)	A₁———B₁	C₁———D₁	E'———F'

TIME

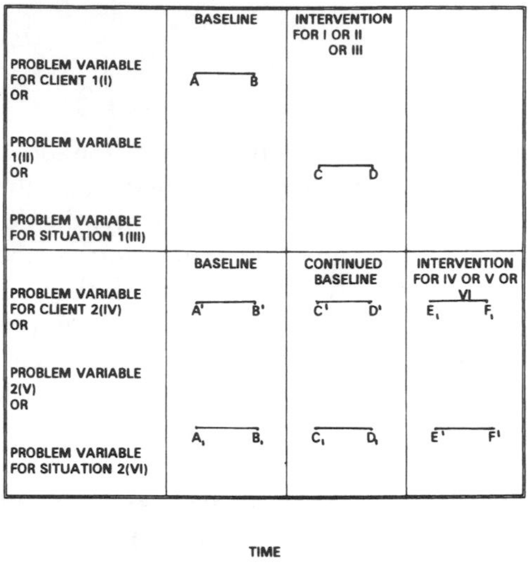

behavior, setting, or individual at the same time, even though some might still be in baseline. On the other hand, if the intervention is accountable for the improvement, then that improvement will occur on each graph at a different point that corresponds to the introduction of the intervention. (pp. 315–316)

This definition is elaborated in Figure 49, which contains idealized data patterns necessary for multiple baseline designs. The terms target behavior, individual, and setting in the preceding definition are synonymous with problem variable, client, and situation, respectively, in Figure 49.

The clinical social worker can simultaneously baseline two or more problem variables, clients, or situations in multiple baseline design. Although some authors (for example, Monette, Sullivan, & DeJong, 1986) recommend that researchers use three or more baselines to increase the internal validity of these designs, it is simply impractical in many clinical situations. Therefore, the generalized multiple baseline model in Figure 49 depicts only two baselines.

In Figure 49, baselines are constructed simultaneously for a problem variable for two different clients, two different problem variables for the same client, or a problem variable in two different situations. Suppose that line AB represents the baseline for problem variable 1 (II); then either line A'B' or line A_1B_1 represents a comparative baseline for problem variable 2 (IV). For example, line AB might represent high consumption of alcohol and line A'B' might indicate high anxiety. The problem variables do not have to be measured in the same units or be of the same magnitude; hence, line A_1B_1 might be the baseline used simultaneously with line AB, and it could refer, for example, to lack of assertiveness. Recall from Chapter 3 that baselines should not show upward or downward trends—that is, they should be horizontally stable as depicted in the idealized version (a straight line in Figure 49).

After establishing baselines, the social worker applies an intervention to one client, problem variable, or situation, but continues to baseline the other client, problem variable, or situation. Hence, line CD shows a change from line AB at intervention, indicating an effective intervention. In contrast, the continued baseline shows no change from baseline—that is, lines A'B' and C'D' and lines A_1B_1 and C_1D_1 show similar patterns. Then, the social worker applies the intervention to the other client problem variable or situation whose baseline is continued. The ideal pattern would represent a significant change from C_1D_1 to E_1F_1 or from C'D' to E'F'.

To achieve a multiple baseline design, the clinical social worker must implement the procedures of simultaneous baselining, applying the intervention to one problem variable, client, or situation while continuing to baseline the other and then applying the intervention to the other problem variable, client, or situation. In addition, to obtain a multiple baseline design, he or she must ensure that the data patterns conform to the idealized patterns shown in Figure 49 (the time series do not have to be straight lines, but they should represent horizontal stability to the x axis on the graph). The social worker can compute C, Sc, and Z to verify conformity to the idealized pattern. Therefore, line AB should be statistically significantly different from line CD; lines A'B' and C'D' or lines A_1B_1 and C_1D_1 should not be statistically significantly different; and lines C'D' and E'F' or lines C_1D_1 and E_1F_1 should be statistically significantly different.

General Guidelines for Using Multiple Baseline Designs

Determine whether there are two different problems, situations, or clients. If this condition is satisfied, the social worker should decide whether to treat the problems, situations, or clients simultaneously. If they are treated simultaneously, then the social worker cannot use multiple baseline. To be used in multiple baseline design, the problem variables, situations, and clients should be independent of each other. This is not problematic when there are two different clients; however, two different problem variables or two different situations might be highly correlated. For example, the problem variables of anxiety and depression might be highly correlated for a particular client: when he or she is depressed or anxious; when he or she is not depressed or not anxious. If the problem variables are highly correlated, then the social worker will not obtain the idealized data pattern for a multiple baseline design because the variables not receiving intervention during the continued baseline (see Figure 49) will also change, not satisfying the requirement that lines A'B' and C'D' or lines A_1B_1 and C_1D_1 should not be significantly different.

Construct simultaneous baselines. The social worker should specify and make systematic the procedures for measurement, in addition to constructing baselines following the guidelines in Chapter 3. He or she might reconstruct baselines from available records, or from client's memories, or construct them using new data. Both baselines should be horizontally stable. Furthermore, the scoring procedures and magnitudes for the graphs can be different, but it is recommended that the social worker take measurements at the same period.

Specify the clinical objectives. The objectives for each of the problem variables, situations, or clients should be compatible. That is, the practitioner should expect changes after the same amount of intervention. The magnitude of changes may not be the same, but the changes should be statistically significantly different to verify adherence to the logic of the multiple baseline design.

Specify the intervention. The intervention should be equivalent for both problem variables, situations, or clients. The structure of interventions that are applied to two different situations or to two different problem variables for the same client should be similar, although the contents might differ. For example, an intervention might include discussion of the problem, focus on the problem, and rewards for solving the problem. When the intervention deals with tardiness in school, it is focused on the reasons for tardiness, rewards for being on time, and so on. Another problem variable of speech anxiety may not be the focus of treatment until the client goes to school on time. When focusing the intervention on speech anxiety, the clinical social worker follows the same structure as with lateness to school (that is, discusses the client's feelings about the problem, provides rewards for reducing the problem, and so forth), but the content varies. To the extent that the interventions are equivalent, the logic of multiple baseline design is applicable. If the interventions differ, the design is not a multiple baseline design; instead, it simply comprises two different, basic single-subject designs.

The simpler the interventions, the easier it is to argue for their similarity. Advice, didactic presentations, use of positive reinforcements, and focused group discussions are examples of interventions that can be similar, differing primarily in focus and contents.

Implement the intervention for one problem variable, client, or situation. The practitioner implements the intervention until the expected change occurs in the problem variable. If no change occurs, the basic requirements for a multiple baseline design are not met.

Continue to baseline for the other problem variable, client, or situation. It is important to show that no changes occur during the continued baseline without intervention, yet, simultaneously, changes should occur in the idealized data pattern of the multiple baseline design when the practitioner provides intervention at the same time for the other problem variable. The occurrence of this pattern provides evidence that changes result from the intervention and not from historical or maturational factors.

Analyze the graphic patterns and perform statistical analyses. The clinician should use graphic analysis and statistical testing to show that changes occur from baseline to interventions for I, II, or III (see Figure 49). In addition, he or she should analyze the differences between baseline and continued baseline to show there are no changes. If these patterns occur, then the clinical social worker can proceed to the next step in the multiple baseline design. Showing no changes between line AB (baseline) and line CD (intervention for I, II, or III) indicates there is no reason to shift the intervention to the other problem variable because it is ineffective with the first problem variable. On the other hand, changes may occur during intervention and during continued baseline (see Figure 49) for the following reasons:

- The intervention for one problem variable generalizes to the other problem variable.
- The problem variables are not independent, that is, they are highly correlated.

- The changes for both problem variables might result from historical or maturational factors or multiple treatment interference.

Withdraw the intervention from problem variable 1 and introduce it for problem variable 2. In Figure 49 it is apparent that the practitioner has withdrawn the intervention from I, II, or III and introduced it for IV, V, or VI. The interventions should be as similar as possible. If they are equivalent, the logic of the multiple baseline design is upheld.

Analyze the new graphic pattern and perform statistical analyses. The social worker should make comparisons between the continued baseline and intervention for IV, V, or VI. That is, in Figure 49, the practitioner should compare line $C'D'$ with line $E'F'$ or line C_1D_1 with line E_1F_1. If there is a statistically significant change, then the criteria for a multiple baseline design have been met. Otherwise, the clinical social worker uses the same strategies for making decisions about the intervention as discussed in chapter 4 when comparing baselines and interventions.

The following are three examples of multiple baseline designs for clients, problem variables, and situations, complete with graphic presentations and statistical analyses. Two of the examples meet all of the criteria for a multiple baseline design; the other example results in two single-subject designs. The guidelines for multiple baseline designs are applied in each example.

Multiple Baseline Design for One Client with Problem Variables of Productivity and Lateness

Determine whether there are two or more different problems, situations, or clients. A client's supervisor referred the client to an EAP. In an assessment, the social worker learns that the client has relationship difficulties with his girlfriend, low self-esteem, has been consistently late to work, and has been performing below productivity standards in his factory job. The clinical social worker's long range goal is to increase the client's self-esteem and to reduce his anxiety through cognitive therapy. Lateness to work and below-standard productivity are shorter term goals, both of which the social worker plans to treat through behavioral therapy; the goals can serve as the intervention objectives in a multiple baseline design that first focuses on lateness and subsequently on work productivity.

Construct simultaneous baselines. The social worker reconstructs both baselines. The client gives the clinical social worker permission to access his productivity and lateness records from his supervisor. Apparently, in a work week that consists of five work days, the client has been below productivity standards five days per week for the past five weeks, and he has been late to work every day for the past five weeks (Figure 50). Both baselines show that the client has major problems with productivity and lateness. In addition, both baselines are horizontally stable, showing no accelerating or decelerating trends.

Specify the clinical objectives. The clinical objectives are as follows:

- reduce lateness to work to no more than one day per week by week 5 of intervention
- focus the intervention on increased productivity when the first objective has been achieved; the objective for productivity is that the number of days that the employee works below the standard productivity rate should be no more than one day per week
- although not immediately relevant for the multiple baseline design, anxiety should be reduced and self-esteem increased after three months of intervention.

Specify the intervention. The practitioner bases the intervention on the provision of one "reward unit" for each day the client is

figure 50

A Multiple Baseline Design for One Client with Problem Variables of Productivity and Lateness

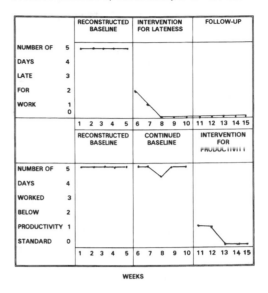

not late. Each reward unit is equivalent to one free meal at a local fast-food restaurant, the client's preferred eatery. The restaurant is participating in the program for the next several months, a plan that the social worker devised. During the first intervention interview, the clinical social worker determined that a free meal would be the most powerful reinforcer for the client.

Implement the intervention for one problem variable, client, or situation. The clinical social worker implements the intervention for lateness, the most immediate employee problem for the factory. The social worker explains the system to the client and indicates it will operate for the next five weeks, the social worker expects the client will reduce his lateness to no more than one time per week.

Continue to baseline for the other problem variable, client, or situation. The clinical social worker uses the lateness and productivity information provided by the client's supervisor each week. The practitioner plots the information on a graph (Figure 50).

Analyze the graphic patterns and perform statistical analyses. Apparently, the clinical social worker has attained the objective of no more than one day of lateness per week (Figure 50). In the five weeks of intervention, the number of days late per week declined from two in week 6 to one in week 7 to three weeks of no days late. Table 26 verifies this shift: it shows a statistically significant shift between the reconstructed baseline and the intervention for lateness.

Simultaneously, the social worker observes no apparent changes between the reconstructed baseline and the continued baseline for productivity. The client performs below the productivity standards every day for five weeks during the reconstructed baseline, and he is below standard every day except one during the five weeks of continued baseline with observations of 5, 5, 4, 5, and 5 for the number of days below productivity recorded on the graph. That

there are no statistically significant differences between reconstructed and continued baselines is evident in Table 27.

Withdraw the intervention for problem variable 1 and introduce it for problem variable 2. The clinical social worker withdraws the intervention for lateness and introduces it for the problem of productivity. The social worker provides the same reinforcer of a free meal for each reward unit. For each day the client performs at or above the standard productivity level, he receives one reward unit. The clinical social worker explains to the client that the same system is operative but now is focused on productivity rather than lateness.

Analyze the new graphic pattern and perform statistical analyses. As shown in Figure 50, the social worker observes 5, 5, 4, 5 and 5 days per week in which the client worked below productivity standards dur-

---

table 26 *Computing C, Sc, and Z for Reconstructed Baseline and Intervention for Lateness Time Series in Figure 50*

x	$x - M$	$(x - M)^2$	x_i	$x - x_i$	$(x - x_i)^2$
5	2.2	4.84	5	0	0
5	2.2	4.84	5	0	0
5	2.2	4.84	5	0	0
5	2.2	4.84	5	0	0
5	2.2	4.84	2	3	9
2	.8	.64	1	1	1
1	−1.8	3.24	0	1	1
0	−2.8	7.84	0	0	0
0	−2.8	7.84	0	0	0
0	−2.8	7.84	—	—	—
$28 = \Sigma x$		$51.60 = SS(x)$			$11 = D^2$

$$M = \frac{\Sigma x}{n} = \frac{28}{10} = 2.8$$

$$C = 1 - \frac{D^2}{2SS(x)} = 1 - \frac{11}{2(51.60)} = .89$$

$$Sc = \sqrt{\frac{n + 2}{(n + 1)(n - 1)}} = \sqrt{\frac{10 + 2}{(10 + 1)(10 - 1)}} = .35$$

$$Z = \frac{C}{Sc} = \frac{.89}{.35} = 2.54$$

NOTE: Because $Z > 1.64$, there are statistically significant differences between the time series for reconstructed baseline and intervention for lateness.

x	$x - M$	$(x - M)^2$	x_i	$x - x_i$	$(x - x_i)^2$
5	0.1	0.01	5	0	0
5	0.1	0.01	5	0	0
5	0.1	0.01	5	0	0
5	0.1	0.01	5	0	0
5	0.1	0.01	5	0	0
5	0.1	0.01	5	0	0
5	0.1	0.01	4	1	1
4	−0.9	0.81	5	−1	1
5	0.1	0.01	5	0	0
5	0.1	0.01	—	—	—
$49 = \Sigma x$		$0.90 = SS(x)$			$2 = D^2$

$$M = \frac{\Sigma x}{n} = \frac{49}{10} = 4.9$$

$$C = 1 - \frac{D^2}{2SS(x)} = 1 - \frac{2}{2(0.90)} = -.11$$

$$Sc = \sqrt{\frac{n + 2}{(n + 1)(n - 1)}} = \sqrt{\frac{10 + 2}{(10 + 1)(10 - 1)}} = .35$$

$$Z = \frac{C}{Sc} = \frac{-.11}{.35} = -.31$$

NOTE: Because $Z < 1.64$, there are no statistically significant differences between the time series at reconstructed baseline and continued baseline.

ing the period of continued baseline. The client's productivity increased during intervention: he worked below productivity standards only 1, 1, 0, 0, and 0 days per week. Furthermore, there is a statistically significant change in the time series from continued baseline to intervention for productivity (Table 28).

The overall graphic patterns and the statistical tests provide evidence that the criteria have been satisfied for the multiple baseline design for two different problem variables. Evidently, the intervention is generalizable across problem variables because in this instance, the intervention is effective for both productivity and lateness. In contrast, Figure 51 shows a data pattern that does not conform to the multiple baseline pattern. The intervention provides a shift from reconstructed baseline to intervention for lateness. However, the same pattern also occurs for productivity in which C'D' is

significantly different from A'B'; this is identical to the pattern observed from AB to CD. Hence, associated with the intervention for lateness are shifts in time series for lateness and for productivity.

Multiple Baseline Design for Two Clients for the Problem Variable of Index of Sexual Satisfaction

This type of design can produce information about the generalizability of an intervention for more than one client. The same logic for the implementation of procedures and the analyses of data patterns is applicable. Because the design involves more than one client, it technically is not a single-subject design. But it is included in this chapter because it is potentially useful when there are two or more clients with the same problem.

Determine whether there are two different problems, situations, or clients. The clini-

table 28 *Computing C, Sc, and Z for Continued Baseline and Intervention for Productivity Time Series in Figure 50*

x	$x - M$	$(x - M)^2$	x_i	$x - x_i$	$(x - x_i)^2$
5	2.4	5.76	5	0	0
5	2.4	5.76	4	1	1
4	1.4	1.96	5	−1	1
5	2.4	5.76	5	0	0
5	2.4	5.76	1	4	16
1	−1.6	2.56	1	0	0
1	−1.6	2.56	0	1	1
0	−2.6	6.76	0	0	0
0	−2.6	6.76	0	0	0
0	−2.6	6.76	—	—	—
$26 = \Sigma x$		$50.40 = SS(x)$			$19 = D^2$

$$M = \frac{\Sigma x}{n} = \frac{26}{10} = 2.6$$

$$C = 1 - \frac{D^2}{2SS(x)} = 1 - \frac{19}{2(50.40)} = .81$$

$$Sc = \sqrt{\frac{n + 2}{(n + 1)(n - 1)}} = \sqrt{\frac{10 + 2}{(10 + 1)(10 - 1)}} = .35$$

$$Z = \frac{C}{Sc} = \frac{.81}{.35} = 2.31$$

NOTE: Because $Z > 1.64$, there is a statistically significant shift in the time series from continued baseline to intervention.

cal social worker is involved in psychotherapy with two clients at a VA mental health clinic. Both clients are being treated for posttraumatic stress resulting from the Vietnam War. The basic intervention for both of them is psychodynamic therapy, including exploration of the past and the clients' feelings about the effects of the war on their environment; the social worker also develops cognitive strategies to deal with the clients' flashbacks of their war experiences. Both clients are married, and a relatively minor problem has been their dissatisfaction with sex. In addition to the ongoing therapy, the social worker decided to provide a program of sex therapy for both clients if the baseline assessments of sexual satisfaction indicated clinical problems.

Construct simultaneous baselines. The practitioner used Hudson's Index of Sexual Satisfaction (ISS) (Corcoran & Fischer,

figure 51

Two Single-Subject Designs for One Client, for Lateness and for Productivity over Time

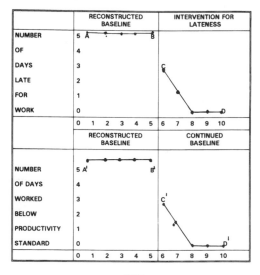

figure 52

A Multiple Baseline for Client 1 (A) and Client 2 (B) for the Problem Variable of Index of Sexual Satisfaction (ISS)

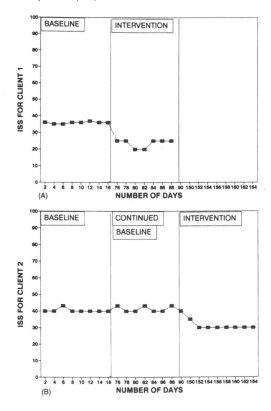

meet the requirements of multiple baseline design.)

Specify the clinical objectives. The clinical objectives are as follows:

- increase sexual satisfaction (significantly lower the average scores in time series at intervention) for client 1

- increase sexual satisfaction for client 2, after achieving it for client 1.

The social worker should achieve these objectives by day 76 to day 90 after the initial baseline contact for client 1 and by day 150 to day 164 after the initial baseline contact for client 2. These objectives are those intended for the multiple baseline design.

Other objectives for both clients are longer term objectives: to decrease the number of "flashbacks," to increase self-esteem, and to decrease anxiety.

Specify the intervention. The clinician bases the intervention on a model of sex therapy, which the therapist provides in an interview each week, with each client and the clients' spouses; this interview is separate from an ongoing weekly interview with each client. The clinician and clients discuss problems, issues, and feelings involved in the clients' sex activities; the social worker offers suggestions for each couple to try in their homes; the couples and the clinician discuss these sexual experiences in subsequent interviews. The focus is on teaching the partners to be aware of and sensitive to their needs, and to overcome fears related to sexual performance.

Implement the intervention for one problem variable, client, or situation. The social worker implements the intervention of sex therapy for client 1 after the last observation in baselines. The clinician plans to continue until day 76 to day 90 since initial contact at baseline.

Continue to baseline for the other problem variable, client, or situation. The clinician

1987a, pp. 100–101) in Appendix 11 to measure sexual satisfaction. ISS is useful because a score above 30 indicates a clinical problem; the lower the score, the greater the degree of sexual satisfaction.

The social worker makes observations every two days on ISS because the practitioner believes that changes in the measure of sexual satisfaction might occur in two days but not in one day. The clinician observes that there are relatively stable horizontal baselines for both clients 1 and 2 (Figure 52). Although the magnitude of the problem is higher for client 2 (40 and above for eight measurements) than for client 1 (for which scores ranged from 35 to 37), both clients have scores that indicate clinical problems. (The observations for both baselines do not have to be equivalent to

continues the baseline for client 2 until day 90 from initial baseline contact.

Analyze the graphic patterns and perform statistical analyses. A reduction in the sexual satisfaction scores for client 1 from baseline to intervention is evident from day 76 to day 90 since initial contact (Figure 52). (The break in the x axis (Figure 52) between 16 and 76 days was necessary to save space.) The reduction is from a range of 35 to 37 at baseline to a range of 20 to 25 at intervention. All of the scores at intervention are below the cutting score of 30, which means a clinical problem no longer is evident (see Appendix 11). In contrast, the observations for baseline and continued baseline for client 2 are similar. At baseline, there are observations of 40, 40,

43, 40, 40, 40, 40, and 40; at continued baseline, the sexual satisfaction scores are slightly higher: 43, 40, 40, 43, 40, 40, 43, and 40.

The trends from baseline to intervention continued downward until the relatively stable pattern shown in intervention for client 1; the trend from baseline to continued baseline was neither upward nor downward, but relatively stable, consistent with the pattern shown for continued baseline for client 2.

Table 29 provides statistical calculations for client 1. There are changes beyond the .05 level of statistical significance between the time series at baseline and at intervention. Further supporting the data pattern

table 29 *Computing C, Sc, and Z for Baseline and Intervention, Client 1, in Figure 52*

x	$x - M$	$(x - M)^2$	x_i	$x - x_i$	$(x - x_i)^2$
36	6.19	38.32	35	1	1
35	5.19	26.94	35	0	0
35	5.19	26.94	36	−1	1
36	6.19	38.32	36	0	0
36	6.19	38.32	37	−1	1
37	7.19	51.70	36	1	1
36	6.19	38.32	36	0	0
36	6.19	38.32	25	11	121
25	−4.81	23.14	25	0	0
25	−4.81	23.14	25	0	0
25	−4.81	23.14	20	5	25
20	−9.81	96.24	20	0	0
20	−9.81	96.24	25	−5	25
25	−4.81	23.14	25	0	0
25	−4.81	23.14	25	0	0
25	−4.81	23.14	—	—	—
477 = Σx		628.50 = $SS(x)$			175 = D^2

$$M = \frac{\Sigma x}{n} = \frac{477}{16} = 29.81$$

$$C = 1 - \frac{D^2}{2SS(x)} = 1 - \frac{175}{2(628.50)} = .86$$

$$Sc = \sqrt{\frac{n + 2}{(n + 1)(n - 1)}} = \sqrt{\frac{16 + 2}{(16 + 1)(16 - 1)}} = .26$$

$$Z = \frac{C}{Sc} = \frac{.86}{.26} = 3.31$$

NOTE: Because $Z > 1.64$, there is a statistically significant shift in the time series from baseline to intervention.

table 30 *Computing C, Sc, and Z for Baseline and Continued Baseline, Client 2, in Figure 52*

x	$x - M$	$(x - M)^2$	x_i	$x - x_i$	$(x - x_i)^2$
40	−.75	.56	40	0	0
40	−.75	.56	43	−3	9
43	2.25	5.06	40	3	9
40	−.75	.56	40	0	0
40	−.75	.56	40	0	0
40	−.75	.56	40	0	0
40	−.75	.56	40	0	0
40	−.75	.56	43	−3	9
43	2.25	5.06	40	3	9
40	−.75	.56	40	0	0
40	−.75	.56	43	−3	9
43	2.25	5.06	40	3	9
40	−.75	.56	40	0	0
40	−.75	.56	43	−3	9
43	2.25	5.06	40	3	9
40	−.75	.56	—	—	—
652 = Σx		26.96 = SS(x)			72 = D²

$$M = \frac{\Sigma x}{n} = \frac{652}{16} = 40.75$$

$$C = 1 - \frac{D^2}{2SS(x)} = 1 - \frac{72}{2(26.96)} = -.34$$

$$Sc = \sqrt{\frac{n + 2}{(n + 1)(n - 1)}} = \sqrt{\frac{16 + 2}{(16 + 1)(16 - 1)}} = .26$$

$$Z = \frac{C}{Sc} = \frac{-.34}{.26} = -1.31$$

NOTE: Because $Z < 1.64$, there are no statistically significant differences.

for a multiple baseline design, Table 30 indicates there are no statistically significant differences in the time series at baseline and at continued baseline for client 2.

Withdraw the intervention for client 1 and introduce it for client 2. The social worker withdraws the intervention of sex therapy for client 1 and introduces it for client 2. Sex therapy for both clients is the same intervention given by the same therapist.

Analyze the new graphic pattern and perform statistical analyses. The observations over time stop at day 90 and continue on day 150 (Figure 52). Again, as in day 16 to day 76, the social worker could have recorded the observations from day 92 to day 148, but did not do so for simplicity in pre-

sentation. Those observations showed a steady downward trend from continued baseline to intervention at 150 days. Furthermore, the magnitude of scores on sexual satisfaction (which means an increase in sexual satisfaction) decreased from 40 to 43 at continued baseline to 35 for one observation and 30 for seven observations at intervention. This shift in time series is statistically significant because Z is greater than 1.64 (Table 31). However, the clinician does not withdraw intervention because the score of 30 still indicates a problem in sexual satisfaction. Although there was a statistically significant change from continued baseline to intervention, indicating effectiveness of the intervention, the clinician can attain more progress until there is no clinical problem. That is, client 2 and his spouse appear to require more sex therapy intervention than do client 1 and his spouse. Nevertheless, their graphic analyses and the statistical analyses provide evidence that the multiple baseline criteria have been met and that sex therapy was effective for both clients.

Two Single-Subject Designs for One Client for Lateness at Home and at School

This example shows the result of an attempt at a multiple baseline design for two situations for one client. The attempt fails, with two resulting single-subject designs instead of the multiple baseline design. It does not meet the criteria of a multiple baseline design because the continued baseline for days late at home is significantly different from the reconstructed baseline (Figure 53).

Determine whether there are two or more different problems, situations, or clients. The client is an adolescent male whom the counseling staff at a public school has identified as a predelinquent; the staff has referred the adolescent to a behavioral therapy project for interventions aimed to reduce school tardiness and the days tardy at home. In addition, the project is designed to increase school attendance, increase grades, increase positive relations at home, and increase the client's self-esteem (Stuart, Jayaratne, & Tripodi, 1976).

table 31 *Computing C, Sc, and Z for Baseline and Intervention, Client 2, in Figure 52*

x	$x - M$	$(x - M)^2$	x_i	$x - x_i$	$(x - x_i)^2$
43	7.12	50.69	40	3	9
40	4.12	16.97	40	0	0
40	4.12	16.97	43	−3	9
43	7.12	50.69	40	3	9
40	4.12	16.97	40	0	0
40	4.12	16.97	43	−3	9
43	7.12	50.69	40	3	9
40	4.12	16.97	35	5	25
35	−.88	0.77	30	5	25
30	−5.88	34.57	30	0	0
30	−5.88	34.57	30	0	0
30	−5.88	34.57	30	0	0
30	−5.88	34.57	30	0	0
30	−5.88	34.57	30	0	0
30	−5.88	34.57	30	0	0
30	−5.88	34.57	—	—	—
574 = Σx		479.68 = $SS(x)$			95 = D^2

$$M = \frac{\Sigma x}{n} = \frac{574}{16} = 35.88$$

$$C = 1 - \frac{D^2}{2SS(x)} = 1 - \frac{95}{2(479.68)} = .90$$

$$Sc = \sqrt{\frac{n + 2}{(n + 1)(n - 1)}} = \sqrt{\frac{16 + 2}{(16 + 1)(16 - 1)}} = .26$$

$$Z = \frac{C}{Sc} = \frac{.90}{.26} = 3.46$$

NOTE: Because $Z > 1.64$, there are statistically significant differences between baseline and intervention.

figure 53

*Two Single-Subject Designs for One Client for
Lateness to School and Arriving at Home*

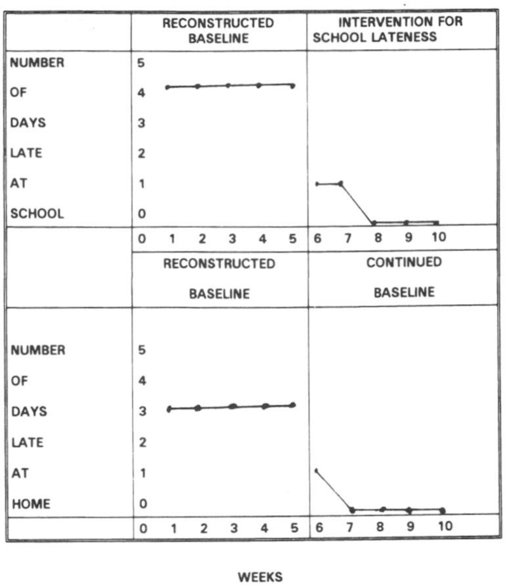

	RECONSTRUCTED BASELINE	INTERVENTION FOR SCHOOL LATENESS

NUMBER OF DAYS LATE AT SCHOOL: 5 4 3 2 1 0 — 0 1 2 3 4 5 6 7 8 9 10

	RECONSTRUCTED BASELINE	CONTINUED BASELINE

NUMBER OF DAYS LATE AT HOME: 5 4 3 2 1 0 — 0 1 2 3 4 5 6 7 8 9 10

WEEKS

Construct simultaneous baselines. The clinical social worker uses school records to show the number of days per week that the client was late for school. Based on an interview with the boy's mother, the clinical social worker reconstructs a baseline for five weeks before social work contact. Evidently, the client has a horizontally stable baseline of being late for school four out of five days per week and a horizontally stable baseline of being late arriving home three out of five days per week (Figure 53). (The two different baselines do not have to have the same magnitude of observations to satisfy the criteria of a multiple baseline design.)

Specify the clinical objectives. The clinical objectives are to significantly reduce the number of days per week late to school by week 5 of intervention (weeks 6 to 10); after achieving that objective, the clinical objective is to significantly reduce the number of days per week late arriving home—these are short-term objectives.

Specify the intervention. The intervention for the short-term objectives is behavioral therapy. The social worker rewards the boy for each week that he is not late more than one day. The social worker bases the reward on what is most meaningful for the boy: money to see movies on weekends.

Implement the intervention for one problem variable, client, or situation. The clinician implements behavioral therapy to reduce the number of days late per week to school. The clinical social worker develops and explains the reward system and discusses with the boy reasons for being late to school and how he might resolve the problem. The practitioner also involves the boy's family in the discussion, which occurs once per week.

Continue to baseline for the other problem variable, client, or situation. The boy's mother provides the clinical social worker with a report of the number of days the boy is late arriving home during school days. The report only covers weekdays to equalize the number of days for home lateness and school lateness.

Analyze the graphic patterns and perform statistical analyses. There is a reduction in number of days late to school from four days per week at reconstructed baseline to one or zero days per week during the intervention (Figure 53). However, there is also a decrease from reconstructed baseline, from three days per week late arriving home to one or zero days per week during the continued baseline. Analyses verify these observations, showing statistically significant changes from reconstructed baseline to intervention for days per week late to school and for reconstructed baseline to continued baseline for days per week late arriving home (Tables 32 and 33).

Hence, the practitioner has attained the clinical objectives both for lateness to school and arriving home. However, it is unclear whether the intervention was effective for school lateness and that generalized to home lateness, or whether the changes resulted from historical or maturational influences or from other forms of intervention such as group therapy.

table 32 *Computing C, Sc, and Z for Reconstructed Baseline and Intervention for School Lateness in Figure 53*

x	$x - M$	$(x - M)^2$	x_i	$x - x_i$	$(x - x_i)^2$
4	1.8	3.24	4	0	0
4	1.8	3.24	4	0	0
4	1.8	3.24	4	0	0
4	1.8	3.24	4	0	0
4	1.8	3.24	1	3	9
1	−1.2	1.44	1	0	0
1	−1.2	1.44	0	1	1
0	−2.2	4.84	0	0	0
0	−2.2	4.84	0	0	0
0	−2.2	4.84	—	—	—
22 = Σx		33.60 = SS(x)			10 = D^2

$$M = \frac{\Sigma x}{n} = \frac{22}{10} = 2.20$$

$$C = 1 - \frac{D^2}{2SS(x)} = 1 - \frac{10}{2(33.60)} = .85$$

$$Sc = \sqrt{\frac{n + 2}{(n + 1)(n - 1)}} = \sqrt{\frac{10 + 2}{(10 + 1)(10 - 1)}} = .35$$

$$Z = \frac{C}{Sc} = \frac{.85}{.35} = 2.43$$

NOTE: Because $Z > 1.64$, there are statistically significant differences in the time series.

table 33 *Computing C, Sc, and Z for Reconstructed Baseline and Continued Baseline for Home Lateness in Figure 53*

x	$x - M$	$(x - M)^2$	x_i	$x - x_i$	$(x - x_i)^2$
3	1.4	1.96	3	0	0
3	1.4	1.96	3	0	0
3	1.4	1.96	3	0	0
3	1.4	1.96	3	0	0
3	1.4	1.96	1	2	4
1	−.6	.36	0	1	1
0	−1.6	2.56	0	0	0
0	−1.6	2.56	0	0	0
0	−1.6	2.56	0	0	0
0	−1.6	2.56	—	—	—
16 = Σx		20.40 = SS(x)			5 = D^2

$$M = \frac{\Sigma x}{n} = \frac{16}{10} = 1.6$$

$$C = 1 - \frac{D^2}{2SS(x)} = 1 - \frac{5}{2(20.40)} = .88$$

$$Sc = \sqrt{\frac{n + 2}{(n + 1)(n - 1)}} = \sqrt{\frac{10 + 2}{(10 + 1)(10 - 1)}} = .35$$

$$Z = \frac{C}{Sc} = \frac{.88}{.35} = 2.51$$

NOTE: Because $Z > 1.64$, there are statistically significant differences in the time series.

GRADUATED INTENSITY DESIGN

The graduated intensity design is similar to the basic single-subject design. It involves baseline followed by an intervention; if the intervention phase is statistically different from baseline but not enough reduction in the problem variable has occurred, the intensity of the intervention is changed. If the time series with increased (or decreased) intervention is statistically significantly different from the time series at the first intervention stage, the resulting data pattern produces the graduated intensity design (Tripodi & Epstein, 1980). The ideal data pattern is depicted in Figure 54. There is a horizontally stable baseline followed by a change in magnitude during the first intervention, which, in turn, is followed by a change in magnitude during the phase in which the social worker has administered the changed intensity of the intervention.

Intensity can refer to the duration of each intervention contact, the number of contacts within a given period, the addition of new intervention components, the extent of the clinical social worker's involvement, or the degree of the client's participation. For example, a one-hour contact is more intense than contact for half an hour; two contacts per week is more intense than one contact per week; cognitive therapy and behavioral techniques combined are more intense than cognitive therapy by itself. One can estimate the degree of involvement of the clinical social worker or the client by the amount of time either spends talking in a therapeutic session. A clinical social worker who by design talks five minutes in an hour-long session could increase his or her intensity by talking 30 minutes, for example.

The graduated intensity design can provide some control over the internal validity threats of history, maturation, and multiple treatment interference. The design is based on the supposition that intensity is related to effectiveness and on the notion that successive statistically significant changes (from baseline to intervention and from intervention to a changed intensity of inter-

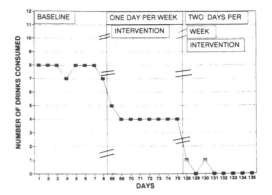

figure 54

Graduated Intensity Design

vention) are more likely to indicate that the changes in magnitude of the problem variable result from the intervention and not extraneous factors (Carter, 1972; Jayaratne & Levy, 1979).

Furthermore, the graduated intensity design fits the practice of many clinical social workers. The social worker may achieve progress with an intervention without attaining the clinical objectives. For example, an alcoholic reduces the amount of his or her drinking, but still drinks; the adolescent reduces the number of days truant from school, but he or she still is truant; the young adult female increases her degree of assertiveness, but she continues to be unassertive in most situations. When the client has made such progress, the clinical social worker can make several possible decisions: continue the same intervention, change the intensity of the intervention, or substitute another intervention. Deciding to change the intensity involves a simple manipulation (for example, doubling the number of contacts per week). If no changes occur with the changed intensity, the graduated intensity design is not produced; rather, the basic baseline plus an intervention phase is evident. Therefore, an unsuccessful graduated intensity design continues to represent two phases of the basic single-subject design model.

The chief disadvantage of using graduated intensity design is that it requires the systematic collection of data over a relatively long time. To the extent that data collection is time-consuming and the data are difficult to collect, the design becomes impractical. However, if the client or the social worker can easily obtain data, the design is quite feasible and advantageous because it provides data directly relevant to the possible manipulations the clinical social worker makes in implementing the intervention. The other major disadvantage is that the ideal data pattern may not materialize; nevertheless, it is still important information for the clinical social worker to know whether changes in the problem variable occur with changes in the implementation of the intervention.

General Guidelines for Implementing the Graduated Intensity Design

Specify the problem variable. The clinical social worker should determine from an assessment of the client and his or her situation whether any problem variables need change. The social worker should operationally define the variable and indicate how he or she will systematically measure it during baseline and intervention.

Obtain a baseline. The practitioner should use procedures previously discussed (see Chapter 3) and analyze the data pattern. The problem variable should be at a high enough magnitude to warrant intervention. A horizontally stable baseline or a baseline with increasing trends indicates that the problem is persistent, which further indicates the need for intervention.

Specify the clinical objectives. The clinician needs to specify how much change he or she desires and when the social worker expects change to occur after introducing the intervention.

Specify the intervention. The practitioner must specify the type of intervention and pay close attention to parameters of intensity, such as length of time for sessions, the number of contacts, client involvement, and so forth. The more specific the intervention is in relation to these parameters, the easier it is for the clinical social worker to change components of the intervention.

Introduce the intervention. The social worker should introduce the intervention after obtaining the baseline. He or she should systematically implement the intervention, for example, with the same duration for each interview and the same number of contacts per week.

Compare the intervention to baseline. The clinical social worker should analyze the data graphically and statistically to determine whether there are significant changes in the desired direction. In addition, he or she should observe whether he or she has attained the clinical objectives. If the social worker has made progress but has not attained the clinical objectives, then he or she needs to proceed to the next step. If the practitioner has not made any progress or if he or she has already attained the clinical objectives, then the social worker has not met the design requirements of the graduated intensity design. The clinical social worker makes the decision that fits his or her clinical practice. For example, if the clinical social worker has achieved the objectives, then he or she may work on other objectives or make arrangements for termination and follow-up.

Change the intervention intensity. Changing the intensity could involve increasing or decreasing the parameters of intensity. Although the clinician bases increasing intensity on the assumption that the level of intensity is directly related to effectiveness, decreasing intensity is predicated on a different assumption: The level of intensity is inversely related to the degree of effectiveness—the more the intervention is reduced, the greater the degree of effectiveness. The clinical social worker bases his or her decision to increase or decrease intensity on judgment stemming from his or her clinical experience, on notions of the intervention applied, and on the assessment of the particular client.

Compare the intervention with changed intensity to the intervention implemented after baseline. The social worker needs to graphically and statistically analyze whether there are changes in the time series. In addition, the social worker must determine the extent to which he or she has realized clinical objectives. If there are statistically significant differences, then the social worker has fulfilled the criteria for the graduated intensity design. The realization of clinical objectives signifies that the clinical social worker can plan for termination and follow-up, assuming there are no other objectives to accomplish.

Example

Specify the problem variable. The client, an adult female, is an alcoholic. She is addicted to drinking Scotch, and she voluntarily sought help from a clinical social worker in private practice. From an assessment interview, the clinical social worker concludes that the client has problems with family as well as with other interpersonal relationships. Although the client, a professor of journalism, is successful at work and in community activities, she has a great deal of difficulty in pursuing and in sustaining intimate relationships. The social worker views the alcoholism as a symptom of more deeply seated problems in the client's relationships with her family. The problem variable is that of the number of drinks of Scotch the client consumes daily. The client indicates that she has been consuming seven to eight glasses of Scotch daily for the past two months, and she is afraid that her work will soon deteriorate because of her excessive drinking.

Obtain a baseline. A baseline of eight consecutive days indicates the client drank eight drinks on six days and seven drinks on the other two days (Figure 54). The problem, as reported by the client to the clinical social worker, is severe; it is of high magnitude and it has been persistent. The baseline verifies the information the client reported in the initial assessment interview.

Specify the clinical objectives. The long-range clinical objectives are to increase the client's understanding of her drinking behavior and to discuss the extent to which the drinking is related to relationship problems with her family. The objective with respect to the drinking of alcohol is that the client stop drinking after two months (60 days) of intervention.

Specify the intervention. The intervention is psychodynamic psychotherapy. Not wanting to reveal her problem to university associates, the client chooses not to enter into an Alcoholics Anonymous program. Both the client and the therapist believe that they need to unravel the client's problems with family relationships. Nevertheless, they also believe they should monitor the problem variable of alcohol consumption because it is a tangible symptom that might indicate overall progress; more important, if the client does not reduce her alcoholic consumption, her career could be in jeopardy. The intervention consists of exploration of family problems and relationships as well as discussion of thoughts, actions, and feelings involved when the need to drink Scotch is manifest. The social worker plans to use techniques of clarification, support, and interpretation to help the client gain perspective on why she needs to drink.

Introduce the intervention. The intervention is of one-hour duration for one session per week. It commenced immediately after the baseline period of eight days ended.

Compare the intervention to baseline. In accordance with the clinical objectives, the practitioner compares the time series at intervention from day 68 to day 75 from initial contact with the client (two months after intervention began) with the baseline. Although not recorded in Figure 54, the client recorded the number of drinks consumed daily and reported those numbers weekly to the clinical social worker. The number of drinks consumed did not depart from the baseline pattern until day 38 since initial client contact; then there was a gradual decline until the social worker obtained the pattern recorded in Figure 54. At baseline the number of drinks consumed range from seven to eight, whereas at intervention, the client consumed four drinks daily for seven days and five drinks for one day. Hence, there was a reduction in the daily number of drinks consumed, but the social worker had not achieved the clinical objective of no drinking.

Computations of C, Sc, and Z statistics to test for statistically significant differences in the problem variable from baseline to intervention one day per week are shown in Table 34. Because Z is greater than 1.64, there are differences beyond the .05 level of statistical significance.

Change the intervention intensity. Because the social worker did not achieve the clinical objectives, he or she believed more progress would be made by increasing the intensity of the intervention from one day to two days per week. Moreover, the prac-

titioner changed the clinical objectives of no drinks per day after two months to no drinks per day after another two months, that is, at day 135 since initial client contact.

Compare the intervention with changed intensity to the intervention implemented after baseline. Figure 54 shows that during the intervention two days per week, the client had one drink daily for two days and no drinks daily for six days. Hence, the social worker did not achieve the clinical objective of no drinks daily. Although not shown in Figure 54, the trend was downward from four drinks at day 75 to one drink at day 128.

Table 35 provides statistical evidence that there were significant changes in the time

---

table 34	Computing C, Sc, and Z, Baseline to Intervention One Day Per Week in Figure 54

x	$x - M$	$(x - M)^2$	x_i	$x - x_i$	$(x - x_i)^2$
8	2.06	4.24	8	0	0
8	2.06	4.24	8	0	0
8	2.06	4.24	7	1	1
7	1.06	1.12	8	−1	1
8	2.06	4.24	8	0	0
8	2.06	4.24	8	0	0
8	2.06	4.24	7	1	1
7	1.06	1.12	5	2	4
5	−.94	0.88	4	1	1
4	−1.94	3.76	4	0	0
4	−1.94	3.76	4	0	0
4	−1.94	3.76	4	0	0
4	−1.94	3.76	4	0	0
4	−1.94	3.76	4	0	0
4	−1.94	3.76	4	0	0
4	−1.94	3.76	—	—	—
$95 = \Sigma x$		$54.88 = SS(x)$			$8 = D^2$

$$M = \frac{\Sigma x}{n} = \frac{95}{16} = 5.94$$

$$C = 1 - \frac{D^2}{2SS(x)} = 1 - \frac{8}{2(54.88)} = .93$$

$$Sc = \sqrt{\frac{n + 2}{(n + 1)(n - 1)}} = \sqrt{\frac{16 + 2}{(16 + 1)(16 - 1)}} = .26$$

$$Z = \frac{C}{Sc} = \frac{.93}{.26} = 3.58$$

NOTE: Because $Z > 1.64$, there are statistically significant differences.

x	$x - M$	$(x - M)^2$	x_i	$x - x_i$	$(x - x_i)^2$
5	2.81	7.90	4	1	1
4	1.81	3.28	4	0	0
4	1.81	3.28	4	0	0
4	1.81	3.28	4	0	0
4	1.81	3.28	4	0	0
4	1.81	3.28	4	0	0
4	1.81	3.28	4	0	0
4	1.81	3.28	1	3	9
1	−1.19	1.42	0	1	1
0	−2.19	4.80	1	−1	1
1	−1.19	1.42	0	1	1
0	−2.19	4.80	0	0	0
0	−2.19	4.80	0	0	0
0	−2.19	4.80	0	0	0
0	−2.19	4.80	0	0	0
0	−2.19	4.80	—	—	—
$35 = \Sigma x$		$62.50 = SS(x)$			$13 = D^2$

$$M = \frac{\Sigma x}{n} = \frac{35}{16} = 2.19$$

$$C = 1 - \frac{D^2}{2SS(x)} = 1 - \frac{13}{2(62.50)} = .90$$

$$Sc = \sqrt{\frac{n + 2}{(n + 1)(n - 1)}} = \sqrt{\frac{16 + 2}{(16 + 1)(16 - 1)}} = .26$$

$$Z = \frac{C}{Sc} = \frac{.90}{.26} = 3.46$$

NOTE: Because $Z > 1.64$, there are statistically significant differences.

series from the one-day-per-week intervention to the two-days-per-week intervention. Thus, the social worker has met the basic requirements of a graduated intensity design with respect to procedures for manipulating intensity of the intervention and to the resulting data patterns. Moreover, Table 36 provides further evidence that the time series at the intervention for two days per week is statistically significantly different than the time series for the problem variable at baseline.

Therefore, the practitioner has met the short-term goals for the client. The clinical social worker decides to continue to monitor alcohol consumption but is now ready to specify more precise objectives with the client for establishing more positive relationships. During the process of psychotherapy, the social worker discovered that the client and her mother spent a great deal of hostile energy in competing for attention from the client's father and the client had been encouraged to seek new relationships, both with men and with women. This discovery illustrates that the client and the social worker may accomplish an objective during the course of therapy and subsequently pursue other objectives. Obviously, with problems such as alcoholism, the danger of relapse is present, particularly with this client, who may revert to drinking behavior if she does not achieve successful new relationships with a clearer understanding of the influence of her familial relationships on her contemporary ones.

x	$x - M$	$(x - M)^2$	x_i	$x - x_i$	$(x - x_i)^2$
8	4	16	8	0	0
8	4	16	8	0	0
8	4	16	7	1	1
7	3	9	8	−1	1
8	4	16	8	0	0
8	4	16	8	0	0
8	4	16	7	1	1
7	3	9	1	6	36
1	−3	9	0	1	1
0	−4	16	1	−1	1
1	−3	9	0	1	1
0	−4	16	0	0	0
0	−4	16	0	0	0
0	−4	16	0	0	0
0	−4	16	0	0	0
0	−4	16	—	—	—
$64 = \Sigma x$		$228 = SS(x)$			$42 = D^2$

$$M = \frac{\Sigma x}{n} = \frac{64}{16} = 4.0$$

$$C = 1 - \frac{D^2}{2SS(x)} = 1 - \frac{42}{2(228)} = .91$$

$$Sc = \sqrt{\frac{n + 2}{(n + 1)(n - 1)}} = \sqrt{\frac{16 + 2}{(16 + 1)(16 - 1)}} = .26$$

$$Z = \frac{C}{Sc} = \frac{.91}{.26} = 3.46$$

NOTE: Because $Z > 1.64$, there are statistically significant differences.

WITHDRAWAL–REVERSAL DESIGN

The withdrawal–reversal design involves four stages; the first three stages are identical to the basic model of baseline, intervention, and follow-up, whereas the last stage calls for the reintroduction of the intervention. First, the social worker establishes a baseline of the problem variable to indicate there is a problem of sufficient magnitude to warrant intervention. Then he or she introduces the intervention; if the time series of the problem variable shows a significant decrease in the problem, the social worker withdraws the intervention. During the follow-up stage, if there is a significant reversal to indicate that the problem is again of sufficient magnitude to warrant inter-

vention, the practitioner reintroduces the intervention. The clinician has fully met the requisites of the withdrawal/reversal design if the time series of the problem variable again show a significant decrease. This idealized pattern is observable in Figure 55: At baseline, there is a problem of noncompliance with a diet regimen; at intervention, the client increases compliance (that is, the problem is decreased); at follow-up or withdrawal of the intervention, the problem recurs; and at the reintroduction of the intervention, the problem again decreases.

This design variation provides a degree of control over the internal validity threats of maturation, history, expectancy, and multiple treatment interference based on the

figure 55

An Idealized Data Pattern for a Withdrawal–Reversal Design

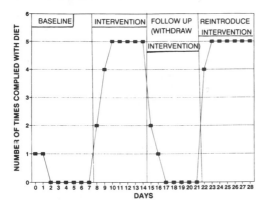

following. During the baseline, the clinician could attribute changes to the intervention and the internal validity threats. However, the increase in the problem during follow-up indicates that the decrease in the problem during intervention probably did not result from the internal validity threats, which are still operative at follow-up when the social worker had withdrawn the intervention. This inference is further substantiated with the reintroduction of the intervention when the problem again is reduced. In effect, the problem is there when the intervention is not; it is diminished when the intervention is present. Hence, this design, which the practitioner only achieves using the procedures of introduction, withdrawal, and reintroduction of the intervention as well as the data pattern described, controls internal validity threats (Monette et al., 1986; Rubin & Babbie 1993; Tripodi & Epstein, 1980).

The chief advantage of this design is that it can occur naturally in clinical social work practice. If all the data patterns from stage to stage do not occur, what remains is a basic design of baseline, intervention, and follow-up. In contrast, the major disadvantage is that it is difficult to reintroduce the exact intervention that was in effect before follow-up. The more complex the intervention, the more unlikely it is that the social worker will reintroduce the same intervention. It is necessary to have the same intervention to control for internal validity threats.

Guidelines for Implementing Withdrawal–Reversal

The design is most practical when the intervention is relatively simple and involves routine, identifiable actions, for example, making a phone call or directly giving advice. In addition, the implementation of the withdrawal–reversal design is most feasible with short-term interventions. It is inadvisable to withdraw intervention unless the social worker has met the clinical objectives for the client; otherwise, such a procedure may be unethical. The following are general guidelines for implementing the withdrawal–reversal design:

- **Specify the problem variable.** The practitioner should define the problem variable, indicating how he or she will measure it. The clinician must use the same measurement procedure throughout all of the stages of the design.

- **Obtain a baseline.** The social worker should obtain a baseline, analyze the data pattern, and determine whether there is a problem of sufficient magnitude to warrant intervention.

- **Specify the clinical objectives.** The clinician should indicate the magnitude of change expected and when he or she expects the changes to occur. If possible, the social worker should estimate how long the changes should persist after withdrawal of the intervention as a result of termination.

- **Specify the intervention.** The clinical social worker needs to specify the intervention so that he or she can easily replicate it following withdrawal.

- **Introduce the intervention.** The social worker should introduce and systematically implement the intervention in accordance with the specified plan.

- **Compare the intervention to baseline.** The practitioner needs to graphically analyze the data patterns and perform statistical tests. If he or she has met the clinical objectives, then the social worker will proceed to the next step.

- **Withdraw the intervention.** The clinician should continue to measure the problem variable and compare the withdrawal stage to the intervention stage. If there are statistically significant differences and the social worker has not met the clinical objectives, then he or she will proceed to the next step.

- **Reintroduce the intervention.** In this step, the clinician obtains measurements of the problem variable and compares the time series in this phase with that of the withdrawal phase. If there are statistically significant differences in the direction of reducing the problem, then the social worker has met the basic criteria for the withdrawal–reversal design. At this point, the clinical social worker

has to decide whether to continue the intervention or to withdraw it again. To avoid the problem of reversal, the clinical social worker may decide to gradually reduce the intervention in small increments, continuing to monitor the problem variable to locate the possibility of another reversal.

Using the Withdrawal–Reversal Design

Specify the problem variable. The client is a male outpatient with diverticulitis. The hospital nutritionist had recommended a plan for a diet regimen that would control the disease and possibly prevent the client's having to undergo surgery. However, the client had difficulty complying with the diet; the nutritionist referred him to the clinical social worker to discuss the psychosocial aspects of his disease, including the change of routine family patterns and

---

table 37 *Computing C, Sc, and Z, Comparing Baseline with Intervention in Figure 55*

x	$x - M$	$(x - M)^2$	x_i	$x - x_i$	$(x - x_i)^2$
1	−1.36	1.85	1	0	0
1	−1.36	1.85	0	1	1
0	−2.36	5.57	0	0	0
0	−2.36	5.57	0	0	0
0	−2.36	5.57	0	0	0
0	−2.36	5.57	0	0	0
0	−2.36	5.57	2	−2	4
2	−.36	0.13	4	−2	4
4	1.64	2.69	5	−1	1
5	2.64	6.97	5	0	0
5	2.64	6.97	5	0	0
5	2.64	6.97	5	0	0
5	2.64	6.97	5	0	0
5	2.64	6.97	—	—	—
$33 = \Sigma x$		$69.22 = SS(x)$			$10 = D^2$

$$M = \frac{\Sigma x}{n} = \frac{33}{14} = 2.36$$

$$C = 1 - \frac{D^2}{2SS(x)} = 1 - \frac{10}{2(69.22)} = .93$$

$$Sc = \sqrt{\frac{n + 2}{(n + 1)(n - 1)}} = \sqrt{\frac{14 + 2}{(14 + 1)(14 - 1)}} = .29$$

$$Z = \frac{C}{Sc} = \frac{.93}{.29} = 3.21$$

NOTE: Because $Z > 1.64$, there are statistically significant differences between baseline and intervention.

---

table 38 *Computing C, Sc, and Z, Comparing Intervention with Intervention Withdrawal in Figure 55*

x	$x - M$	$(x - M)^2$	x_i	$x - x_i$	$(x - x_i)^2$
2	−.43	.18	4	−2	4
4	1.57	2.46	5	−1	1
5	2.57	6.60	5	0	0
5	2.57	6.60	5	0	0
5	2.57	6.60	5	0	0
5	2.57	6.60	5	0	0
5	2.57	6.60	2	3	9
2	−.43	.18	1	1	1
1	1.13	2.04	0	1	1
0	−2.43	5.90	0	0	0
0	−2.43	5.90	0	0	0
0	−2.43	5.90	0	0	0
0	−2.43	5.90	0	0	0
0	−2.43	5.90	—	—	—
$34 = \Sigma x$		$67.36 = SS(x)$			$16 = D^2$

$$M = \frac{\Sigma x}{n} = \frac{34}{14} = 2.43$$

$$C = 1 - \frac{D^2}{2SS(x)} = 1 - \frac{16}{2(67.36)} = .88$$

$$Sc = \sqrt{\frac{n + 2}{(n + 1)(n - 1)}} = \sqrt{\frac{14 + 2}{(14 + 1)(14 - 1)}} = .29$$

$$Z = \frac{C}{Sc} = \frac{.88}{.29} = 3.03$$

NOTE: Because $Z > 1.64$, there are statistically significant differences between the time series at intervention and intervention withdrawal.

the necessity to adhere to the regimen prescribed in the diet. Essentially, the client was to eat five times per day and he was to avoid fried foods, alcohol, coffee, uncooked vegetables, and spicy foods. The nutritionist prescribed a menu for the client. The problem variable is compliance with the diet—this means compliance with all five prescribed meals daily.

Obtain a baseline. The social worker obtains a baseline for one week and instructs the client's wife to observe whether he complied with the requirements of each meal, because he remained at home using his home as a business office. The social worker tells the wife to offer the client the food, but not to nag him about eating desirable foods and to avoid eating and drinking nonprescribed foods and liquids. The baseline observed in Figure 55 indicates that after the first two days of complying with only one out of five meals, he did not comply to any meals for five straight days. Thus, apparently an intervention is warranted.

Specify the clinical objectives. The short-term clinical objective is to immediately help the client comply with the diet regimen. From the assessment interview, the social worker observes that the client does not realize the seriousness of his illness and the importance of adhering to his diet. Hence, the clinical social worker has the longer range objective of helping him understand the nature of his illness and how he can adapt to it. The social worker be-

table 39 *Computing C, Sc, and Z, Comparing Intervention Withdrawal with Reintroduction of Intervention in Figure 55*

x	x − M	(x − M)²	x_i	x − x_i	(x − x_i)²
2	−0.64	.41	1	1	1
1	−1.64	2.69	0	1	1
0	−2.64	6.97	0	0	0
0	−2.64	6.97	0	0	0
0	−2.64	6.97	0	0	0
0	−2.64	6.97	0	0	0
0	−2.64	6.97	4	−4	16
4	1.36	1.85	5	−1	1
5	2.36	5.57	5	0	0
5	2.36	5.57	5	0	0
5	2.36	5.57	5	0	0
5	2.36	5.57	5	0	0
5	2.36	5.57	5	0	0
5	2.36	5.57	—	—	—
37 = Σx		73.22 = SS(x)			19 = D²

$$M = \frac{\Sigma x}{n} = \frac{37}{14} = 2.6$$

$$C = 1 - \frac{D^2}{2SS(x)} = 1 - \frac{19}{2(73.22)} = .87$$

$$Sc = \sqrt{\frac{n + 2}{(n + 1)(n - 1)}} = \sqrt{\frac{14 + 2}{(14 + 1)(14 - 1)}} = .29$$

$$Z = \frac{C}{Sc} = \frac{.87}{.29} = 3.00$$

NOTE: Because $Z > 1.64$, there are statistically significant differences between the intervention withdrawal and reintroduction of intervention.

lieves that once the client has achieved full compliance (five meals a day), he will continue to comply with the diet for an unlimited period.

Specify the intervention. The intervention for the short-term goal is a phone call the clinical social worker makes to the client one time each day at noon. The phone call is brief; the social worker asks how the client is doing with his diet and stresses how important it is for him to comply with it.

Introduce the intervention. The practitioner introduces the intervention the next day after completing the baseline. Furthermore, the social worker continues to make telephone calls every day of the week at exactly the same time.

Compare the intervention to baseline. The time series at intervention contains five straight days of full compliance after the first two days of two and four times complied (Figure 55). This is a dramatic change from baseline to intervention, reflected in Table 37, which shows statistically significant changes from baseline to intervention.

Withdraw the intervention. The clinical social worker ceases making telephone calls from day 15 to day 21. Instead of continuing to maintain the diet as the clinical social worker had predicted, the client reverts to the baseline pattern with no compliance from day 17 to day 21 (see Figure 55). Statistical analysis reveals significant differences from intervention to intervention withdrawal (Table 38).

The clinical social worker speaks with the client on day 21. The social worker learns that the client believes that sticking to the diet is unimportant because the social worker quit calling him. The social worker explains to him that it is very important, indicating why the client should continue on his diet. She resumes the telephone intervention on day 22.

Reintroduce the intervention. The social worker reintroduces the intervention and maintains it for the next seven days. The client again fully complies with the diet regimen; in fact, he was in full compliance for six out of the seven days (Figure 55). Again, there was a dramatic increase from follow-up to the reintroduction of the intervention. The statistical analysis verifies this increase, indicating a significant shift in the time series (Table 39).

OTHER VARIATIONS

Readers who wish to learn about other variations should consult the following references: Barlow and Hersen (1984), whose book is the most authoritative text on variations of single-subject designs. The examples are from behavioral psychology and the interventions are of short-term duration. It is difficult to read, but is most comprehensive in the variety of designs presented. Also, the Bloom et al. (1993) book presents a number of variations on single-subject design. Its focus is on the evaluation of practice in social work; it includes many technical procedures and statistical analytic strategies. In addition, the text by Blythe et al. (1994) contains many designs and research procedures that social workers in human services agencies can use. It also includes a number of statistical techniques for analyzing the results of research.

Those books include a number of references that should enable students to gain a detailed knowledge of single-subject designs. It is hoped that the basic concepts presented in this book will serve as a useful introduction in considering the applicability of single-subject designs for clinical social workers.

APPENDIXES

INDEX OF SELF-ESTEEM (ISE)

INDEX OF SELF-ESTEEM (ISE)

Name: _____   Today's Date: _____

Context: _____

This questionnaire is designed to measure how you see yourself. It is not a test, so there are no right or wrong answers. Please answer each item as carefully and as accurately as you can by placing a number beside each one as follows.

> 1 = None of the time
> 2 = Very rarely
> 3 = A little of the time
> 4 = Some of the time
> 5 = A good part of the time
> 6 = Most of the time
> 7 = All of the time

---

1. ____ I feel that people would not like me if they really knew me well.
2. ____ I feel that others get along much better than I do.
3. ____ I feel that I am a beautiful person.
4. ____ When I am with others I feel they are glad I am with them.
5. ____ I feel that people really like to talk with me.
6. ____ I feel that I am a very competent person.
7. ____ I think I make a good impression on others.
8. ____ I feel that I need more self-confidence.
9. ____ When I am with strangers I am very nervous.
10. ____ I think that I am a dull person.
11. ____ I feel ugly.
12. ____ I feel that others have more fun than I do.
13. ____ I feel that I bore people.
14. ____ I think my friends find me interesting.
15. ____ I think I have a good sense of humor.
16. ____ I feel very self-conscious when I am with strangers.
17. ____ I feel that if I could be more like other people I would have it made.
18. ____ I feel that people have a good time when they are with me.
19. ____ I feel like a wallflower when I go out.
20. ____ I feel I get pushed around more than others.
21. ____ I think I am a rather nice person.
22. ____ I feel that people really like me very much.
23. ____ I feel that I am a likeable person.
24. ____ I am afraid I will appear foolish to others.
25. ____ My friends think very highly of me.

3, 4, 5, 6, 7, 14, 15, 18, 21, 22, 23, 25.

Reproduced by permission of WalMyr Publishing Co., Tempe, AZ.

MICHIGAN ALCOHOLISM SCREENING TEST (MAST)

MICHIGAN ALCOHOLISM SCREENING TEST (MAST)

Please circle either Yes or No for each item as it applies to you.

Yes No (2)   1. Do you feel you are normal drinkers?

Yes No (2)   2. Have you ever awakened the morning after some drinking the night before and found that you could not remember a part of the evening before?

Yes No (1)   3. Does your wife (or do your parents) ever worry or complain about your drinking?

Yes No (2)   4. Can you stop drinking without a struggle after one or two drinks?

Yes No (1)   5. Do you ever feel bad about your drinking?

Yes No (2)   6. Do friends or relatives think you are a normal drinker?

Yes No (0)   7. Do you ever try to limit your drinking to certain times of the day or to certain places?

Yes No (2)   8. Are you always able to stop drinking when you want to?

Yes No (5)   9. Have you ever attended a meeting of Alcoholics Anonymous (AA)?

Yes No (1)   10. Have you gotten into fights when drinking?

Yes No (2)   11. Has drinking ever created problems with you and your wife?

Yes No (2)   12. Has your wife (or other family member) ever gone to anyone for help about your drinking?

Yes No (2)   13. Have you ever lost friends or girlfriends/boyfriends because of drinking?

Yes No (2)   14. Have you ever gotten into trouble at work because of drinking?

Yes No (2)   15. Have you ever lost a job because of drinking?

Yes No (2)   16. Have you ever neglected your obligations, your family, or your work for two or more days in a row because you were drinking?

Yes No (1)   17. Do you ever drink before noon?

Yes No (2)   18. Have you ever been told you have liver trouble? Cirrhosis?

Yes No (5)   19. Have you ever had delirium tremens (DTs), severe shaking, heard voices, or seen things that weren't there after heavy drinking?

Yes No (5)   20. Have you ever gone to anyone for help about your drinking?

Yes No (5)   21. Have you ever been in a hospital because of drinking?

Yes No (2)   22. Have you ever been a patient in a psychiatric hospital or on a psychiatric ward of a general hospital where drinking was part of the problem?

Yes No (2)   23. Have you ever been seen at a psychiatric or mental health clinic, or gone to a doctor, social worker, or clergyman for help with [an] emotional problem in which drinking had played a part?

Yes No (2)   24. Have you ever been arrested, even for a few hours, because of drunk behavior?

Yes No (2)   25. Have you ever been arrested for drunk driving after drinking?

Source: Selzer, M.L. (1971). The Michigan Alcoholism Screening Test: The quest for a new diagnostic instrument. *American Journal of Pyschiatry, 127,* 89–94. Copyright 1994, the American Psychiatric Association. Reprinted by permission.

CLIENT QUESTIONNAIRE TO MONITOR CLINICAL SOCIAL WORKER'S IMPLEMENTATION OF POSTHOSPITAL PLANNING

1. Were insurance and discharge forms filled out by the social worker?
   Yes __ No __ Don't know __
2. Did the social worker discuss medication with you?
   Yes __ No __ Don't know __
   With your family?
   Yes __ No __ Don't know __
3. Did the social worker discuss what your living arrangements with your family will be after you leave the hospital?
   Yes __ No __ Don't know __
4. Did the social worker discuss different community living arrangements for you?
   Yes __ No __ Don't know __
5. Did the social worker talk with your family?
   Yes __ No __ Don't know __
6. Did the social worker refer you to another social worker in the community?
   Yes __ No __ Don't know __
7. Did the social worker discuss employment with you?
   Yes __ No __ Don't know __
8. Did the social worker discuss education with you?
   Yes __ No __ Don't know __
9. Did the social worker make an appointment to see you after you leave the hospital?
   Yes __ No __ Don't know __

FOLLOW-UP QUESTIONNAIRE

Since you stopped receiving help from the social worker:

Have you received help from other resources or persons?
    Yes ___ No ✓
      If yes, please explain _____

Have you had any recurrences of the major problem for which you received help?
    Yes ___ No ✓
      If yes, please explain _____

Have you changed any of your daily habits?
    Yes ___ No ✓
      If yes, please explain _____

Have there been any changes in your living circumstances?
    Yes ___ No ✓
      If yes, please explain _____

Have you been ill?
    Yes ___ No ✓
      If yes, please explain _____

Have any of your family members been sick?
    Yes ___ No ✓
      If yes, please explain _____

Have there been any changes in your personal relationships with family and friends?
    Yes ✓ No ___
      If yes please explain *I am dating women more often.* _____

Have any other major problems occurred?
    Yes ___ No ✓
      If yes, please explain _____

Have there been any unexpected positive or negative changes resulting from the services you received from the social worker?
    Yes ✓ No ___
      If yes, please explain *I have felt more energetic.* _____

FOLLOW-UP QUESTIONNAIRE FOR TOM AND HIS RELATIONSHIP TO JERRY

Does Jerry try to pick fights with you?
Yes __ No __
    If yes, indicate how often he does this:
    Once a week __ Two to three times per week __
    Four to five times per week __
    Six to seven times per week __
Do you try to pick fights with Jerry?
Yes __ No __
    If yes, indicate how often you do this:
    Once a week __ Two to three times per week __
    Four to five times per week __
    Six to seven times per week __
Have you argued with Jerry in the past week?
Yes __ No __
    If yes, indicate about how many arguments you had:
    One __ Two to five __ Six to eight __
    Nine or more __
To what extent do you believe you are responsible for the arguments and fights with Jerry?
    Not at all responsible __ Somewhat responsible __
    Completely responsible __
To what extent do you believe Jerry is responsible for arguments and fights with you?
    Not at all responsible __ Somewhat responsible __
    Completely responsible __
Do you believe your father:
    Likes you and Jerry about the same __ Favors you __
    Favors Jerry __
Do you believe your mother:
    Likes you and Jerry about the same __ Favors you __
    Favors Jerry __
Do you like or dislike Jerry?
    Dislike __ Like __ Neither like nor dislike __
Does Jerry like or dislike you?
    Dislike __ Like __ Neither like nor dislike __
In the past week, have Jerry and you gone places together to have a good time (such as the movies, a baseball game, a tennis match, sailing)?
    Yes __ No __
        If yes, indicate how many times __
Please describe the nature of your relationship with Jerry _____
Has your relationship with Jerry changed since you have had contacts with the social worker?
    Yes __ No __
        If yes, please explain _____
How could the relationship between you and Jerry be improved? _____

FOLLOW-UP QUESTIONNAIRE ABOUT THE INTERVENTION AND THE CLINICAL SOCIAL WORKER

To what extent has the social worker been sensitive to your needs as expressed in interviews?

    Very sensitive __ Moderately sensitive __

    Neither sensitive nor insensitive __

    Moderately insensitive __ Very insensitive __

Did the social worker meet with you on time for your appointments?

    All of the time __ Most of the time __

    Some of the time __ Not at all __

Did the social worker review progress with you?

    Yes __ No __

      If yes, how often?

      Every session __ Every other session __

      Every third session __

      At least every fourth session __

Did the social worker provide you with graphic information about your progress?

    Yes __ No __

Did the social worker explain how to make self-ratings of anxiety?

    Yes __ No __

Did the social worker explain how to use the standardized instrument for measuring depression?

    Yes __ No __

Did the social worker help you identify the problem(s) you worked on?

    Yes __ No __

      If yes, please describe the problem(s) _____

Did the social worker provide you with good advice that you could use on everyday practical problems?

    Yes __ No __

Did the social worker help you to understand when and why you become anxious?

    Yes __ No __

Did the social worker use role playing of interpersonal situations in your sessions?

    Yes __ No __

Were you comfortable discussing your personal problems with the social worker?

    Yes __ No __

      If no, what could the social worker have done to make you more comfortable?

    _____

Did the social worker give you homework assignments after each session?

    Yes __ No __

      If yes, to what extent were these assignments helpful?

        Very helpful __ Helpful __

        Moderately helpful __ Not at all helpful __

Was the social worker helpful to you?

    Yes __ No __

      Please describe _____

CLIENT SATISFACTION QUESTIONNAIRE (CSQ-8)

CLIENT SATISFACTION QUESTIONNAIRE (CSQ-8)

Please help us improve our program by answering some questions. We are interested in your honest opinions, whether they are positive or negative. *Please answer all of the questions.* We also welcome your comments and suggestions. Thank you very much; we really appreciate your help.

Circle your answer:

1. How would you rate the quality of service you have received?

4	3	2	1
Excellent	Good	Fair	Poor

2. Did you get the kind of service you wanted?

1	2	3	4
No, definitely	Not really	Generally yes	Yes, definitely

3. To what extent has our program met your needs?

4	3	2	1
Almost all of my needs have been met	Most of my needs have been met	Only a few of my needs have been met	None of my needs has been met

4. If a friend were in need of similar help, would you recommend our program to him or her?

1	2	3	4
No, definitely not	No, I don't think so	Yes, I think so	Yes, definitely

5. How satisfied are you with the amount of help you have received?

1	2	3	4
Quite dissatisfied	Indifferent or mildly dissatisfied	Mostly satisfied	Very satisfied

6. Have the services you received helped you to deal more effectively with your problems?

4	3	2	1
Yes, they helped a great deal	Yes, they helped somewhat	No, they really didn't help	No, they seemed to make things worse

7. In an overall general sense, how satisfied are you with the service you have received?

4	3	2	1
Very satisfied	Mostly satisfied	Indifferent or mildly dissatisfied	Quite satisfied

8. If you were to seek help again, would you come back to our program?

1	2	3	4
No, definitely not	No, I don't think so	Yes, I think so	Yes, definitely

FOLLOW-UP QUESTIONNAIRE FOR CLIENT: ASSERTIVE BEHAVIORS

Have you failed to be assertive in interpersonal situations in which you should have been assertive?

    Yes ___ No ✓

        If yes, please explain _____

Have other problems occurred for you since you finished your work with the social worker?

    Yes ___ No ✓

        If yes, please explain _____

Do you understand why you should be assertive in certain situations?

    Yes ✓ No ___

        If yes, did you acquire this understanding in your work with the social worker?

            Yes ✓ No ___

        If no, how should the social worker have helped you acquire this understanding? ___
_____

Did you discuss with the social worker interpersonal situations in which you should be assertive?

    Yes ✓ No ___

        If no, should you have discussed these situations with the social worker?

            Yes ___ No ___

Have you made progress in being assertive since your first contact with the social worker?

    Yes ✓ No ___

        If yes, please explain *I have understood my reluctance to be assertive, and I have overcome my hesitation to be assertive by practicing with the social worker.*

Have you received professional help from other persons since you finished your work with the social worker?

    Yes ___ No ✓

        If yes, please explain _____

Have you felt a need to continue to work with the social worker on assertiveness or on other problems?

    Yes ___ No ✓

        If yes, please explain _____

Have any events occurred recently that facilitated your assertiveness?

    Yes ___ No ✓

        If yes, please explain _____

Have any events occurred recently that prevented you from being assertive?

    Yes ___ No ✓

        If yes, please explain _____

Have you reported the daily number of times you were assertive in a consistent manner?

    Yes ✓ No ___

        If no, please explain _____

Did the social worker help you to become more assertive?

    Yes ✓ No ___

        If no, how could the social worker have helped? _____

FOLLOW-UP QUESTIONNAIRE FOR CLIENT: EXCESSIVE COFFEE CONSUMPTION

Have you been drinking more than two cups of coffee per day?
     Yes ✓ No __
     If yes, please explain *I've been upset.*

Have other problems occurred for you since you finished your work with the social worker?
     Yes ✓ No __
     If yes, please explain *My wife was diagnosed as having cancer, and she's very tired during the day.*

Do you understand why you should not drink more than two cups of coffee per day?
     Yes ✓ No __
          If no, should the social worker try to help you understand?
               Yes __ No __

Have you made progress in drinking less coffee since your first contact with the social worker?
     Yes ✓ No __
          Please explain *At first there was progress when I was able to go on excursions with my wife. But then I drank a lot more after I learned about her illness.*

Have you received professional help from other persons since you finished your work with the social worker?
     Yes __ No ✓
     If yes, please explain _____

Have you felt a need to continue to work with the social worker on reducing your coffee consumption or on other problems?
     Yes ✓ No __
     If yes, please explain *I need to control my coffee drinking when I get upset.*

Have any events occurred recently that facilitated your reduction in coffee consumption?
     Yes __ No ✓
     If yes, please explain _____

Have any events occurred recently that prevented you from reducing your coffee consumption?
     Yes ✓ No __
     If yes, please explain *My wife is ill, diagnosed as having cancer.*

Have you reported the daily number of cups of coffee consumed in a consistent manner?
     Yes ✓ No __
     If no, please explain _____

Have you been able to substitute decaf for regular coffee?
     Yes __ No ✓
     If no, please explain *It doesn't taste as good as regular coffee.*

Have you had frequent stomachaches in the past two weeks?
     Yes ✓ No __

Have you had any other illness in the past two weeks?
     Yes ✓ No __
     If yes, please explain *I've had headaches and feelings of nausea.*

Did the social worker help you to drink fewer cups of coffee?
     Yes ✓ No __
          If no, how could the social worker have helped?
          She helped by having my wife and I go on excursions, but I wasn't prepared for illness. I need to be able to deal with my wife's illness as well as control my coffee drinking.

FOLLOW-UP QUESTIONNAIRE FOR JACK: REDUCTION OF NEGATIVE REMARKS TO HIS FATHER

Have you made unwarranted negative remarks to your father?
    Yes ✓ No ___
        If yes, please explain *I have made a few negative comments, but they were not as negative as before.*
Have other problems occurred for you since you finished your individual work with the social worker?
    Yes ___ No ✓
        If yes, please explain _____
Do you understand what leads you to make negative remarks to your father?
    Yes ✓ No ___
        If yes, did you acquire this understanding in your work with the social worker?
            Yes ✓ No ___
        If no, how should the social worker have helped you acquire this understanding? ___
_____

Did you discuss with the social worker interpersonal situations in which you should reduce your negative remarks to your father?
    Yes ✓ No ___
        If no, should you have discussed these situations with the social worker? _____
Have you made progress in reducing unwarranted negative remarks to your father since your first contact with the social worker?
    Yes ✓ No ___
        Please explain. *I've decreased the number of negative remarks to my father.*
Have any events occurred recently that facilitated a reduction in unwarranted negative remarks to your father?
    Yes ✓ No ___
        If yes, please explain *My father has spent more time with me in recreational activities.*
Have any events occurred recently that prevented you from reducing unwarranted negative remarks to your father?
    Yes ___ No ✓
        If yes, please explain _____
Did the social worker help you to reduce the daily number of negative remarks to your father?
    Yes ✓ No ___
        If no, how could the social worker have helped? _____

INDEX OF SEXUAL SATISFACTION (ISS)

INDEX OF SEXUAL SATISFACTION (ISS)

Name: _____   Today's Date: _____

This questionnaire designed to measure the degree of satisfaction you have in the sexual relationship with your partner. It is not a test. so there are no right or wrong answers. Answer each item as carefully and as accurately as you can by placing a number beside each one as follows.

1 = None of the time
2 = Very rarely
3 = A little of the time
4 = Some of the time
5 = A good part of the time
6 = Most of the time
7 = All of the time

1. _____ I feel that my partner enjoys our sex life.
2. _____ Our sex life is very exciting.
3. _____ Sex is fun for my partner and me.
4. _____ Sex with my partner has become a chore for me.
5. _____ I feel that our sex is dirty and disgusting.
6. _____ Our sex life is monotonous.
7. _____ When we have sex it is too rushed and hurriedly completed.
8. _____ I feel that my sex life is lacking in quality.
9. _____ My partner is sexually very exciting.
10. _____ I enjoy the sex techniques that my partner likes or uses.
11. _____ I feel that my partner wants too much sex from me.
12. _____ I think that out sex is wonderful.
13. _____ My partner dwells on sex too much.
14. _____ I try to avoid sexual contact with my partner.
15. _____ My partner is too rough or brutal when we have sex.
16. _____ My partner is a wonderful sex mate.
17. _____ I feel that sex is a normal function of our relationship.
18. _____ My partner does not want sex when I do.
19. _____ I feel that our sex life really adds a lot to our relationship.
20. _____ My partner seems to avoid sexual contact with me.
21. _____ It is easy for me to get sexually excited by my partner.
22. _____ I feel that my partner is sexually pleased with me.
23. _____ My partner is very sensitive to my sexual needs and desires.
24. _____ My partner does not satisfy me sexually.
25. _____ I feel that my sex life is boring.

1. 2, 3, 9, 10, 12, 16, 17, 19, 21, 22, 23.

REFERENCES

American Psychiatric Association. (1994). *Diagnostic and statistical manual of mental disorders—Fourth Edition*. Washington, DC: Author.

Barlow, D. H., & Hersen, M. (1984). *Single case experimental design. Strategies for studying behavior change* (2nd ed.). Tarrytown, NY: Pergamon Press.

Berlin, S. B., & Marsh, J. C. (1993). *Informing practice decisions*. New York: Macmillan.

Bloom, M., & Fischer, J. (1982). *Evaluating practice: Guidelines for the accountable professional*. Englewood Cliffs, NJ: Prentice Hall.

Bloom, M., Fischer, J., & Orme, J. (1993). *Evaluating practice: Guidelines for the accountable professional* (2nd ed.). Englewood Cliffs, NJ: Prentice Hall.

Blythe, B. J., & Briar, S. (1985). Developing empirically based models of practice. *Social Work, 30*, 483–488.

Blythe, B. J., & Tripodi, T. (1989). *Measurement in direct practice*. Newbury Park, CA: Sage Publications.

Blythe, B. J., Tripodi, T., & Briar, S. (1994). *Direct practice research in human service agencies*. New York: Columbia University Press.

Burns, D. D., & deJong, M. D. (1980). *The feeling good handbook*. New York: Penguin Books.

Campbell, D., & Stanley, J. (1963). *Experimental and quasi-experimental designs for research*. Chicago: Rand McNally.

Carter, R. (1972). *Designs and data patterns in intensive experimentation* (Course Monographs: Research in Interpersonal Influence). Ann Arbor: University of Michigan School of Social Work.

Cook, T. D., & Campbell, D. T. (1979). *Quasi-experimentation: Design and analysis issues for field settings*. Chicago: Rand McNally.

Corcoran, K., & Fischer, J. (1987a). *The clinical measurement package: A field manual*. Chicago: Dorsey Press.

Corcoran, K., & Fischer, J. (1987b). *Measures for clinical practice: A sourcebook*. New York: Free Press.

Epstein, I., & Tripodi, T. (1977). *Research techniques for program planning, monitoring, and evaluation*. New York: Columbia University Press.

Fowler, F. J., Jr. (1988). *Survey research methods* (rev. ed.). Newbury Park, CA: Sage Publications.

Gambrill, E. D., & Barth, R. P. (1980). Single-case study designs revisited. *Social Work Research & Abstracts, 16*, 15–20.

Grasso, A. J., & Epstein, I. (Eds.). (1992). *Research utilization in the social services: Innovations for practice and administration*. New York: Haworth Press.

Hayes, S. C. (1992). Single-case experimental design and empirical clinical practice. In A. E. Kazdin (Ed.), *Methodological issues and strategies in clinical research* (pp. 491–522). Washington, DC: American Psychological Association.

Hersen, M., & Barlow, D. H. (1976). *Single case experimental designs*. Tarrytown, NY: Pergamon Press.

Hudson, W. W., & Thyer, B. A. (1987). Research measures and indices in direct practice. In A. Minahan (Ed.-in-Chief), *Encyclopedia of social work* (18th ed., pp. 487–498). Silver Spring, MD: National Association of Social Workers.

Ivanoff, A., Blythe, B. J., & Tripodi, T. (1994). *Research based practice with involuntary clients*. New York: Aldine de Gruyter.

Jayaratne, S. (1977). Single-subject and group designs in treatment evaluation. *Social Work Research & Abstracts, 13*(3), 35–42.

Jayaratne, S., & Levy, R. L. (1979). *Empirical clinical practice*. New York: Columbia University Press.

Kazdin, A. E. (Ed.). (1992). *Methodological issues and strategies in clinical research*. Washington, DC: American Psychological Association.

McCubbin, H. I., & Thompson, A. I. (Eds.). (1987). *Family assessment inventories for research and practice*. Madison: University of Wisconsin Press.

Minahan, A. (Ed.-in-Chief). (1987). *Encyclopedia of social work* (18th ed.). Silver Spring, MD: National Association of Social Workers.

Monette, D. R., Sullivan, T. J., & DeJong, C. R. (1986). *Applied social research: Tool for the human services*. New York: Holt, Rinehart & Winston.

National Association of Social Workers. (1994). *NASW code of ethics*. Washington, DC: Author.

Nurius, P. S., Wedenoja, M., & Tripodi, T. (1987). Prescriptions, proscriptions, and generalizations in social work practice literature. *Social Casework, 68,* 589–596.

Rubin, A., & Babbie, E. (1993). *Research methods for social work* (2nd ed.). Monterey, CA: Brooks/Cole.

Siegel, D. (1984). Defining empirically based practice. *Social Work, 29,* 325–331.

Stuart, R. B., Jayaratne, S., & Tripodi, T. (1976). Changing adolescent deviant behavior through reprogramming the behaviour of parents and teachers: An experimental evaluation. *Canadian Journal of Behavioral Science, 8*(2), 132–144.

Thomas, E. J. (1978). Research and service in single-case experimentation: Conflicts and choices. *Social Work Research & Abstracts, 14*(4), 20–31.

Tripodi, T. (1983). *Evaluative research for social workers.* Englewood Cliffs, NJ: Prentice Hall.

Tripodi, T., & Epstein, I. (1980). *Research techniques for clinical social workers.* New York: Columbia University Press.

Tryon, W. W. (1982). A simplified time-series analysis for evaluating treatment interventions. *Journal of Applied Behavioral Analysis, 15,* 423–429.

Videka-Sherman, L., & Reid, W. J. (Eds.). (1990). *Advances in clinical social work research.* Silver Spring, MD: National Association of Social Workers.

INDEX

implementing, 68–70
location of, 67
making decisions about, 82–83
measurement during, 70–72, 74
monitoring implementation in, 69
in multiple baseline design, 109–110
purpose of, 64
specifying, 66–68
topology for considering changes in, 83–85
in withdrawal–reversal design, 126
without baseline, 72–74
Interviewing schedules, 28

K

Knowledge
  causal, 80–82
    and use of single-subject design methodology, 12, 13
  correlational, 9, 79
    inferences about, 79–80
    and use of single-subject design methodology, 11–12
  descriptive, 9, 10
    and use of single-subject design methodology, 11–12
  levels of, 9–10

L

Location of intervention, 67

M

Maintenance as change objective, 65
Marital Happiness Scale, 30–31
Maturation in single-subject design methodology, 81–82
Measurement
  arguments against, 27–28
  arguments for, 26–27
  characteristics of useful variables, 20–25
  developing, 29
    during intervention, 70–72
    questionnaires, 34–38
    rating scales, 30–33
    self-anchored rating scales, 29–30
    systematic observations, 33–34
  graphing measures, 72–83
  relationship of variables to assessment and evaluation, 19–20
  standardized instruments in, 28–29
  types of variables in, 18

Measurement scales, 16–18
Michigan Alcoholism Screening Test (MAST), 136
Multiple baseline design, 51–56, 107–109
  establishing baseline in, 108
  general guidelines for using, 109–110
  for one client with problem variables, 110–113
  statistical analyses in, 110, 112–113, 116, 117–118, 119
  for two clients with problem variables, 113–118
  two single-subject designs for one client, 118–119
Multiple treatment interference, 82

N

National Association of Social Workers (NASW)
  in defining clinical social work, 2–4
  standards for clinical social workers, 1
Negative change, 75–76
No change, examples of, 75–76
Nominal scale, 16–17
  measurement of, 26
Nonreactivity of variables, 25

O

Objectivity, 26
  measurement in enhancing, 26–27
Observation forms, 28
Observations in obtaining information for baselines, 41–44
Open-ended question, 36
Ordinal measurement scales, 17

P

Paper-and-pencil tests, 28
Positive change, 76
Potential indicators, 16
Precision, 26
Predictive validity, 25
Prescriptions, definition of, 64
Prevention as change objective, 65
Problem duration in graphing, 49
Problem existence in graphing, 48
Problem frequency in graphing, 48–49
Problem severity or magnitude, 19
Proscriptions, definition of, 64

ABOUT THE AUTHOR

Tony Tripodi, MSW, DWS, ACSW, is director, doctoral program, associate director and professor, School of Social Work, Florida International University, North Miami. He has conducted research on many subjects of interest to social workers, including clinical judgment, juvenile delinquency, psychotherapy, program evaluation, research methodology, and use of research methods by social workers.

Dr. Tripodi has served as a research and evaluation consultant for national and international organizations such as the European Common Market and the Zancan Foundation in Padova, Italy. He was a member of the Task Force on Social Work Research, National Institute of Mental Health; currently, he is a member of the National Research Advisory Committee, Boysville, Michigan; a member of the Board of Visitors to the President of Clark Atlanta University; and a participant in setting a research agenda for comprehensive school-linked services for children and families, sponsored by the Office of Educational Research, U.S. Department of Education.

Dr. Tripodi was editor-in-chief of *Social Work Research & Abstracts* from 1980 to 1984. He serves on the editorial boards of several professional journals. He has written or co-authored 15 textbooks on research and evaluation, co-edited six books, and published extensively in social work, psychology, public health, and interdisciplinary evaluation journals and books. Among his most recent publications (with others) are *Involuntary Clients in Social Work Practice: A Research-Based Approach* (1994), *Direct Practice Research in Human Service Agencies* (1994), and *Metodi di Misurazione Nelle Attivita de Servizo Sociale: A Conttato Diretto Con L'utenze* (1993).

A Primer on Single-Subject Design for
Clinical Social Workers

Cover and interior design by Ethel Kessler Design, Inc.

Graphic illustrations by Dr. Suzanne Stonbely

This book was composed by Graphic Composition Inc., and printed by Boyd Printing Co., Inc.

RESEARCH TOOLS FOR SOCIAL WORKERS FROM NASW PRESS

A Primer on Single-Subject Design for Clinical Social Workers, *by Tony Tripodi.* This practical guide demonstrates how to build the single-subject design model into your practice without disruption and then use it easily to make key clinical decisions, monitor the effectiveness of treatment, promote client understanding, and demonstrate accountability in clinical practice.

ISBN: 0-87101-238-3. 1994. Item #2383. $29.95

Advances in Mental Health Research: Implications for Practice, *edited by Janet B. W. Williams and Kathleen Ell, cofunded by the National Institute of Mental Health.* This book provides the latest scientific knowledge for treating the wide range of conditions and issues encountered in social work practice. Public policy deliberations and the health care reimbursement system are creating an urgent need to prove that social work mental health practice is based on scientific knowledge. This book will help you work toward that goal.

ISBN: 0-87101-291-X. 1998. Item #291X, $27.95

Practitioner–Researcher Partnerships: Building Knowledge from, in, and for Practice, *edited by Peg McCartt Hess and Edward J. Mullen.* This book meets the long-term demand for ways to forge more successful and effective partnerships between the worlds of social work practice and social work research. This valuable resource explains how to deal successfully with differing outlooks on approaches and methods.

ISBN: 0-87101-252-9. 1995. Item #2529. $31.95

Ethical Standards in Social Work: A Critical Review of the *NASW Code of Ethics,* **by** *Frederic G. Reamer.* Here is the first comprehensive, in-depth examination of the code of ethics of the social work profession. With this practical guide, which includes many case examples, you'll have a firm foundation for making ethical decisions and minimizing malpractice and liability risk.

ISBN: 0-87101-293-6. 1998. Item #2936. $24.95

Advances in Clinical Social Work Research, *edited by Lynn Videka-Sherman and William J. Reid.* This book offers contributions from 54 noted researchers. With four expansive sections, the reader is provided with skills, techniques, and methods that can be used to help clients in any setting.

ISBN: 0-87101-186-7. 1990. Item #1867. $31.95

Social Work Research

This quarterly journal publishes exemplary research to advance the development of knowledge and inform social work practice. Includes analytic reviews of research, theoretical articles pertaining to social work research, evaluation studies, and diverse research studies that contribute to knowledge about social work issues.

ISSN: 1070-5309. Published March, June, September, and December. Yearly subscriptions: NASW members, $40.00; NASW student members, $28.00; individual nonmembers, $63.00; libraries/institutions, $87.00.

(Order form on reverse side)

ORDER FORM

	Title	Item #	Price	Total
__	A Primer on Single-Subject Design	2383	$29.95	_____
__	Advances in Mental Health Research	291X	$27.95	_____
__	Practitioner–Researcher Partnerships	2529	$31.95	_____
__	Ethical Standards in Social Work	2936	$24.95	_____
__	Advances in Clinical Social Work Research	1867	$31.95	_____
__	Social Work Research (Member)	7001	$40.00	_____
__	Social Work Research (Student Member)	7101	$28.00	_____
__	Social Work Research (Individual Nonmember)	7201	$63.00	_____
__	Social Work Research (Library/Institution)	7301	$87.00	_____
			Subtotal	_____
		+ 10% postage and handling		_____
			Total	_____

☐   I've enclosed my check or money order for $ _____.

☐   Please charge my   ☐ NASW Visa*   ☐ Other Visa   ☐ MasterCard

_____   _____

Credit Card Number   Expiration Date

Signature _____

Use of this card generates funds in support of the social work profession.

Name_____

Address _____

City _____ State/Province _____

Country _____ Zip _____

Phone _____ E-mail _____

NASW Member # (if applicable) _____

(Please make checks payable to NASW Press. Prices are subject to change.)

NASW PRESS

P. O. Box 431
Annapolis JCT, MD 20701
USA

Credit card orders call
1-800-227-3590
(In the Metro Wash., DC, area, call 301-317-8688)
Or fax your order to 301-206-7989
Or order online at http://www.naswpress.org

Visit our Web site at http://www.naswpress.org.   SSBI98